THE APOCRYPHAL JESUS

The Apocryphal Jesus

Legends of the Early Church

─────────── ✧ ───────────

J. K. ELLIOTT

OXFORD UNIVERSITY PRESS
1996

Oxford University Press, Walton Street, Oxford OX2 6DP

Oxford New York
Athens Auckland Bangkok Bombay
Calcutta Cape Town Dar es Salaam Delhi
Florence Hong Kong Istanbul Karachi
Kuala Lumpur Madras Madrid Melbourne
Mexico City Nairobi Paris Singapore
Taipei Tokyo Toronto
and associated companies in
Berlin Ibadan

Oxford is a trade mark of Oxford University Press

Published in the United States
by Oxford University Press Inc., New York

©J. K. Elliott 1996

British Library Cataloguing in Publication Data
Data available

Library of Congress Cataloging in Publication Data
Data available

ISBN 0–19–826385–6
0–19–826384–8 (Pbk)

1 3 5 7 9 10 8 6 4 2

Typeset by Best-set Typesetter Ltd., Hong Kong
Printed in Great Britain on acid-free paper by
Biddles Ltd., Guildford and King's Lynn

Contents

⟡

Introduction   1

A. STORIES RELATING TO THE PERIOD
    OF THE NEW TESTAMENT GOSPELS   7

1. The Birth of Jesus   9

2. The Childhood of Jesus   19

3. Jesus' Parents   31
   (a) Mary   31
   (b) Joseph   44

4. The Ministry of Jesus   51
   (a) Stories about Jesus' Ministry   51
   (b) 'Secret' Sayings of Jesus   55
   (c) Jesus' Physical Appearance   57
   (d) Other Stories about Jesus' Ministry   59
   (e) A Letter from Jesus   64

5. The Death and Resurrection of Jesus   66

6. Pilate   89

7. Jesus in the Underworld   97

8. Veronica   109

9. Zacharias   112

B. STORIES RELATING TO THE GROWTH
    OF THE CHURCH   115

10. Peter   117

11. Paul   130
    (*a*) Paul's Missionary Journey   130
    (*b*) Paul's Letters   143

12. John   147

13. Thomas   161

14. Andrew   175

C. STORIES RELATING TO LIFE AFTER DEATH   187

15. Heaven and Hell   189

16. The End Time   205

Epilogue   209

Indexes
    1. Apocryphal Texts Cited   213
    2. General Index   214

Introduction

—————————— ✧ ——————————

Christians from the second–third centuries onwards seem to have been avid readers. Not only did they study the twenty-seven writings that later were to be collected together to form the New Testament, but they also heard and read other stories and sayings about Jesus and the founders of the church which were not in the New Testament. Many of the early stories about Jesus, his parents, and his disciples were supplemented and expanded as the church developed. Secular romances, the novels of their day, provided precedents on which the burgeoning Christian literary tradition drew. The curiosity of pious Christians about the origins of their faith was increasingly satisfied by a growing number of Gospels, Acts, and other types of literature.

Much of this writing provided the popular reading matter of a significant number of believers. These second–third-century inventions may be judged as crudely sensational, magical, or superstitious. Little of this literature maintains the restrained spirituality of the earlier writings that eventually formed the New Testament. Nor do these 'popular' books match the highly intellectual theology of the church father's treatises that are contemporaneous with them. Yet these lively supplementary Gospels, Acts, Epistles, and Apocalypses testify to a vigorous folk religion which was sometimes deviant, even unorthodox, when compared to the mainstream Christianity that established itself, but which, in general, was perfectly normal and orthodox, albeit reflecting an uncritical, simple, even ascetic, faith. These writings characterized and stimulated a significant number of early Christians.

Once the church authorities decided to control the flood of writings by selecting approved, canonical, texts, authorized for the faithful to read, then those writings which failed to qualify were rejected. The popularity of some of the rejected books ensured their continued circulation, albeit in clandestine or censored versions. It is these secondary texts that are now commonly referred to as New Testament apocrypha. The term does not signify that we are dealing with 'hidden' writings (which is what the word 'apocrypha' should properly mean); rather, that these are texts branded by the authorities as spurious or of dubious value in comparison with the approved, canonical, scriptures which were promoted as the foundation documents of the Christian faith.

Given the ecclesiastical disapprobation, it is surprising that so many of these apocrypha survived at all. Many not only survived but were extensively distributed, frequently copied, and widely known and revered.

Some of these rejected texts remained best-sellers. Many copies, some very early, have survived to our own day. Apocryphal Gospels, and other texts, that had their origin in the second or third centuries were still being copied several centuries later. Not only were apocryphal books enduring but they had a widespread circulation throughout Christendom, East and West. Tales composed in Greek were commonly translated into Latin, Syriac, and Coptic. Revisions were made. Versions and adaptations in Ethiopic or Slavonic were produced. Some of the stories of Jesus' infancy, for example, are to be found nowadays in a large number of manuscripts of early date in a wide range of languages. For some texts of course we are not so lucky with the quantity of manuscripts that have chanced to survive: some early apocryphal Gospels, for instance, are known to us in just one isolated, fragmentary, copy. However, the vast number of apocryphal Gospels, Acts, and other genres of literature of this type and the large number of copies and translations of many of them testify to the ongoing interest in and appetite for these books in the ancient and medieval church.

The collections of this material which have been made and printed in modern times usually represent a mere sample of the huge variety of texts that may qualify to appear under an umbrella title such as 'The Apocryphal New Testament'. Strictly, the title and designation 'New Testament Apocrypha' should be applied to writings composed in imitation of the type of writing in the New Testament itself (Gospels, Acts, etc.), or which concern themselves with the characters, including 'fringe' characters, of the New Testament. Jesus, his parents, and the disciples are the usual *dramatis personae* of many apocryphal texts, but others like Nicodemus, the good and bad thieves, Pilate's wife, Thomas, Andrew, John, and other apostles gain prominence. The stories betray an insatiable interest in these characters' miracles, and pronouncements, their travels and, increasingly, their deaths. Believers' curiosity about these persons fuelled a creative literary urge. It is the writings resulting from that impetus which are drawn upon for the present selection.

Inevitably, in fluid writing of this type, additions were constantly made as the stories were repeated and copied; more and more secondary details were invented and added out of oral sources, as well as from previously written accounts elsewhere. Conversely, some of the longer books were subjected to contraction, and this is especially true after the church at large castigated their contents. In the case of the apocryphal Acts, often only the accounts of the apostles' martyrdom remained; these portions were permitted to survive in a catholicized and expurgated form as acceptable hagiographies. Nevertheless, the original contents of several of the early Acts and other texts can be reconstructed from extant remnants that survived.

These apocryphal books are of importance as historical witnesses to the beliefs, prayers, practices, and interests of the society that produced and preserved them. There may be little in their contents to encourage the modern faithful, but, as literary sources that inspired much in Christianity, they have an unrivalled importance. It is in these apocrypha that art, sculpture, poetry, and drama often found inspiration. Dante's *Inferno*, the Harrowing of Hell in the medieval English religious dramas known as mystery (or miracle) plays, and the works of Milton can often only be understood against a background of the New Testament apocryphal legends. Likewise, the earliest literary expression of common Christian teaching on the perpetual virginity of Mary or her Assumption is in this corpus. The well-known story of Veronica and her kerchief, used for a Station of the Cross, occurs only in this apocryphal literature. The credal formula 'He descended into Hell' is amplified in and was probably inspired by the so-called Acts of Pilate. Popular tales like Paul's baptizing a lion, the *Quo Vadis?* scene (in which Peter, prior to his own crucifixion, encounters and questions Jesus outside Rome), and the account of Jesus' birth in a cave all occur in the apocryphal, not the canonical, New Testament. The deeds of Joseph of Arimathaea, the evangelization of India, and the accounts of Pilate's death are all found here too.

Many of the apocryphal books are repetitive and turgid in style but there are occasional purple passages and some well-crafted and memorable scenes. Certainly, many episodes influenced later generations of Christians. It is the more significant and readable of these texts that are to be found in this present collection.

Modern scholarship identifies frequent linguistic and textual problems involved in the reconstruction and editing of these texts. Many literary and palaeographical issues require specialist scholarly attention before we can be sure of reading a definitive edition of some of the apocrypha, but outstanding difficulties are being tackled by a growing army of scholars. Interest and research into this literature have grown rapidly in the last decade, and improved editions of the texts are being published. Even now, enough work has already been done to satisfy general readers. We find good and reliable versions of most of the texts. These literary and textual problems are described in my *Apocryphal New Testament* (Oxford: Clarendon Press, 1993). In this book is to be found a comprehensive collection of early texts in translation. The introductions and bibliographies in that volume should point the way forward to those who wish to investigate this literature in more detail.

In the meantime, this short digest of the highlights of the New Testament apocrypha should serve as an introductory insight into their contents and character. Even though many extracts here are taken out of context, I trust the flavour of the texts has been preserved. Introductory comments are intended to set the scene and to say something about the importance of the passages. My selection is divided into three: the first part, A, deals with Jesus' career—birth, childhood, ministry, death, and descent to the underworld, as well as with the stories that concern his parents. The section also has chapters on Pilate, and on two minor characters, Veronica and Zacharias. Part B draws on stories that feature the missionary activities of the apostles, Peter, Paul, John, Thomas, and Andrew, all of whom are working in Jesus' name. The third part, C, includes accounts about the end of the world and descriptions of hell and paradise.

SUGGESTED FURTHER READING

J. K. Elliott, *The Apocryphal New Testament* (Oxford: Clarendon Press, 1993).

W. Schneemelcher, *New Testament Apocrypha,* English translation of the 5th–6th German edition edited by R. McL. Wilson, 2 vols. (Cambridge: Clarke, 1991 and 1992).

H. Koester, *Ancient Christian Gospels: Their History and Development* (London: SCM and Philadelphia: Fortress, 1990).

R. I. Pervo, *Profit with Delight: the Literary Genre of the Acts of the Apostles* (Philadelphia: Fortress, 1987).

R. Cameron, *The Other Gospels: Non-Canonical Gospel Texts* (Philadelphia: Fortress, 1983).

A

Stories relating to the Period of the New Testament Gospels

✧

In this section stories about Jesus' birth, childhood, ministry, death, and descent to Hades are included. The main focus of apocryphal literature seems to have been concentrated on his nativity and infancy. Comparatively little in the apocryphal tradition covers the period of Jesus' earthly ministry or his death—although stories and sayings that probably belong to the time of his ministry were written, and some surviving texts are included here. Also in this section are legends about Jesus' parents, Joseph and Mary, and about Mary's parents, Joachim and Anna. One chapter is given to Pilate, who figures in a long cycle of apocryphal works.

Other *dramatis personae* from the New Testament Gospels who reappear in apocryphal legends include Zacharias, the father of John the Baptist, and the woman with the issue of blood of Mark 5: 25 (named Veronica in the later traditions). These two merit a short chapter apiece as a postscript to this section.

1

The Birth of Jesus

✧

The Christmas story in the New Testament is found only in the opening chapters of Matthew's and Luke's Gospels. The earliest Gospel (Mark) and the earliest writings in the New Testament (Paul's letters) do not show any knowledge of the circumstances of Jesus' birth. So, already within the period when the New Testament was being written (say, AD 50 to AD 100), there was a developing interest in describing the beginning of Jesus' life. It was a process that continued into the second–third century, when many apocryphal legends about his nativity originated.

As far as the account in Matthew is concerned, we read there that Joseph learns in a dream that his fiancée, Mary, is pregnant by the Holy Spirit. At his birth Jesus is honoured by the astrologers (magi), who disobey King Herod the Great's command that they should report to him the whereabouts of the new-born Messiah. Joseph is warned in a second dream to escape with Mary and Jesus to Egypt in order to avoid the wholesale slaughter of infants (the Massacre of the Innocents) initiated by Herod. Only after Herod's death does the Holy Family leave Egypt and settle in Nazareth.

In Luke's version we read of the journey of Joseph and Mary to Bethlehem for a census, Jesus' birth there, the adoration by shepherds, and the presentation of Jesus in the Jerusalem Temple. Luke's account contains the parallel story of the birth of John the Baptist, who is said to be a kinsman of Jesus. It is in these first two chapters of Luke that we find within the birth stories early hymns, such as the Nunc Dimittis, the Magnificat, and the Benedictus, which have retained a prominent place in Christian public worship.

Modern nativity plays and scenes depicted on Christmas

cards continue to popularize the account of Jesus' birth. These modern expressions of popular piety are of a piece with medieval mystery plays and with much religious art, especially of the Byzantine period. All of them regularly draw on details found in apocryphal accounts of the events surrounding the birth, as well as on the Biblical stories. The apocryphal influences can usually be traced to two texts, the Protevangelium of James and the Gospel of Pseudo-Matthew. Apocryphal accounts like these were particularly prolific. Other versions may be seen in the Arabic or Armenian infancy stories as well as in various Latin texts.

The aim of the ancient apocryphal accounts is, as is usual in this type of literature, to expand the New Testament story, although some elements in the birth stories are clearly there to enhance the role of Mary, to tell of her background, and to propagate the belief in her perpetual virginity. Details about Mary's physical condition after the birth of Jesus are described in some of the accounts. Examples follow (under (1) and (2)). Another characteristic theme in some of the stories shown in the examples below is that the physical reality of Jesus' incarnation is underplayed. These descriptions, which are somewhat mystical, may have been due to Docetic or other heretical tendencies. Docetists (whose name is derived from the Greek verb 'to seem') taught that Jesus' earthly body only *seemed* to be physical: it was in effect a phantom body. We find other examples of this teaching: in descriptions of what Jesus looked like (in Chapter 4 below) we see Docetist influence at work; in Chapter 5 we have another example of Docetism in the account of the death of Jesus. Such descriptions would have been attractive to those unable to accept that the Son of God (of all people) could have adopted sinful human flesh.

Three extracts from apocryphal nativity Gospels are given below.

The first example (from the second-century Protevangelium of James) elaborates the account of the journey to Bethlehem. This seems to be the earliest reference to Jesus' birth in a cave. The narrative continues with a famous monologue by Joseph, who describes the wonders that accompanied Jesus' birth—in particular, the cessation of natural phenomena. The apocryphal writer obviously believed that the arrival on earth of the universal saviour demanded cosmic recognition. The moving star in the Biblical account was not sufficient: for this developed tradition the catalepsy of nature was introduced as an appropriate accompaniment to the birth. In this, of course, parallels can be drawn with the cosmic events that accompanied Jesus' departure from earth, notably the eclipse and the earthquake at the time of his crucifixion (Matthew 27: 51-2; Mark 15: 33).

A variation of the stories in the Protevangelium is to be seen in the later Gospel of Pseudo-Matthew, which in its present form may date from the eighth century, although it drew on much earlier material. Here Jesus' birth is acknowledged not only by the shepherds and the wise men, but also by animals. In the extract below (2) will be seen the episode in which the ox and the ass adore Jesus. This popular scene, which has survived through the centuries, is due to the influence of the Old Testament, in particular Isaiah 1: 3 and Habakkuk 3: 2. This represents an ongoing tradition in which various Biblical passages were read as Messianic prophecies that were then said to have been fulfilled in the life of Jesus. Pseudo-Matthew's use of Old Testament citations continues a Christian tradition as old as the New Testament itself.

Extract (3) is from the medieval Latin nativity story known as Arundel manuscript number 404. The cessation of nature at Jesus' birth is found here too. But the extract from Arundel 404 is given below for the description of the actual birth, which is the most Docetic in character in any of these apocryphal Gospels and appears to reflect second-century interests. Here in the birth story Jesus only *seems* to be human. His physical appearance on earth in the Arundel text is described as only a manifestation of divine light.

(1) *Protevangelium of James* 17-21

17. 1. Now there went out a decree from the king Augustus that all those in Bethlehem in Judaea should be enrolled. And Joseph said, 'I shall enrol my sons, but what shall I do with this child? How shall I enrol her? As my wife? I am ashamed to do that. Or as my daughter? But all the children of Israel know that she is not my daughter. On this day of the Lord the Lord will do as he wills.' 2. And he saddled his she-ass and sat her on it; his son led, and Joseph followed. And they drew near to the third milestone. And Joseph turned round and saw her sad and said within himself, 'Perhaps the child within her is paining her.' Another time Joseph turned round and saw her laughing and said to her, 'Mary, why is it that I see your face at one moment laughing and at another sad?' And Mary said to Joseph, 'I see with my eyes two peoples, one weeping and lamenting and one rejoicing and exulting.' 3. And having come half-way, Mary said to him, 'Joseph, take me down from the she-ass, for the child within me presses me to come forth.' And he took her down from the she-ass and said to her, 'Where shall I take you and hide your shame? For the place is desert.'

18. 1. And he found a cave there and brought her into it, and left her in the care of his sons and went out to seek for a Hebrew midwife in the region of Bethlehem. 2. Now I, Joseph, was walking, and yet I did not walk, and I looked up to the air and saw the air in amazement. And I looked up at the vault of heaven, and saw it standing still and the birds of the heaven motionless. And I looked down at the earth, and saw a dish placed there and workmen reclining, and their hands were in the dish. But those who chewed did not chew, and those who lifted up did not lift, and those who put something to their mouth put nothing to their mouth, but everybody looked upwards. And behold, sheep were being driven and they did not come forward but stood still; and the shepherd raised his hand to strike them with his staff but his hand remained upright. And I looked at the flow of the river, and saw the mouths of the kids over it and they did not drink. And then suddenly everything went on its course.

19. 1. And behold, a woman came down from the hill-country and said to me, 'Man, where are you going?' And I said, 'I seek a Hebrew midwife.' And she answered me, 'Are you from Israel?' And I said to her, 'Yes.' And she said, 'And who is she who brings forth in the cave?' And I said, 'My betrothed.' And she said to me, 'Is she not your wife?' And I said to her, 'She is Mary, who was brought up in the temple of the Lord, and I received her by lot as my wife, and she is not my wife, but she has conceived by the Holy Spirit.' And the midwife said to him, 'Is this true?' And Joseph said to her, 'Come and see.' And she went with him. 2. And they stopped at the entrance to the cave, and behold, a bright cloud overshadowed the cave. And the midwife said, 'My soul is magnified today, for my eyes have seen wonderful things: for salvation is born to Israel.' And immediately the cloud disappeared from the cave and a great light appeared, so that our eyes could not bear it. A short time afterwards that light withdrew until the baby appeared, and it came and took the breast of its mother Mary. And the midwife cried, 'This day is great for me, because I have seen this new sight.' 3. And the midwife came out of the cave, and Salome met her. And she said to her, 'Salome, Salome. I have a new sight to tell you about; a virgin has brought forth, a thing which her condition does not allow.' And Salome said, 'As the Lord my God lives, unless I insert my finger and test her condition, I will not believe that a virgin has given birth.'

20. 1. And the midwife went in and said to Mary, 'Make yourself ready, for there is no small contention concerning you.' And Salome inserted her finger to test her condition. And she cried out, saying, 'Woe for my wickedness and my unbelief; for I have tempted the living God; and behold, my hand falls away from me, consumed by fire!' 2. And she bowed her knees before the Lord saying, 'O God of my fathers, remember me; for I am the seed of Abraham, Isaac, and Jacob; do not make me pilloried for the children of Israel, but restore me to the poor. For you know, Lord, that in your name I perform my duties and from you I have received my hire.' 3. And behold, an angel of the Lord appeared and said to her, 'Salome, Salome, the Lord God has heard your prayer. Bring your hand to the child and touch him and salvation and joy will be yours.' 4. And Salome came near and touched him, saying, 'I will worship him, for a great king has been born to Israel.' And Salome was healed as she had requested, and she went out of the cave. And, behold, an angel of the Lord cried, 'Salome, Salome, do not report what marvels you have seen, until the child has come to Jerusalem.'

21. 1. And behold, Joseph was ready to go to Judaea. And there took place a great tumult in Bethlehem of Judaea. For there came wise men saying, 'Where is the new-born king of the Jews? For we have seen his star in the east and have come to worship him.' 2. When Herod heard this he was troubled and sent officers to the wise men, and sent for the high priests and questioned them, 'How is it written concerning the Messiah? Where is he born?' They said to him, 'In Bethlehem of Judaea; for thus it is written.' And he let them go. And he questioned the wise men and said to them, 'What sign did you see concerning the new-born king?' And the wise men said, 'We saw how an indescribably greater star shone among these stars and dimmed them, so that the stars no longer shone; and so we knew that a king was born for Israel. And we have come to worship him.' And Herod said, 'Go and seek, and when you have found him, tell me, that I also may come to worship him.' 3. And the wise men went out. And behold, the star which they had seen in the east, went before them until they came to the cave. And it stood over the head of the cave. And the wise men saw the young child with Mary his mother, and they took out of their pouch gifts: gold, and frankincense, and myrrh. 4. And having been warned by the angel that they should not go into Judaea, they went to their own country by another route.

(2) *Gospel of Pseudo-Matthew* 13–14

13. And it came to pass some little time after, that an enrolment was made according to the edict of Caesar Augustus for all the world to be enrolled, each man in his native place. This enrolment was made by Cyrinus, the governor of Syria. It was necessary, therefore, that Joseph should enrol with Mary in Bethlehem, because they came from there, being of the tribe of Judah and of the house and family of David. When, therefore, Joseph and Mary were going along the road which leads to Bethlehem, Mary said to Joseph, 'I see two peoples before me, the one weeping, and the other rejoicing.' And Joseph answered, 'Sit still on your beast, and do not speak superfluous words.' Then there appeared before them a beautiful boy, clothed in white raiment, who said to Joseph, 'Why did you say that the words which Mary spoke about the two peoples were superfluous? For she saw the people of the Jews weeping

because they have departed from their God; and the people of the Gentiles rejoicing, because they have now approached and are near to the Lord, in accordance with what he promised to our fathers Abraham, Isaac, and Jacob: for the time is at hand when in the seed of Abraham a blessing should be bestowed on all nations.'

And when he had said this, the angel ordered the beast to stand, for the time when she should bring forth was at hand; and he commanded Mary to come down from the animal, and go into an underground cave, in which there never was light, but always darkness, because the light of day could not reach it. And when Mary had gone into it, it began to shine with as much brightness as if it were the sixth hour of the day. The light from God so shone in the cave that neither by day nor night was light wanting as long as Mary was there. And there she brought forth a son, and the angels surrounded him when he was being born. And as soon as he was born he stood upon his feet, and the angels adored him saying, 'Glory to God in the highest, and on earth peace to men of good will.' Now, when the birth of the Lord was at hand, Joseph had gone away to seek midwives. And when he had found them, he returned to the cave and found with Mary the infant which she had brought forth. And Joseph said to Mary, 'I have brought two midwives, Zelomi and Salome; and they are standing outside by the entrance to the cave, not daring to come in because of the intense brightness.' And when Mary heard this she smiled; and Joseph said to her, 'Do not smile, but be prudent and allow them to visit you, in case you should require them for medication.' Then she ordered them to come to her. And when Zelomi had come in, she said to Mary, 'Allow me to touch you.' And when she had permitted her to make an examination the midwife cried out with a loud voice and said, 'Lord, Lord Almighty, mercy on us! It has never been heard or thought of that any one should have her breasts full of milk and that the birth of a son should show his mother to be a virgin. But there has been no spilling of blood in his birth, no pain in bringing him forth. A virgin has conceived, a virgin has brought forth, and a virgin she remains.' And hearing these words, the other midwife with the name Salome said, 'I will not believe what I have heard unless I also examine her.' And Salome entered and said to Mary, 'Allow me to handle you, and prove whether Zelomi has spoken the truth.' And Mary allowed her to handle her. And when she had withdrawn her hand from handling her it dried up, and through excess of pain she began to weep bitterly and to be in great distress, crying out and saying, 'O Lord God, you know that I have always feared you, and that without recompense I have cared for all the poor; I have taken nothing from the widow and the orphan, and the needy have I not sent empty away. And, behold, I am made wretched because of my unbelief, since without a cause I wished to test your virgin.'

And while she was speaking, there stood by her a young man in shining garments saying, 'Go to the child and worship him and touch him with your hand, and he will heal you, because he is the Saviour of the world and of all that hope in him.' And she went to the child with haste and worshipped him and touched the fringe of the clothes in which he was wrapped, and instantly her hand was cured. And going out she began to cry aloud and to tell the wonderful things which she had seen and which she had suffered and how she had been cured, so that many believed through her preaching.

And some shepherds also affirmed that they had seen angels singing a hymn at midnight, praising and blessing the God of heaven and saying, 'The Saviour of all, who is Christ the Lord has been born. Salvation shall be brought back to Israel through him.'

A great star, larger than any that had been seen since the beginning of the world, shone over the cave from the evening till the morning. And the prophets who were in Jerusalem said that this star pointed out the birth of Christ who should restore the promise not only to Israel but to all nations.

14. And on the third day after the birth of our Lord Jesus Christ, Mary went out of the cave and, entering a stable, placed the child in the manger, and an ox and an ass adored him. Then was fulfilled that which was said by Isaiah the prophet, 'The ox knows his owner, and the ass his master's crib.' Therefore, the animals, the ox and the ass, with him in their midst, incessantly adored him. Then was fulfilled that which was said by Habakkuk the prophet, saying, 'Between two animals you

are made manifest.' Joseph remained in the same place with Mary for three days.

(3) *Arundel 404* 72–4

72. In that hour, a great silence descended with fear. For even the winds stopped, they made no breeze; there was no movement of the leaves on the trees, nor sound of water heard; the streams did not flow; there was no motion of the sea. All things born in the sea were silent; no human voice sounded and there was a great silence. For the pole itself ceased its rapid course from that hour. The measure of time almost stopped. Everyone was overwhelmed with great fear and kept silent; we were expecting the advent of the most high God, the end of the world.

73. As the time drew near, the power of God showed itself openly. The maiden stood looking into heaven; she became like a vine. For now the end of the events of salvation was at hand. When the light had come forth, Mary worshipped him whom she saw she had given birth to. The child himself, like the sun, shone brightly, beautiful and most delightful to see, because he alone appeared as peace, bringing peace everywhere. In that hour when he was born the voice of many invisible beings proclaimed in unison, 'Amen.' And that light, which was born, was multiplied and it obscured the light of the sun itself by its shining rays. The cave was filled with the bright light and with a most sweet smell. The light was born just as the dew descends from heaven to the earth. For its perfume is fragrant beyond all the smell of ointments.

74. I [= midwife], however, stood stupefied and amazed. Fear seized me. I was gazing at the intense bright light which had been born. The light, however, gradually shrank, imitated the shape of an infant, then immediately became outwardly an infant like a child born normally. I became bold and leaned over and touched him. I lifted him in my hands with great awe, and I was terrified because he had no weight like other babies who are born. I looked at him; there was no blemish in him, but his whole body was shining, just as the dew of the most high God. He was light to carry, radiant to see. For a while I was amazed at him because he did not cry as new-born infants

are accustomed to cry. While I held him, looking into his face, he smiled at me with a most joyful smile, and, opening his eyes, he looked at me intently, and suddenly a great light came forth from his eyes like a brilliant flash of lightning.

2

The Childhood of Jesus

✧

Except for one story in Luke's Gospel (the episode of Jesus in the Temple at the age of 12 in Luke 2: 41–50) the New Testament writings leave a tantalizing gap in the life of Jesus between his birth and his baptism at the beginning of the public ministry. Inevitably, the developing literary tradition, taking its cue from the childhood story in Luke, created a series of incidents that tell of events in Jesus' boyhood. Their main theme is to show Jesus' precocious awareness of his supernatural origin and his power over life, death, and nature.

Such belief in Jesus' divinity is clearly orthodox in Christian doctrine, but the often sensational manifestations of his supernatural abilities displayed in the numerous childhood stories in apocryphal Gospels tend to distort that belief. Extracts below from the second–third-century Infancy Gospel of Thomas, given under (1), have the effect of portraying the child Jesus as an *enfant terrible*. Modern readers are struck less by the piety underlying the stories than by the destructiveness of many of Jesus' actions. Such a negative theme may be paralleled in the New Testament story of Jesus' blasting the fig-tree (Mark 11: 12–14, 20–4), but the recurrence of the theme makes it the dominant feature of the Infancy Gospel of Thomas, as well as other apocryphal texts, such as the Gospel of Pseudo-Matthew. Several of the stories in the Infancy Gospel of Thomas are reproduced below. Among them we read the episode of the schoolteacher, which was a particularly popular theme that recurs in different places. It would seem that the childhood story in Luke, where the 12-year-old Jesus confounds the teachers of the Jewish Law, was the inspiration behind the apocryphal versions. However, the mystical interpretation of the shape of the letters in the Greek alphabet is obscure in the account in the Infancy Gospel of Thomas and obviously does not derive from Luke's story.

Clearly, for believers from earlier centuries, these stories struck a favourable chord and were not seen as alien to their Christological teachings.

Extracts from the later Gospel of Pseudo-Matthew (2) and from the Arabic Infancy Gospel under (3) tell stories of the baby Jesus performing miracles during the Holy Family's exile in Egypt. It will be seen that one of the stories includes the robbers who thirty years later are to be crucified alongside Jesus. These characters reappear, differently named, in other apocryphal texts and some of those stories are found below in Chapters 5 and 7. Other comparable stories about baby Jesus may be seen in Chapter 3 with reference to Mary.

Both Pseudo-Matthew and the Arabic Gospel include tales of Jesus as an older child, and examples are given below.

(1) *Infancy Gospel of Thomas* 2–11

2. 1. When this boy Jesus was five years old he was playing at the crossing of a stream, and he gathered together into pools the running water, and instantly made it clean, and gave his command with a single word. 2. Having made soft clay he moulded from it twelve sparrows. And it was the sabbath when he did these things. And there were also many other children playing with him. 3. When a certain Jew saw what Jesus was doing while playing on the sabbath, he at once went and told his father Joseph, 'See, your child is at the stream, and he took clay and moulded twelve birds and has profaned the sabbath.' 4. And when Joseph came to the place and looked, he cried out to him, saying, 'Why do you do on the sabbath things which it is not lawful to do?' But Jesus clapped his hands and cried out to the sparrows and said to them, 'Be gone!' And the sparrows took flight and went away chirping. 5. The Jews were amazed when they saw this, and went away and told their leaders what they had seen Jesus do.

3. 1. Now the son of Annas the scribe was standing there with Joseph; and he took a branch of a willow and with it dispersed the water which Jesus had collected. 2. When Jesus saw what he had done he was angry and said to him, 'You insolent, godless ignoramus, what harm did the pools and the water do to you? Behold, now you also shall wither like a tree and shall bear neither leaves nor root nor fruit.' 3. And immediately that child withered up completely; and Jesus departed and went into Joseph's house. But the parents of the boy who was withered carried him away, bemoaning his lost youth, and brought him to Joseph and reproached him. 'What kind of child do you have, who does such things?'

4. 1. After this he again went through the village, and a child ran and knocked against his shoulder. Jesus was angered and said to him, 'You shall not go further on your way', and immediately he fell down and died. But some, who saw what took place, said, 'From where was this child born, since his every word is an accomplished deed?' 2. And the parents of the dead child came to Joseph and blamed him and said, 'Since you have such a child, you cannot dwell with us in the village; teach him to bless and not to curse. For he is killing our children.'

5. 1. And Joseph called the child to him privately and admonished him saying, 'Why do you do such things? These people suffer and hate us and persecute us.' But Jesus replied, 'I know that these words are not yours; nevertheless for your sake I will be silent. But these people shall bear their punishment.' And immediately those who had accused him became blind. 2. And those who saw it were greatly afraid and perplexed, and said concerning him, 'Every word he speaks, whether good or evil, was a deed and became a miracle.' And when they saw that Jesus had done this, Joseph arose and took him by the ear and pulled it violently. 3. And the child was angry and said to him, 'It is fitting for you to seek and not to find, and you have acted most unwisely. Do you not know that I am yours? Do not vex me.'

6. 1. Now a certain teacher, Zacchaeus by name, who was standing in a certain place, heard Jesus saying these things to his father, and marvelled greatly that, being a child, he voiced such things. 2. And after a few days he came near to Joseph and said to him, 'You have a clever child, and he has understanding. Come, hand him over to me that he may learn letters, and I will teach him with the letters all knowledge, and how to address all the older people and to honour them as forefathers and fathers, and to love those of his own age.' 3. And he told him all the letters from Alpha to Omega distinctly, and with much questioning. But he looked at Zacchaeus the teacher and said to him. 'How do you, who do not know the Alpha according to its nature, teach others the Beta? Hypocrite, first if you know it, teach the Alpha, and then we shall believe you concerning the Beta.' Then he began to question the teacher about the first letter, and he was unable to answer him. 4. And in the hearing of many the child said to Zacchaeus, 'Hear, teacher, the arrangement of the first letter, and pay heed to this, how it has lines and a middle stroke which goes through the pair of lines which you see, (how these lines) converge, rise, turn in the dance, three signs of the same kind, subject to and supporting one another, of equal proportions; here you have the lines of the Alpha'.

7. 1. Now when Zacchaeus the teacher heard so many such allegorical descriptions of the first letter being expounded by the child, he was perplexed at such a reply and at his teaching and said to those who were present, 'Woe is me, I am in difficulties wretch that I am; I have brought shame to myself in drawing to myself this child. 2. Take him away, therefore, I beseech you, brother Joseph. I cannot endure the severity of his gaze, I cannot make out his speech at all. This child is not earth-born; he can even subdue fire. Perhaps he was begotten even before the creation of the world. What belly bore him, what womb nurtured him I do not know. Woe is me, my friend, he confuses me, I cannot attain to his understanding. I have deceived myself, thrice wretched man that I am. I desired to get a pupil, and have found I have a teacher. 3. My friends, I am filled with shame, that I, an old man, have been defeated by a child. I suffer despair and death because of this child, for I cannot in this hour look him in the face. And when all say that I have been conquered by a small child, what have I to say? And what can I tell concerning the lines of the first letter of which he spoke to me? I do not know, my friends, for I know neither beginning nor end of it. 4. Therefore I beg you, brother Joseph, take him away to your house. Whatever great thing he is, a god or an angel I do not know what I should say.

8. 1. And while the Jews were trying to console Zacchaeus, the child laughed aloud and said, 'Now let those who are yours bear fruit, and let the blind in heart see. I have come from above to curse them and to call them to the things above, as he who sent me ordained for your sakes.' 2. And when the child had ceased speaking, immediately all those who had fallen under his curse were saved. And no one after that dared to provoke him, lest he should curse him, and he should be maimed.

9. 1. Now after some days Jesus was playing in the upper story of a house, and one of the children who were playing with him fell down from the house and died. And when the other children saw it they fled, and Jesus remained alone. 2. And the parents of the one who was dead came and accused him. But they threatened him. 3. Then Jesus leaped down from the roof and stood by the corpse of the child, and cried with a loud voice, 'Zeno'—for that is what he was called—'arise and tell me, did I throw you down?' And he arose at once and said, 'No, Lord, you did not throw me down, but raised me up.' And when they saw it they were amazed. And the parents of the child glorified God for the sign that had happened and worshipped Jesus.

10. 1. After a few days a certain man was cleaving wood in a corner, and the axe fell and split the sole of his foot, and he was losing so much blood that he was about to die. 2. And there was a clamour, a crowd gathered, and the child Jesus also ran there, forced his way through the crowd, and took the injured foot, and it was healed immediately. And he said to the young man, 'Arise now, cleave the wood and remember me.' And when the crowd saw what happened, they worshipped the child, saying, 'Truly the spirit of God dwells in this child.'

11. 1. When he was six years old, his mother gave him a pitcher and sent him to draw water and bring it into the house. 2. But in the crowd he stumbled, and the pitcher was broken. But Jesus spread out the garment he was wearing, filled it with water and brought it to his mother. And when his mother saw the miracle, she kissed him, and kept to herself the mysteries which she had seen him do.

(2) *Gospel of Pseudo-Matthew* 18–24, 35, 36, 40

18. And having come to a certain cave, and wishing to rest in it, Mary dismounted from her beast, and sat down with the child Jesus in her lap. And on the journey there were with

Joseph three boys, and with Mary a girl. And behold, suddenly there came out of the cave many dragons; and when the boys saw them they cried out in great terror. Then Jesus got down from his mother's lap and stood on his feet before the dragons; and they worshipped Jesus and then departed. Then was fulfilled that which was said by David the prophet, 'Praise the Lord from the earth, dragons, and all you ocean depths.' And the child Jesus, walking before them, commanded them to hurt no one. But Mary and Joseph were very much afraid lest the child should be hurt by the dragons. And Jesus said to them, 'Do not be afraid, and do not consider me to be a child, for I am and always have been perfect; and all the beasts of the forest must needs be docile before me.'

19. Likewise, lions and panthers adored him and accompanied them in the desert. Wherever Joseph and Mary went, they went before them showing them the way and bowing their heads; they showed their submission by wagging their tails, they worshipped him with great reverence. Now at first, when Mary saw the lions and the panthers and various kinds of wild beasts surrounding them, she was very much afraid. But the infant Jesus looked into her face with a joyful countenance and said, 'Be not afraid, mother, for they come not to do you harm, but they make haste to serve both you and me.' With these words he drove all fear from her heart. And the lions kept walking with them, and with the oxen and the asses and the beasts of burden, which carried what they needed, and did not hurt a single one of them, though they remained with them; they were tame among the sheep and the rams which they had brought with them from Judaea and which they had with them. They walked among wolves and feared nothing; and not one of them was hurt by another. Then was fulfilled that which was spoken by the prophet, 'Wolves shall feed with lambs; lion and ox shall eat straw together.' There were two oxen and a waggon in which they carried their necessities, and the lions directed them in their path.

20. And it came to pass on the third day of their journey, while they were walking, that Mary was fatigued by the excessive heat of the sun in the desert; and, seeing a palm-tree she said to Joseph, 'I should like to rest a little in the shade of this tree.' Joseph therefore led her quickly to the palm and

made her dismount from her beast. And as Mary was sitting there, she looked up to the foliage of the palm and saw it full of fruit and said to Joseph, 'I wish it were possible to get some of the fruit of this palm.' And Joseph said to her, 'I am surprised that you say so, for you see how high the palm-tree is, and that you think of eating its fruit. I am thinking more of the want of water because the skins are now empty, and we have nothing with which to refresh ourselves and our cattle.' Then the child Jesus, reposing with a joyful countenance in the lap of his mother, said to the palm, 'O tree, bend your branches and refresh my mother with your fruit.' And immediately at these words the palm bent its top down to the very feet of Mary; and they gathered from it fruit with which they all refreshed themselves. And after they had gathered all its fruit it remained bent down, waiting the order to rise from him who had commanded it to bend down. Then Jesus said to it, 'Raise yourself, O palm, and be strong and be the companion of my trees which are in the paradise of my Father; and open from your roots a vein of water which is hidden in the earth and let the waters flow, so that we may quench our thirst.' And it rose up immediately, and at its root there began to gush out a spring of water exceedingly clear and cool and sparkling. And when they saw the spring of water, they rejoiced greatly and were all satisfied, including their cattle and their beasts and they gave thanks to God.

21. And on the day after, when they were setting out from there, and at the hour in which they began their journey, Jesus turned to the palm and said, 'This privilege I give you, O palm-tree, that one of your branches be carried away by my angels, and planted in the paradise of my Father. And this blessing I will confer upon you, that it shall be said to all who shall be victorious in any contest, "You have attained the palm of victory." ' And while he was speaking, behold, an angel of the Lord appeared and stood upon the palm tree and, taking off one of its branches, flew to heaven with the branch in his hand. And when they saw this, they fell on their faces and were like dead men. And Jesus said to them, 'Why are your hearts possessed with fear? Do you not know that this palm, which I have caused to be transferred to paradise, shall be prepared for all the saints in the place of blessedness, as it has been prepared

for us in this desert place?' And they were filled with joy; and being strengthened, they all arose.

22. After this, while they were going on their journey, Joseph said to Jesus, 'Lord, the heat is roasting us; if it please you, let us go by the sea-shore that we may be able to rest in the cities on the coast.' Jesus said to him, 'Fear not, Joseph; I will shorten the way for you, so that what you would have taken thirty days to traverse you shall accomplish in this one day.' And while they were speaking, behold, they looked ahead and began to see the mountains and cities of Egypt.

And rejoicing and exulting, they came into the regions of Hermopolis and entered into a certain city of Egypt, which is called Sotinen; and because they knew no one there from whom they could ask hospitality, they went into a temple, which was called the Capitol of Egypt. And in this temple there had been set up three hundred and sixty-five idols, to each of which on its own day divine honours and sacred rites were paid.

23. And it came to pass that, when Mary went into the temple with the child, all the idols prostrated themselves on the ground, so that all of them were lying on their faces shattered and broken to pieces; and thus they plainly showed that they were nothing. Then was fulfilled that which was said by the prophet Isaiah, 'Behold, the Lord will come upon a swift cloud and will enter Egypt, and all the handiwork of the Egyptians shall be moved before his face.'

24. When this was told to Affrodosius, governor of that city, he went to the temple with his whole army. And when the priests of the temple saw Affrodosius coming into the temple with all his army, they thought they would see him take vengeance on those who had caused the gods to fall down. But when he came into the temple and saw all the gods lying prostrate on their faces, he went up to Mary, who was carrying the Lord in her bosom, and worshipped him and said to his whole army and all his friends, 'Unless this were the God of our gods, our gods would not have fallen on their faces before him, nor would they be lying prostrate in his presence: therefore they silently confess that he is their Lord. Unless we do what we have seen our gods doing, we may run the risk of his anger and all come to destruction, just as it happened to Pharaoh

king of the Egyptians who, not believing in powers so mighty, was drowned in the sea with all his army.' Then all the people of the city believed in the Lord God through Jesus Christ.

35. There is a road going out of Jericho and leading to the river Jordan, to the place where the children of Israel crossed; and there the ark of the covenant is said to have rested. And Jesus was eight years old, and he went out of Jericho and went towards the Jordan. And there was beside the road, near the bank of the Jordan, a cave where a lioness was nursing her whelps; and no one was safe to walk that way. Jesus, coming from Jericho, and knowing that in that cave the lioness had brought forth her young, went into it in the sight of all. And when the lions saw Jesus, they ran to meet him and worshipped him. And Jesus was sitting in the cavern and the lion's whelps ran round his feet, fawning and playing with him. And the older lions, with their heads bowed, stood at a distance and worshipped him and fawned upon him with their tails. Then the people who were standing afar off and who did not see Jesus, said, 'Unless he or his parents had committed grievous sins, he would not of his own accord have exposed himself to the lions.' And when the people were reflecting within themselves and were overcome with great sorrow, behold, suddenly in the sight of the people Jesus came out of the cave and the lions went before him, and the lion's whelps played with each other before his feet. And the parents of Jesus stood afar off with their heads bowed and they watched; likewise also the people stood at a distance on account of the lions, for they did not dare to come close to them. Then Jesus began to say to the people, 'How much better are the beasts than you, seeing that they recognize their Lord and glorify him; while you men, who have been made in the image and likeness of God, do not know him! Beasts know me and are tame; men see me and do not acknowledge me.'

36. After these things Jesus crossed the Jordan in the sight of them all with the lions; and the water of the Jordan was divided on the right hand and on the left. Then he said to the lions so that all could hear, 'Go in peace and hurt no one; neither let man injure you, until you return to the place where you have come from.' And they, bidding him farewell, not only

with their voices but with their gestures, went to their own place. But Jesus returned to his mother.

40. After these things Joseph departed with Mary and Jesus to go into Capernaum by the sea-shore, on account of the malice of his adversaries. And when Jesus was living in Capernaum, there was in the city a man named Joseph, exceedingly rich. But he had wasted away under his infirmity and died, and was lying dead in his couch. And when Jesus heard people in the city mourning and weeping and lamenting over the dead man, he said to Joseph, 'Why do you not grant the benefit of your favour to this man, seeing that he is called by your name?' And Joseph answered him, 'How have I any power or ability to grant him a benefit?' And Jesus said to him, 'Take the kerchief which is upon your head, go and put it on the face of the dead man and say to him, "Christ save you", and immediately the dead man will be healed and will rise from his couch.' And when Joseph heard this, he went away at the command of Jesus and ran and entered the house of the dead man, and put the kerchief, which he was wearing on his head, upon the face of him, who was lying in the couch and said, 'Jesus save you.' And forthwith the dead man rose from his bed and asked who Jesus was.

(3) *Arabic Infancy Gospel* 17, 23, 24, 37, 40

17. On the day after, a woman took scented water to wash the Lord Jesus; and after she had washed him, she took the water with which she had done it, and poured some of it upon a girl who was living there and whose body was white with leprosy, and washed her with it. And as soon as this was done, the girl was cleansed from her leprosy. And the townspeople said, 'There is no doubt that Joseph and Mary and this child are gods, not men.' And when they were ready to leave them, the girl who had suffered from the leprosy came up to them, and asked them to take her with them.

23. And departing from this place, they came to a desert; and hearing that it was infested by robbers, Joseph and the Lady Mary decided to cross this region by night. But on their way,

behold, they saw two robbers lying in wait on the road, and with them a great number of robbers, who were their associates, sleeping. Now those two robbers into whose hands they had fallen were Titus and Dumachus. Titus therefore said to Dumachus, 'I beseech you to let these persons go free, so that our comrades do not see them.' And as Dumachus refused, Titus said to him again, 'Take forty drachmas from me, and have them as a pledge.' At the same time he held out to him the belt which he had had about his waist, that he should not open his mouth or speak. And the Lady Mary, seeing that the robber had done them a kindness, said to him, 'The Lord God will sustain you with his right hand, and will grant you remission of your sins.' And the Lord Jesus answered, and said to his mother, 'Thirty years hence, O my mother, the Jews will crucify me at Jerusalem, and these two robbers will be raised upon the cross along with me, Titus on my right hand and Dumachus on my left; and after that day Titus shall go before me into paradise.' And she said, 'God keep this from you, my son.' And they went from there towards a city of idols, which, as they came near it, was transformed into sand-hills.

24. From there they went to that sycamore which is now called Matarea, and the Lord Jesus brought forth in Matarea a fountain in which the Lady Mary washed his shirt. And from the sweat of the Lord Jesus which he let drop there, balsam was produced in that region.

37. One day, when Jesus was running about and playing with some children, he passed by the workshop of a dyer called Salem. They had in the workshop many cloths which he had to dye. The Lord Jesus went into the dyer's workshop, took all the pieces of cloth and put them into a tub full of indigo. When Salem came and saw that the cloths were spoiled, he began to cry aloud and asked the Lord Jesus, saying, 'What have you done to me, son of Mary? You have ruined my reputation in the eyes of all the people of the city; for everyone orders a colour to suit himself, but you have come and spoiled everything.' And the Lord Jesus replied, 'I will change for you the colour of any cloth which you wish to be changed', and he immediately began to take the cloths out of the tub, each of them dyed in the colour the dyer wished, until he had taken

them all out. When the Jews saw this miracle and wonder, they praised God.

40. On another day the Lord Jesus went out into the road, and seeing some boys who had met to play, he followed them; but the boys hid themselves from him. The Lord Jesus, therefore, having come to the door of a certain house, and seen some women standing there, asked them where the boys had gone; and when they answered that there was no one there, he said again, 'Who are these whom you see in the archway?' They replied that they were young goats of three years old. And the Lord Jesus cried out and said, 'Come out, O goats, to your Shepherd.' Then the boys, in the form of goats, came out, and began to skip round him; and the women, seeing this, were very much astonished, and were seized with trembling, and speedily supplicated the Lord Jesus, saying, 'O our Lord Jesus, son of Mary, you are truly that good Shepherd of Israel; have mercy on your handmaidens who stand before you, and who have never doubted: for you have come, O our Lord, to heal, and not to destroy.' And when the Lord Jesus answered that the sons of Israel were like the Ethiopians among the nations, the women said, 'You, O Lord, know all things, nor is anything hid from you; now, indeed, we beseech you, and ask you of your mercy to restore these boys, your servants, to their former condition.' The Lord Jesus therefore said, 'Come, boys, let us go and play.' And immediately, while these women were standing by, the kids were changed into boys.

3

Jesus' Parents

———————————— ✧ ————————————

This chapter marks a step backwards chronologically as it includes stories about Mary and Joseph which precede Jesus' birth. However, as it also contains accounts of the parents' deaths, the chapter is out of the chronological sequence of the section by jumping forward! The chapter is divided into two parts: (*a*) Mary, (*b*) Joseph.

(*a*) MARY

The earliest of the four New Testament Gospels, Mark, refers only once to Jesus' mother by name. She is not an active participant in any of Mark's stories. It is only when the other canonical Gospels were written a decade or more later than Mark that we find Mary's role enhanced. The birth stories in Matthew and Luke obviously make her the most prominent character apart from Jesus himself. A summary of those nativity accounts prefaces our introductory notes in Chapter 1. The Annunciation scene (Luke 1: 26–38), in which Mary is addressed by the angelic visitor with the words 'Blessed are you among women', both reflects and itself encouraged Mariology and Mariolatry. It is in Luke also that Mary delivers the hymn known as the Magnificat. Outside the birth stories, Matthew and Luke, like Mark, have no further active part for Mary to play. In the Fourth Gospel, however, she is present at the wedding in Cana (John 2: 1–10) and she appears at her son's crucifixion. Later (according to Acts 1: 14), she seems to have been a prominent member of the Jerusalem church. No details about this period of her life are forthcoming. The New Testament gives no information about Mary's parentage, birth, or death. It is left to writings from later centuries to fill those gaps.

The New Testament's emphasis on Mary as the mother of Jesus is also apparent in the apocryphal tradition, as may be seen in Chapter 1 ('The Birth of Jesus'). But Mary also features in her own right, especially in the Protevangelium of James, extracts from which appear under (1) below. The first half of that Gospel is concerned with Mary's parents, her birth, and her upbringing prior to her meeting Joseph. The Protevangelium (the 'prior Gospel') is so named because it tells of the events that pre-date the birth of Jesus told in the canonical Gospels. The church, East and West, made Mary's parents, Joachim and Anna, saints. Their story, taken from the Protevangelium and texts derived from it, and the story of Mary's childhood have been the inspiration for many paintings. Perhaps the most significant of these is Giotto's cycle in the Arena Chapel in Padua, but other representations, including many in stained glass, are frequently to be seen. The commemoration of Mary's presentation in the Temple at the age of 3, founded on the story in the Protevangelium, is a major festival in the Christian calendar. For the Eastern church the Presentation of Mary is one of the Twelve Great Feasts alongside Easter and Christmas. Several incidents from the Protevangelium are abstracted below (under 1), including Anna's lament over her childlessness, her subsequent miraculous conception (but note that the early apocryphal tradition does not speak specifically of the immaculate conception of Mary), and Mary's birth. Stories concerning Mary's life in the Temple are included. Her being nurtured at the hands of an angel is also regularly depicted in medieval art, as too is the story of Mary, the veil-maker. The apocryphal account of the Annunciation is included in this chapter: it is interesting to compare it with the New Testament version.

Another attribute of Mary found in this apocryphal tradition which had a tremendous impact on Christian belief and practice is that she was able to perform miracles. A sequence of miracle stories (below (2)) associated with Mary during the Holy Family's sojourn in Egypt is taken from the Arabic Infancy Gospel. The efficacy of Mary's miracle-working encouraged intercessional prayer to Mary, and this practice became commonplace in Christian worship.

Section (3) below includes stories taken from Greek and Coptic sources concerning the death of Mary and her being taken up bodily into heaven (a translating known as Assumption). There are various and varying accounts of Mary's Assumption (or 'Dormition' to use the term preferred in the Eastern churches' tradition) and all are likely to have originated in the fourth century. Accounts of her passing had a profound influence on Christian doctrine and practice; the stories reflected the growing veneration of Mary and of course they themselves helped to encourage further Mariolatry. In the Coptic legends there is an emphasis on the interval between Mary's death and Assumption. The Coptic tradition includes the presence of Peter and John, and has Jesus warn his mother of her impending death. In the tradition represented below by the Greek version (taken from 'The discourse of St John the Divine concerning the Falling Asleep of the Holy Mother of God'), which agrees also with the Latin and Syriac stories, Mary's death is announced by an angel. All the apostles are summoned to be at her side—accounts of their arrival occupy much of the central part of the 'Discourse' but these are not included in the extracts below. In this Greek version Mary's corporeal Assumption occurs shortly after death. The recurrent anti-Jewish character of much apocryphal writing is apparent in this story.

Both Eastern and Western Christianity have widely celebrated the Assumption on 15 August for many centuries. The Roman Catholic church defined the doctrine only in 1950.

(1) *Protevangelium of James* 2–8, 10–12

2. Now the great day of the Lord drew near, and the children of Israel were bringing their gifts. And Reuben stood up and said, 'It is not lawful for you to offer your gifts first, because you have begotten no offspring in Israel.' 3. Then Joachim became very sad, and went to the record-book of the twelve tribes of the people and said, 'I will look in the register to see whether I am the only one who has not begotten offspring in

Israel', and he found that all the righteous had raised up off-spring in Israel. And he remembered the patriarch Abraham to whom in his last days God gave a son, Isaac. 4. And Joachim was very sad, and did not show himself to his wife, but went into the wilderness; there he pitched his tent and fasted forty days and forty nights, saying to himself, 'I shall not go down either for food or for drink until the Lord my God visits me; my prayer shall be food and drink.'

2. 1. Anna his wife sang two dirges and gave voice to a twofold lament:

> 'I will mourn my widowhood,
> and grieve for my childlessness.'

2. Now the great day of the Lord drew near, and Judith her maid said, 'How long do you intend to humble your soul, because the great day of the Lord is near and it is not lawful for you to mourn. But take this headband, which the mistress of work gave me; it is not right for me to wear it because I am a servant and it bears a royal cipher.'

3. But Anna said, 'Get away from me! I shall never do it. The Lord has greatly humbled me. Who knows whether a deceiver did not give it to you, and you have come to make me share in your sin!' Judith answered, 'Why should I curse you?' The Lord God has shut up your womb to give you no fruit in Israel.'

4. And Anna was very sad, but she took off her mourning garments, washed her head, put on her bridal garments, and about the ninth hour went into her garden to walk there. And she saw a laurel tree and sat down beneath it and implored the Lord saying, 'O God of our fathers, bless me and heed my prayer, just as you blessed the womb of Sarah and gave her a son, Isaac.'

3. 1. And Anna sighed towards heaven and saw a nest of sparrows in the laurel tree and she sang a dirge to herself:

> 'Woe is me, who gave me life
> What womb brought me forth?
> For I was born a curse before them all and before the
>   children of Israel,
> And I was reproached, and they mocked me and thrust
>   me out of the temple of the Lord.

2. Woe is me, to what am I likened?
I am not likened to the birds of the heaven;
for even the birds of the heaven are fruitful before you, O
   Lord.
Woe is me, to what am I likened?
I am not likened to the beasts of the earth;
for even the beasts of the earth are fruitful before you, O
   Lord.
3. Woe is me, to what am I likened?
I am not likened to these waters;
for even these waters are fruitful before you, O Lord.
Woe is me, to what am I likened?
I am not likened to this earth;
for even this earth brings forth its fruit in its season and
   praises you, O Lord.'

4. 1. And behold an angel of the Lord appeared to her and said, 'Anna, Anna, the Lord has heard your prayer. You shall conceive and bear, and your offspring shall be spoken of in the whole world.' And Anna said, 'As the Lord my God lives, if I bear a child, whether male or female, I will bring it as a gift to the Lord my God, and it shall serve him all the days of its life.'
2. And behold there came two angels, who said to her, 'Behold, Joachim your husband is coming with his flocks for an angel of the Lord had come down to him and said to him, "Joachim, Joachim, the Lord God has heard your prayer. Go down from here; behold, your wife Anna shall conceive."' 3. And Joachim went down and called his herdsmen and said, 'Bring me here ten female lambs without blemish and without spot; they shall be for the Lord my God. And bring me twelve tender calves and they shall be for the priests and council of elders, and a hundred young he-goats for the whole people.' 4. And, behold, Joachim came with his flocks, and Anna stood at the gate and saw Joachim coming and ran immediately and threw her arms around his neck saying, 'Now I know that the Lord God has greatly blessed me; for behold the widow is no longer a widow, and I, who was childless, shall conceive.'
And Joachim rested the first day in his house.

5. 1. The next day he offered his gifts, saying to himself, 'If the Lord God is gracious to me the frontlet of the priest will make it clear to me.'

And Joachim offered his gifts and observed the priest's frontlet when he went up to the altar of the Lord; and he saw no sin in himself. And Joachim said, 'Now I know that the Lord God is gracious to me and has forgiven all my sins.' And he came down from the temple of the Lord justified, and went to his house.

2. And her months were fulfilled; in the ninth month Anna gave birth. And she said to the midwife, 'What have I brought forth?' And she said, 'A female.' And Anna said, 'My soul is magnified this day.' And she lay down. And when the days were completed, Anna purified herself and gave suck to the child, and called her Mary.

6. 1. Day by day the child grew strong; when she was six months old her mother stood her on the ground to see if she could stand. And she walked seven steps and came to her bosom. And she took her up saying, 'As the Lord my God lives, you shall walk no more upon this earth until I bring you into the temple of the Lord.' And she made a sanctuary in her bedroom and did not permit anything common or unclean to pass through it. And she summoned the undefiled daughters of the Hebrews, and they served her.

2. On the child's first birthday Joachim made a great feast, and invited the chief priests and the priests and the scribes and the elders and all the people of Israel. And Joachim brought the child to the priests, and they blessed her saying, 'O God of our fathers, bless this child and give her a name eternally renowned among all generations.' And all the people said, 'So be it, so be it, Amen.' And they brought her to the chief priests, and they blessed her saying, 'O God of the heavenly heights, look upon this child and bless her with a supreme blessing which cannot be superseded.' And her mother carried her into the sanctuary of her bedroom and gave her suck. And Anna sang this song to the Lord God:

'I will sing a praise to the Lord my God,
  for he has visited me and removed from me the reproach
    of my enemies.

And the Lord gave me the fruit of his righteousness,
  unique yet manifold before him.
Who will proclaim to the sons of Reuben that Anna gives
  suck?'

And she laid her down to rest in the bedroom of her sanctuary,
and went out and served them. When the feast was ended they
went down rejoicing and glorifying the God of Israel.

7. 1. The months passed, and the child grew. When she was
two years old Joachim said, 'Let us take her up to the temple of
the Lord, so that we may fulfil the promise which we made, lest
the Lord send some evil to us and our gift be unacceptable.'
And Anna replied, 'Let us wait until the third year, that the
child may then no more long for her father and mother.' And
Joachim said, 'Let us wait.' 2. And when the child was three
years old Joachim said, 'Call the undefiled daughters of the
Hebrews, and let each one take a torch, and let these be
burning, in order that the child may not turn back and her
heart be tempted away from the temple of the Lord.' And they
did so until they had gone up to the temple of the Lord. And the
priest took her and kissed her and blessed her, saying, 'The
Lord has magnified your name among all generations; because
of you the Lord at the end of the days will reveal his redemp-
tion to the sons of Israel.' 3. And he placed her on the third
step of the altar, and the Lord God put grace upon her and she
danced with her feet, and the whole house of Israel loved her.

8. 1. And her parents returned marvelling, praising the
Lord God because the child did not turn back. And Mary was
in the temple of the Lord nurtured like a dove and received
food from the hand of an angel.

10. 1. Now there was a council of the priests saying, 'Let us
make a veil for the temple of the Lord.' And the priest said, 'Call
to me pure virgins of the tribe of David.' And the officers
departed and searched and they found seven virgins. And the
priest remembered the child Mary, that she was of the tribe of
David and was pure before God. And the officers went and
fetched her. 2. Then they brought them into the temple of the
Lord and the priest said, 'Cast lots to see who shall weave
the gold, the amiantus, the linen, the silk, the hyacinth-blue,

the scarlet, and the pure purple'. The pure purple and scarlet fell by lot to Mary. And she took them and went home. At that time Zacharias became dumb, and Samuel took his place until Zacharias was able to speak again. Mary took the scarlet and spun it.

11. 1. And she took the pitcher and went out to draw water, and behold, a voice said, 'Hail, highly favoured one, the Lord is with you, you are blessed among women.' And she looked around to the right and to the left to see where this voice came from. And, trembling, she went to her house and put down the pitcher and took the purple and sat down on her seat and drew out the thread. 2. And behold, an angel of the Lord stood before her and said, 'Do not fear, Mary; for you have found grace before the Lord of all things and shall conceive by his Word.' When she heard this she considered it and said, 'Shall I conceive by the Lord, the living God, and bear as every woman bears?' 3. And the angel of the Lord said, 'Not so, Mary; for the power of the Lord shall overshadow you; wherefore that holy one who is born of you shall be called the Son of the Most High. And you shall call his name Jesus; for he shall save his people from their sins.' And Mary said, 'Behold, (I am) the handmaid of the Lord before him: be it to me according to your word.'

12. 1. And she made ready the purple and the scarlet and brought them to the priest. And the priest blessed her and said, 'Mary, the Lord God has magnified your name, and you shall be blessed among all generations of the earth'. 2. And Mary rejoiced and went to Elizabeth her kinswoman and knocked on the door. When Elizabeth heard it, she put down the scarlet and ran to the door and opened it, and when she saw Mary she blessed her and said, 'How is it that the mother of my Lord should come to me? For behold, that which is in me leaped and blessed you.' But Mary forgot the mysteries which the archangel Gabriel had told her, and raised a sigh towards heaven and said, 'Who am I, Lord, that all generations of the earth count me blessed?' 3. And she remained three months with Elizabeth. Day by day her womb grew, and Mary was afraid and went into her house and hid herself from the children of Israel. And Mary was sixteen years old when all these mysterious things happened.

(2) *Arabic Infancy Gospel* 13–15, 27

13. Going out from there, they came to a place where there were robbers who had plundered many men of their baggage and clothes, and had bound them. Then the robbers heard a great noise, like the noise of a magnificent king going out of his city with his army, and his chariots and his drums; and at this the robbers were terrified, and left all that they had stolen. And their captives rose up, loosed each other's bonds, recovered their baggage, and went away. And when they saw Joseph and Mary coming up to the place, they said to them, 'Where is that king? When the robbers heard the magnificent sound of his approach they left us, and we have escaped safe?' Joseph answered them 'He will come behind us.'

14. Then they came into another city, where there was a demoniac woman whom the accursed and rebellious Satan had attacked when she had gone out by night for water. She could neither bear clothes, nor live in a house; and as often as they tied her up with chains and thongs, she broke them, and fled naked into desert places; and, standing in cross-roads and cemeteries, she threw stones at people, and brought great calamities upon her friends. And when the Lady Mary saw her, she pitied her; and immediately Satan left her, and fled away in the form of a young man, saying, 'Woe to me from you, Mary, and from your son.' So that woman was cured of her torment, and being restored to her senses, she blushed on account of her nakedness; and shunning the sight of men, went home to her friends. And after she put on her clothes, she gave an account of the matter to her father and her friends; and as they were the chief men of the city, they received the Lady Mary and Joseph with the greatest honour and hospitality.

15. On the day after, being supplied by them with provision for their journey, they went away, and on the evening of that day arrived at another town, in which a marriage was being celebrated; but, by the arts of accursed Satan and the work of enchanters, the bride had become dumb, and could not speak a word. And after the Lady Mary entered the town, carrying her son the Lord Christ, the dumb bride saw her, and stretched out her hands towards the Lord Christ, and drew him to her, and took him into her arms, and embraced him closely and

kissed him, and leaned over him, rocking his body back and forwards. Immediately the knot of her tongue was loosened, and her ears were opened; and she gave thanks and praise to God, because he had restored her to health. And that night the inhabitants of the town rejoiced, and thought that God and his angels had come down to them.

27. Thereafter, going into the city of Bethlehem, they saw there many and grievous diseases infesting the eyes of the children, who were dying in consequence. And a woman was there with a sick son, whom, being very near to death, she brought to the Lady Mary, who saw him as she was washing Jesus Christ. Then the woman said to her, 'O my Lady Mary, look upon this son of mine, who is suffering with a grievous disease.' And the Lady Mary listened to her, and said, 'Take a little of that water in which I have washed my son, and sprinkle him with it.' She therefore took a little of the water, as the Lady Mary had told her, and sprinkled it over her son. And when this was done his illness abated; and after sleeping a little, he awoke safe and sound. His mother rejoiced at this, and took him again to the Lady Mary. And she said to her, 'Give thanks to God, because he has healed your son.'

(3a) *Homily of Evodius of Rome* VII–XVIII (summary)

VII. On the twenty-first of Tobi Jesus returned, on the chariot of the cherubim, with thousands of angels, and David the sweet singer. We besought him to tell what the great offering was to be, and he told them that it was his mother whom he was to take to himself.

VIII. We all wept, and Peter asked if it was not possible that Mary should never die, and then if she might not be left to them for a few days. But the Lord said that her time was accomplished.

IX. The women, and also Mary, wept, but Jesus consoled her. She said, 'I have heard that Death has many terrible faces. How shall I bear to see them?' He said, 'Why do you fear his divine shape when the Life of all the world is with you?' And he kissed her, and blessed them all, and bade Peter look upon the altar for heavenly garments which the Father had sent to shroud Mary in.

x. Mary arose and was arrayed in the garments, and turned to the east and uttered a prayer in the language of heaven, and then lay down, still facing eastward.

Jesus made us stand for the prayer, and the virgins also who used to minister in the temple and had come to wait on Mary after the Passion. We asked them why they left it. They said, 'When we saw the darkness at the crucifixion we fled into the holy of holies and shut the door. We saw a mighty angel come down with a sword, and he rent the veil in two; and we heard a great voice saying, "Woe to you, Jerusalem, who kill the prophets." The angel of the altar flew up into the canopy of the altar with the angel of the sword; and we knew that God had left his people, and we fled to his mother.'

xi. The virgins stood about Mary singing, and Jesus sat by her. She besought him to save her from the many terrors of the next world—the accusers of Amente, the dragon of the abyss, the river of fire that proves the righteous and the wicked.

xii. He comforted her and said to the apostles, 'Let us withdraw for a little while, for Death cannot approach while I am here.' And they went out, and he sat on a stone and looked up to heaven and groaned and said, 'I have overcome you, O Death, who dwell in the storehouses of the south. Come, appear to my virgin mother but not in a fearful shape.' He appeared, and when she saw him her soul leaped into the bosom of her son—white as snow, and he wrapped it in garments of fine linen and gave it to Michael.

All the women wept; Salome ran to Jesus and said, 'Behold, she whom you love is dead.' David the singer rejoiced and said, 'Very dear in the sight of the Lord is the death of his saints.'

xiii. They re-entered the house and found her lying dead, and Jesus blessed her.

xiv. Jesus shrouded the body in the heavenly garments, and they were fastened to it. He bade the apostles take up the body, Peter bearing the head and John the feet, and carry it to a new tomb in the field of Jehoshaphat, and watch it for three and a half days.

David rejoiced, saying, 'She shall be brought to the king' and, 'Arise, O Lord, into your resting place'.

xv. Jesus ascended with Mary's soul in the chariot of the Cherubim. We took up the body, and when we came to the field of Jehoshaphat, the Jews heard the singing and came out intending to burn the body. But a wall of fire encompassed us, and they were blinded; and the body was laid in the tomb and watched for three and a half days.

xvi. The Jews were in terror and confessed their sin and asked pardon. Their eyes were opened and they sought but did not find the body; and they were amazed, and confessed themselves guilty.

xvii. At midday on the fourth day all were gathered at the tomb. A great voice came, saying, 'Go every one to his place till the seventh month, for I have hardened the heart of the Jews, and they will not be able to find the tomb or the body till I take it up to heaven. Return on the 16th of Mesore.' We returned to the house.

In the seventh month after the death, on the 15th of Mesore, we reassembled at the tomb and spent the night in watching and singing.

xviii. At dawn on the 16th of Mesore, Jesus appeared. Peter said, 'We are grieved that we have not seen your mother since her death.' Jesus said, 'She shall now come.' The chariot of the Cherubim appeared with the Virgin seated in it. There were greetings. Jesus bade the apostles go and preach in all the world. He spent all that day with us and with his mother, and gave us the salutation of peace and went up to heaven in glory.

(3b) Discourse of Saint John the Divine concerning the Falling Asleep of the Holy Mother of God 1–3, 44–50

1. When the all-holy glorious mother of God and ever-virgin Mary, according to her custom, went to the holy sepulchre of our Lord to burn incense, and bowed her holy knees, she besought Christ our God who was born of her to come and abide with her.

2. And when the Jews saw her resorting to the holy sepulchre they came to the chief priests saying, 'Mary goes every day to the sepulchre.' And the chief priests called the

watchmen who were charged by them not to allow anybody to pray at the holy sepulchre, and enquired of them if it were so in truth. But the watch answered and said that they saw no such thing; for God did not allow them to see her venerable presence.

3. Now on one day, which was Friday, the holy Mary came as usual to the sepulchre, and as she prayed the heavens were opened and the archangel Gabriel came down to her and said, 'Hail, you who bore Christ our God; your prayer has passed through the heavens to him who was born of you and has been accepted, and henceforth according to your petition you shall leave the world and come to the heavenly places to your Son, to the true life that has no successor.'

44. And the Lord turned and said to Peter, 'The time has come to begin the song of praise.' And when Peter began the song of praise, all the powers of the heavens answered 'Alleluia.' And then the countenance of the mother of the Lord shone above the light. And she rose up and with her own hand blessed every one of the apostles, and all of them gave glory to God; and the Lord spread forth his unstained hands and received her holy and spotless soul. 45. And at the going forth of her spotless soul the place was filled with sweet odour and light unspeakable, and lo, a voice from heaven was heard, saying, 'Blessed are you among women.' And Peter ran, and I, John, and Paul, and Thomas, and embraced her precious feet to receive sanctification; and the twelve apostles laid her honourable and holy body upon a bed and carried it out.

46. And behold, as they carried her, a certain Hebrew named Jephonias, mighty of body, ran forth and attacked the bed as the apostles carried it, and lo, an angel of the Lord with invisible power struck his two hands from off his shoulders with a sword of fire and left them hanging in the air beside the bed. 47. And when this miracle came to pass, all the people of the Jews who beheld it cried out, 'Verily he is the true God who was born of you, Mary, mother of God, ever-virgin.' And Jephonias himself, being commanded by Peter that the wonderful works of God might be shown, stood up behind the bed and cried, 'Holy Mary, who bore Christ who is God, have mercy on me.' And Peter turned and said to him, 'In the name

of him who was born of her your hands which were taken from you shall be joined back on.' And immediately at the word of Peter the hands that were hanging beside the bed of our lady went back and joined Jephonias; and he also believed and glorified Christ, the God, who was born of her.

48. And after this miracle the apostles carried the bed and laid her precious and holy body in Gethsemane in a new tomb. And lo, an odour of sweet savour came out of the holy sepulchre of our lady the mother of God: and until three days were past the voices of invisible angels were heard glorifying Christ our God who was born of her. And when the third day was fulfilled the voices were no more heard, and thereafter we all perceived that her spotless and precious body was translated into paradise.

49. Now after it was translated, lo, we beheld Elizabeth, the mother of the holy John the Baptist, and Anna the mother of our lady, and Abraham and Isaac and Jacob, and David singing 'Alleluia', and all the choirs of the saints worshipping the precious body of the mother of the Lord, and we saw a place of light, than which light nothing is brighter, and a great fragrance came from that place to which her precious and holy body was translated in paradise, and a melody of those who praised him who was born of her; and to virgins only is it given to hear that sweet melody wherewith no man can be sated.

50. We, therefore, the apostles, while we beheld the sudden translation of her holy body, glorified God who had shown to us his wonders at the departure of the mother of our Lord Jesus Christ, by the prayer and intercession of whom may we all be accounted worthy to come into her protection and succour and guardianship, both in this world and in that which is to come; at all times and in all places glorifying her only-begotten Son, with the Father and the Holy Ghost, world without end. Amen.

(b) JOSEPH

The Biblical references to Joseph in the birth narratives are minimal. In Matthew's Gospel Joseph is the recipient of a dream conveying the message that Mary is pregnant; in another dream he learns of King Herod the Great's plot to have Jesus killed. In Luke's account Joseph's role is even more passive; there it is Mary herself who learns of her conception. In neither Gospel does Joseph figure outside these opening chapters. This dearth of information about Joseph was tantalizing for Christians curious about Jesus' family.

It is, therefore, not surprising to see that the apocryphal writings enhance Joseph's role and tell us more about his background. In the Protevangelium of James he is introduced as an old widower with grown-up children from his first marriage. Those children appear in the apocryphal Gospels. Such background information was clearly of apologetic benefit for those needing to preach Mary's perpetual virginity and to explain the relationship of those called Jesus' brothers and sisters in the New Testament to Jesus himself. One explanation that satisfied some in the early church was to say, as the Protevangelium does, that these siblings were Jesus' half-brothers and half-sisters.

In the Protevangelium Joseph is elected as the ward of the 12-year-old Mary by the priests, who up to that time had maintained her in the Temple. He reluctantly accepts the wardship. Joseph in this story is no mere carpenter but a wealthy contractor. Having returned from a sojourn inspecting his building works, he finds his charge pregnant. To exonerate himself from culpability in the eyes of the priests Joseph submits himself to a 'trial of bitter water'. Mary, to avoid shame, does likewise. This story of the truth-revealing drink administered by the priests is bizarre, but the intention and the effect of it is to prove the parents' honesty. This test is portrayed in various artistic representations, including decorations on a splendid fourth-century sarcophagus in Ravenna. Extracts from Joseph's story are given below (1).

Other incidents involving Joseph are found in Chapter 1 'The Birth of Jesus'.

Stories of the deaths of various Biblical characters are commonplace in the apocryphal tradition. As far as Joseph is concerned, his death is retailed at length in the fourth–fifth-century History of Joseph the Carpenter, extracts from which are given below (2). The whole narrative is put into Jesus' mouth. Much of the narrative concerns Jesus' report of the dying days of Joseph and the subsequent mourning. In some parts of Christendom Joseph, as well as being the patron saint of workers, is venerated as the patron of good death.

(1) *Protevangelium of James* 8–9, 13–16

8. 2. When she was twelve years old, there took place a council of the priests saying, 'Behold, Mary has become twelve years old in the temple of the Lord. What then shall we do with her lest she defile the temple of the Lord?' And they said to the high priest, 'You stand at the altar of the Lord; enter the sanctuary and pray concerning her, and that which the Lord shall reveal to you we will indeed do.' 3. And the high priest took the vestment with the twelve bells and went into the Holy of Holies and prayed concerning her. And behold, an angel of the Lord appeared and said to him, 'Zacharias, Zacharias, go out and assemble the widowers of the people, and to whomsoever the Lord shall give a sign she shall be a wife.' And the heralds went forth through all the country round about Judaea; the trumpet of the Lord sounded, and all came running.

9. 1. And Joseph threw down his adze and went out to their meeting. And when they were gathered together, they took the rods and went to the high priest. He took the rods from them all, entered the temple, and prayed. When he had finished the prayer he took the rods, and went out and gave them to them; but there was no sign on them. Joseph received the last rod, and behold, a dove came out of the rod and flew on to Joseph's head. And the priest said to Joseph, 'You have been chosen by lot to receive the virgin of the Lord as your ward.' 2. But Joseph answered him, 'I have sons and am old; she is but a girl. I object lest I should become a laughing-stock to the sons of Israel.' And the priest said to Joseph, 'Fear the Lord your God, and remember what God did to Dathan, Abiram, and Korah, how the earth was split in two and they were all swallowed up because of their rebellion. And now beware, Joseph, lest these things happen in your house too.' And Joseph was afraid and received her as his ward. And Joseph said to Mary, 'I have received you from the temple of the Lord, and now I leave you in my house and go away to build my buildings. I will return to you; the Lord will guard you.'

13. 1. Now when she was in her sixth month, behold, Joseph came from his buildings and entered his house and found her with child. And he struck his face, threw himself down on the ground on sackcloth and wept bitterly saying, 'With what countenance shall I look towards the Lord my God? What prayer shall I offer for this maiden? For I received her as a virgin out of the temple of the Lord my God and have not protected her. Who has deceived me? Who has done this evil in my house and defiled the virgin? Has the story of Adam been repeated in me? For as Adam was absent in the hour of his prayer and the serpent came and found Eve alone and deceived her, so also has it happened to me.' 2. And Joseph arose from the sackcloth and called Mary and said to her, 'You who are cared for by God, why have you done this and forgotten the Lord your God? Why have you humiliated your soul, you who were brought up in the Holy of Holies and received food from the hand of an angel?' 3. But she wept bitterly, saying, 'I am pure, and know not a man.' And Joseph said to her, 'Whence is this in your womb?' And she said, 'As the Lord my God lives, I do not know whence it has come to me.'

14. 1. And Joseph feared greatly and parted from her, pondering what he should do with her. And Joseph said, 'If I conceal her sin, I shall be found to be in opposition to the law of the Lord. If I expose her to the children of Israel, I fear lest that which is in her may be from the angels and I should be found delivering innocent blood to the judgement of death. What then shall I do with her? I will put her away secretly.' And the night came upon him. 2. And behold, an angel of the Lord appeared to him in a dream, saying, 'Do not fear this child. For that which is in her is of the Holy Spirit. She shall bear a son, and you shall call his name Jesus; for he shall save his people from their sins.' And Joseph arose from sleep and glorified the God of Israel who had bestowed his grace upon him, and he guarded her.

15. 1. And Annas the scribe came to him and said to him, 'Joseph, why have you not appeared in our assembly?' And Joseph said to him, 'Because I was weary from the journey and I rested the first day.' And Annas turned and saw that Mary was pregnant. 2. And he went running to the priest and said to him, 'Joseph, for whom you are a witness, has grievously transgressed.' And the high priest said, 'In what way?' And he said, 'The virgin, whom he received from the temple of the Lord, he has defiled, and has secretly consummated his marriage with her, and has not disclosed it to the children of Israel.' And the priest said to him, 'Has Joseph done this?' And Annas said to him, 'Send officers, and you will find the virgin pregnant.' And the officers went and found as he had said, and brought her and Joseph to the court. And the priest said, 'Mary, why have you done this? Why have you humiliated your soul and forgotten the Lord your God, you who were brought up in the Holy of Holies and received food from the hand of an angel, and heard hymns, and danced before him? Why have you done this?' But she wept bitterly saying, 'As the Lord my God lives, I am pure before him and I know not a man.' And the priest said to Joseph, 'Why have you done this?' And Joseph said, 'As the Lord my God lives, I am pure concerning her.' And the priest said, 'Do not give false witness, but speak the truth. You have consummated your marriage in secret, and have not disclosed it to the children of Israel, and have not bowed your head under the mighty hand in order that your seed might be blessed.' And Joseph was silent.

16. 1. And the priest said, 'Give back the virgin whom you have received from the temple of the Lord.' And Joseph began to weep. And the priest said, 'I will give you both to drink the water of the conviction of the Lord, and it will make your sins manifest in your eyes.' 2. And the priest took it and gave it to Joseph to drink and sent him into the hill-country, and he returned whole. And he made Mary drink also, and sent her into the hill-country, and she returned whole. And all the people marvelled, because sin did not appear in them. And the priest said, 'If the Lord God has not revealed your sins, neither do I judge you.' And he released them. And Joseph took Mary and departed to his house, rejoicing and glorifying the God of Israel.

(2) *History of Joseph the Carpenter* 10, 11, 17, 23

10. At length, by increasing years, the old man arrived at an advanced age. He did not, however, labour under any bodily weakness, nor had his sight failed, nor had any tooth perished from his mouth nor, for the whole time of his life, was he ever

insane; but like a boy he always showed youthful vigour in his business and his limbs remained unimpaired, and free from all pain. His life, then, in total, amounted to one hundred and eleven years, his old age being prolonged to the utmost limit.

11. Now Justus and Simeon, the elder sons of Joseph, were married and had families of their own. Both the daughters were likewise married and lived in their own houses. So there remained in Joseph's house Judas and James the Less, and my virgin mother. I [= Jesus] also lived with them, just as if I had been one of his sons. I passed all my life without fault. I called Mary my mother, and Joseph father, and I obeyed them in all that they said; nor did I ever resist them, but complied with their commands, just as other men whom earth produces are wont to do; nor did I at any time arouse their anger, or give any word or answer in opposition to them. On the contrary, I cherished them with great love, like the apple of my eye.

17. I now went in beside him and found his soul exceedingly troubled, for he was in great anguish. And I said to him, 'Hail! my father Joseph, you righteous man; how are you?' And he answered me, 'All hail! my well-beloved son. Indeed, the agony and fear of death have already surrounded me; but as soon as I heard your voice my soul was at rest. O Jesus of Nazareth! Jesus, my Saviour! Jesus, the deliverer of my soul! Jesus, my protector! Jesus! O sweetest name in my mouth, and in the mouth of all those that love it! O eye which sees, and ear which hears, hear me! I am your servant; this day I most humbly venerate you, and before your face I pour out my tears. You are my God; you are my Lord, as the angel has told me on many occasions, and especially on that day when my soul was tossed about with perverse thoughts about the pure and blessed Mary, who was carrying you in her womb, and whom I was thinking of secretly sending away. And while I was thus meditating, behold, there appeared to me in my sleep angels of the Lord, in a wonderful mystery, saying to me, "O Joseph, son of David, fear not to take Mary as your wife; and do not grieve, nor speak unbecoming words of her conception, because she is with child of the Holy Spirit, and shall bring forth a son, whose name shall be called Jesus, for he shall save his people from their sins." Do not for this cause wish me evil, O Lord! for I was

ignorant of the mystery of your birth. I call to mind also, my Lord, that day when the boy died of the bite of the serpent. And his relations wished to deliver you to Herod, saying that you had killed him; but you raised him from the dead, and restored him to them. Then I went up to you, and took hold of your hand, saying, "My son, take care of yourself." But you said to me in reply, "Are you not my father after the flesh? I shall teach you who I am." Now therefore, O Lord and my God, do not be angry with me, or condemn me on account of that hour. I am your servant, and the son of your handmaiden; but you are my Lord, my God and Saviour, most surely the Son of God.'

23. Therefore Michael and Gabriel came to the soul of my father Joseph, and took it, and wrapped it in a shining cloth. Thus he committed his spirit into the hands of my good Father, and he bestowed upon him peace. But as yet none of his children knew that he had fallen asleep. And the angels preserved his soul from the demons of darkness which were in the way, and praised God until they conducted it into the dwelling-place of the pious.

4

The Ministry of Jesus

❖

The bulk of the four canonical Gospels is concerned with the period of Jesus' public ministry from his baptism to his death. These New Testament Gospels are full of the teachings, miracles, and travels of Jesus. By contrast, the post-Biblical traditions seem to have been less interested in amplifying or supplementing such material.

Nevertheless, several apocryphal texts do concern themselves with the period of Jesus' earthly ministry. We find in them sayings and miracles. Some of these are related to the material in the canonical New Testament, but many are quite new and different. Even those sayings close to the New Testament are usually not identical in content or language, and this suggests a degree of independence.

This chapter is divided into five sections: (*a*) stories about Jesus' ministry from apocryphal Gospels; (*b*) isolated sayings attributed to Jesus; (*c*) accounts of Jesus' physical appearance; (*d*) stories about Jesus from the apocryphal Acts; (*e*) a letter from Jesus.

(*a*) STORIES ABOUT JESUS' MINISTRY

The existence of additional stories and 'secret sayings' (to use this conventional, but erroneous, description) need not surprise us. The New Testament authors themselves did not claim to give a complete record of everything that Jesus did and said. The Gospel writers made a selection of the material available to them in the oral tradition or in earlier written accounts (see for instance John 20: 30–1). Some sayings of Jesus are known to us outside the Gospels in Acts 20: 35, or in Paul's letters (for example 1 Corinthians 7: 10; 9: 14; 1 Thessalonians 4: 15 ff.). It may well be that some of the sayings or stories of Jesus known to us from later accounts—the writings of a church father or, as here, in the apocryphal texts—may be as authentic and as 'historic' as those in the New Testament itself. Some modern scholars are even prepared to argue for a first-century origin of some of the following apocryphal stories and sayings. The Epilogue, at the end of this book, returns to this issue.

Three selections of stories are given. The first extract (1) is from an incomplete, one-page, fragment, originally part of a miniature book. It was discovered in 1905 during archaeological excavations at Oxyrhynchus (a city in Middle Egypt that flourished in the Roman Empire and which is now part of the modern town of Behnesa). The manuscript is now known as Oxyrhynchus Papyrus number 840. Most scholars date it third century, although the text it preserves may of course be much older.

The fragments, from which the extracts following (2) have been deciphered, come from a papyrus book, dated by the experts *c.* AD 150. They are housed in the British Library, where they are classified as Egerton Papyrus number 2. This dating makes it (together with the tiny fragment of John's Gospel in Manchester) the oldest Christian writing extant.

The third text contains a strange tale which comes from the so-called Secret Gospel of Mark, for which some recent writers have made great claims, stating that this 'secret' Gospel was originally a larger and earlier version of our canonical Mark. Knowledge of this 'secret' Gospel comes only from one source—a letter, purporting to be by the second–third-century Christian writer Clement of Alexandria, and found written on the endpapers of a seventeenth-century printed book recently discovered in Mar Saba monastery near Jerusalem. It is an extract from that letter which I reproduce here (3).

(1) *Oxyrhynchus Papyrus 840*

Then he took them with him and brought them into the place of purification itself, and was walking in the temple. A Pharisee, a chief priest named Levi, met them and said to the Saviour, 'Who gave you permission to walk in this place of purification and look upon these holy vessels when you have not bathed and your disciples have not washed their feet? But you have walked in this temple in a state of defilement, whereas no one else comes in or dares to view these holy vessels without having bathed and changed his clothes.' Thereupon the Saviour stood with his disciples and answered him. 'Are you then clean, here in the temple as you are?' He said, 'I am clean, for I have bathed in the pool of David and have gone down by one staircase and come up by the other, and I have put on clean white clothes. Then I came and viewed the holy vessels.' 'Alas,' said the Saviour, 'you blind men who cannot see! You have washed in this running water, in which dogs and pigs have wallowed night and day, and you have washed and scrubbed your outer skin, which harlots and flute-girls also anoint and wash and scrub, beautifying themselves for the lusts of men while inwardly they are filled with scorpions and unrighteousness of every kind. But my disciples and I, whom you charge with not having bathed, have bathed ourselves in the living water which comes down from heaven.'

(2) *Egerton Papyrus 2*

And Jesus said to the lawyers, 'Punish every wrong-doer and transgressor, and not me . . . what he does as he does it.' Then, turning to the rulers of the people, he spoke this word, 'Search the scriptures, in which you think you have life; it is they which bear witness to me. Do not think that I have come to accuse you to my Father; your accuser is Moses, on whom you have set your hope.' When they said, 'We know well that God spoke to Moses; but as for you, we do not know where you come from.' Jesus said in reply, 'Now your unbelief is exposed to the one who was witnessed to by him. If you had believed [in Moses] you would have believed me, because he wrote to your fathers about me . . .'

The rulers sought to lay their hands on him in order to arrest him and hand him over to the crowd; but they could not arrest him, because the hour of his betrayal had not yet come. The Lord himself, passing out through their midst, escaped from them.

And behold, a leper approached him and said, 'Teacher Jesus, while journeying with lepers and eating with them in the inn, I myself also became a leper. If, therefore, you are willing, I am cleansed.' The Lord said to him, 'I am willing: be cleansed.' And immediately the leprosy departed from him, and the Lord said, 'Go, show yourself to the priests and make an offering for your cleansing as Moses commanded, and sin no more . . .'

. . . came to him to tempt him, saying, 'Teacher Jesus, we know that you have come from God, for the things which you do bear witness beyond all the prophets. Tell us then: Is it lawful to render to kings what pertains to their rule? Shall we render it to them or not?' But Jesus, knowing their mind, said to them in indignation, 'Why do you call me teacher with your mouth, when you do not do what I say? Well did Isaiah prophesy of you when he said: This people honours me with its lips, but their heart is far from me; in vain do they worship me, teaching as doctrines merely human commandments.'

(3) *Secret Gospel of Mark*

And they came to Bethany, and there was a woman there whose brother had died. She came and prostrated herself before Jesus and said to him, 'Son of David, pity me.' The disciples rebuked her, and Jesus in anger set out with her for the garden where the tomb was. Immediately a loud voice was heard from the tomb, and Jesus approached and rolled the stone away from the entrance to the tomb. And going in immediately where the young man was he stretched out his hand and raised him up, taking him by the hand. The young man looked on him and loved him, and began to beseech him that he might be with him. They came out of the tomb and went into the young man's house, for he was rich. After six days Jesus laid a charge upon him, and when evening came the young man came to him, with a linen robe thrown over his naked body; and he stayed with him that night, for Jesus was teaching him the mystery of the kingdom of God. When he departed thence, he returned to the other side of the Jordan.

(b) 'SECRET' SAYINGS OF JESUS

There are many isolated sayings attributed to Jesus in various sources, in the works of the church fathers, in apocryphal texts, or in Biblical manuscripts. Discussion about their historical value and theological character has spawned a vast secondary literature. The largest single collection (over one hundred sayings) is in the Coptic Gospel of Thomas, discovered in 1945 in Nag Hammadi, a site near the village of al-Qasr (ancient Chenoboskion) in Upper Egypt. Some of the sayings of Jesus in this Gospel of Thomas are new, others closely parallel similar sayings in Matthew and Luke. Several seem to be Gnostic,[1] a multifaceted heresy which plagued the orthodox Christians of the second–third centuries. (In Gnostic teachings the creator God was distinct from the supreme Divine Being; and man, through *gnosis* 'knowledge', sought to aspire to that Being.) My small selection below contains some of the better known sayings.

(1) Found after Luke 6: 4 in the New Testament manuscript Codex Bezae Cantabrigiensis:

The same day, seeing a certain man working on the sabbath, he said to him, 'Man, if indeed you know what you are doing, happy are you; but if not, you are accursed and a transgressor of the law.'

(2) Quoted by Clement of Alexandria as a saying by Jesus: 'Be competent money-changers.'

(3) *Gospel of Thomas* 15, 18, 19, 27, 28, 49–53

15. Jesus said, 'When you see him who was not born of woman, prostrate yourselves on your faces and worship him: that one is your father.'

18. The disciples said to Jesus, 'Tell us in which way our end will occur.' Jesus said, 'Have you indeed discovered the

---

[1] There are many thoroughgoing Gnostic texts, some of them concerning Jesus and his pronouncements. In general, Gnostic literature is not included within collections of New Testament apocryphal writings. A convenient place to read much of it is J. M. Robinson, *The Nag Hammadi Library in English* (Leiden: Brill, 3rd edn. 1988).

beginning, that you search for the end? In the place where the beginning is, there the end will be. Blessed is he who will stand at the beginning: he will know the end and he will not taste death.'

19. Jesus said, 'Blessed is he who existed before he was created. If you become my disciples and you hear my words, these stones shall serve you. For you have five trees in paradise which do not move in summer or winter and their leaves do not fall. Whoever knows them shall not taste death.'

27. [Jesus said], 'If you do not fast with respect to the world, you will not find the Kingdom; if you do not keep the Sabbath as Sabbath, you will not see the Father.'

28. Jesus said, 'I stood in the midst of the world, and I appeared to them in the flesh. I found all of them drunk; I did not find any of them thirsting. And my soul was pained for the sons of men because they are blind in their heart, and they do not see that they came empty into the world; they seek to go empty out of the world. Now they are drunk. When they have shaken off their wine, then they will repent.'

49. Jesus said, 'Blessed are the solitary and the chosen for you will find the kingdom. Because you have come from it you will go there again.'

50. Jesus said, 'If they say to you, "Where did you come from?", say to them, "We have come from the light, the place where the light came into existence alone of its own accord and revealed itself in their image." If they say to you, "Who are you?", say to them, "We are his sons and we are the chosen of the living Father." If they ask you, "What is the sign of your Father who is in you?", say to them, "It is a movement and a repose."'

51. His disciples said to him, 'On what day will the repose of the dead occur and when does the new world come?' He said to them, 'That repose you look for has come, but you have not recognized it.'

52. His disciples said to him, 'Twenty-four prophets spoke in Israel and all of them spoke in you.' He said to them, 'You have neglected the Living One in your presence and you have spoken only about the dead.'

53. His disciples said to him, 'Is circumcision profitable or not?' He said to them, 'If it were profitable, their father would beget them already circumcised from their mother. Rather true circumcision in the Spirit has become completely useful.'

(c) JESUS' PHYSICAL APPEARANCE

It is noteworthy that the period of Jesus' ministry did not seem to attract the same level of apocryphal literary activity as, say, his childhood and death. Nevertheless, curiosity about Jesus' career resulted in descriptions of his physical appearance.

The first extracts (1) come from the second-century Acts of John. It may be thought that the descriptions here reflect heretical, Docetic, teachings about the nature of Jesus' body, but they could parallel the Biblical accounts of Jesus' Transfiguration during his ministry, or those post-Easter accounts in which Jesus is described as having passed through closed doors or having left the sealed tomb.

The polymorphous nature of Christ, encountered in these extracts, is a recurring theme in the apocrypha. Bizarre as the images may strike modern readers, they need not be unorthodox, but merely be attempts to dramatize the belief that Jesus, particularly in his role as risen Lord, is all-pervasive and ever-present. Jesus in the guise of a gardener at the end of John's Gospel could provide a Biblical precedent for this kind of portrayal.

The second, more conventional, portrayal of Jesus (extract 2) comes from the medieval Letter of Lentulus. The description here is likely to reflect, and itself to have influenced, Christian iconography.

(1) Acts of John 88–9, 93

(88.) 'For when he had chosen Peter and Andrew, who were brothers, he came to me and to my brother James, saying, "I have need of you, come unto me." And my brother said, "John, this child on the shore who called to us, what does he want?" And I said, "What child?" He replied, "The one who is beckoning to us." And I answered, "Because of our long watch that we

kept at sea you are not seeing straight, brother James: but do
you not see the man who stands there, fair and comely and of
a cheerful countenance?" But he said to me, "Him I do not see,
brother; but let us go and we shall see what it means." And so
when we had landed the ship, we saw him helping us to beach
the ship.

89. 'And when we left the place, wishing to follow him again,
he again appeared to me, bald-headed but with a thick and
flowing beard; but to James he appeared as a youth whose
beard was just starting. We were perplexed, both of us, as to
the meaning of what we had seen. But when we followed him,
we both became gradually more perplexed as we thought on
the matter. Yet to me there appeared a still more wonderful
sight; for I tried to see him as he was, and I never at any time
saw his eyes closing but only open. And sometimes he appeared to me as a small man and unattractive, and then again
as one reaching to heaven. Also there was in him another
marvel; when I sat at table he would take me upon his breast
and I held him; and sometimes his breast felt to me to be
smooth and tender, and sometimes hard, like stone, so that I
was perplexed in myself and said, "What does this mean?"

93. 'Another glory I will tell you, brethren. Sometimes when I
meant to touch him, I met a material and solid body; and at
other times again when I felt him, the substance was imma-
terial and bodiless and as if it were not existing at all.'

(2) *Letter of Lentulus*

In these days there appeared, and there still is, a man of great
power named Jesus Christ, who is called by the Gentiles the
prophet of truth, whom his disciples call the Son of God,
raising the dead and healing diseases—a man in stature mid-
dling tall, and comely, having a reverend countenance, which
those who look upon may love and fear; having hair of the hue
of an unripe hazel-nut and smooth almost down to his ears,
but from the ears in curling locks somewhat darker and more
shining, flowing over his shoulders; having a parting at the
middle of the head according to the fashion of the Nazareans;
a brow smooth and very calm, with a face without wrinkle or

any blemish, which a moderate red colour makes beautiful; with the nose and mouth no fault at all can be found; having a full beard of the colour of his hair, not long, but a little forked at the chin; having an expression simple and mature, the eyes grey, flashing, and clear; in rebuke terrible, in admonition kind and lovable, cheerful yet keeping gravity; sometimes he has wept, but never laughed; in stature of body tall and straight, with hands and arms fair to look upon; in talk grave, reserved and modest, fairer than the children of men.

(d) OTHER STORIES ABOUT JESUS' MINISTRY

Two further, significant, apocryphal stories about Jesus come not from a Gospel-type book but, again, from the Acts of John. The extracts are from a section of these Acts in which John is reminiscing about his contact with Jesus during the ministry. The first extract (1) gives an account of the Transfiguration, different from that in the New Testament. The second extract (2) contains the dance of Christ; this was set to music by Gustav Holst as a choral work under the title 'The Hymn of Jesus'. After the dance is a speech which is Docetic in character, apparently denying the corporeality of Jesus and implying that the body being crucified was merely a phantom.

(1) *Acts of John* 90–1

90. 'At another time he took me and James and Peter to the mountain, where he used to pray, and we beheld such a light on him that it is not possible for a man who uses mortal speech to describe what it was like. Again in a similar way he led us three up to the mountain saying, "Come with me." And we went again and saw him at a distance praying. Now I, because he loved me, went to him quietly as though he should not see, and stood looking upon his back. And I saw that he was not dressed in garments, but was seen by us as naked and not at all like a man; his feet were whiter than snow, so that the ground there was lit up by his feet, and his head reached to heaven; so that I was afraid and cried out, and he turned and appeared as a man of small stature, and took hold of my beard and pulled

it and said to me, "John, be not unbelieving, but believing, and not inquisitive." And I said to him, "What have I done, Lord?" And I tell you brethren, I suffered such pain for thirty days at the place where he took hold of my beard, that I said unto him, "Lord, if your playful tug has given me so much pain, what if you had given me a beating?" And he said to me, "Let it be your concern from henceforth not to tempt him who is not to be tempted."

91. 'But Peter and James were angry because I spoke with the Lord and beckoned me to come to them and leave the Lord alone. And I went, and they both said to me, "Who was speaking to the Lord when he was on top of the mountain, for we heard both of them speaking?" And I, when I considered his great grace and his unity which has many faces, and his wisdom which without ceasing looked upon us, said, "This you shall learn if you ask him."'

(2) *Acts of John* 94–102

94. 'Now, before he was arrested by the lawless Jews, who received their law from a lawless serpent, he gathered us all together and said, "Before I am delivered up to them, let us sing a hymn to the Father, and go forth to what lies before us." So he commanded us to make a circle, holding one another's hands, and he himself stood in the middle. He said, "Respond Amen to me." He then began to sing a hymn, and to say:

"Glory be to you, Father!"

And we circling him said, "Amen".

"Glory be to you, Word! Glory be to you, Grace!" "Amen."
"Glory be to you, Spirit! Glory be to you, Holy One! Glory be to the glory!" "Amen."
"We praise you, O Father. We give thanks to you, light, in whom darkness does not abide." "Amen."
95. "Now we give thanks, I say:
I will be saved, and I will save." "Amen."
"I will be loosed, and I will loose." "Amen."
"I will be pierced, and I will pierce." "Amen."
"I will be born, and I will bear." "Amen."

"I will eat, and I will be eaten." "Amen."
"I will hear, and I will be heard." "Amen."
"I will be understood, being wholly understanding."
  "Amen."
"I will be washed, and I will wash." "Amen."

Grace is dancing.

"I will pipe, dance all of you!" "Amen."
"I will mourn, lament all of you!" "Amen."
"An Ogdoad is singing with us." "Amen."
"The Twelfth number is dancing above." "Amen."
"The whole universe takes part in the dancing." "Amen."
"He who does not dance, does not know what is being
  done." "Amen."
"I will flee and I will stay." "Amen."
"I will adorn, and I will be adorned." "Amen."
"I will be united, and I will unite." "Amen."
"I have no house, and I have houses." "Amen."
"I have no place, and I have places." "Amen."
"I have no temple, and I have temples." "Amen."
"I am a lamp to you who see me." "Amen."
"I am a mirror to you who perceive." "Amen."
"I am a door to you who knock on me." "Amen."
"I am a way to you, wayfarer." "Amen."

96. ' "Now if you respond to my dancing, see yourself in me
who speak; and when you have seen what I do, keep silence
about my mysteries! You who dance, perceive what I do; for
yours is this passion of mankind which I am to suffer! For you
could not at all have comprehended what you suffer if I had
not been sent to you as the Word by the Father. When you saw
what I suffer, you have seen me as one suffering; and seeing
that, you have not stood firm but were wholly moved. Moved to
become wise, you have me for a support. Rest upon me! Who
am I? You shall know when I go away. What I am now seen to
be, that I am not. You shall see when you come. If you knew
how to suffer, you would have had the power not to suffer.
Learn suffering, and you shall have the power not to suffer.
That which you do not know, I will teach you. I am your God,
not that of the betrayer. I will that there be prepared holy souls
for me. Know the word of wisdom! Say again with me:

Glory be to you, Father; glory be to you, Word;
Glory be to you, Holy Ghost!

Now concerning me, if you would know what I was: with a
word I once deceived all things, and was not put to shame at
all. I have leaped; but understand the whole, and having understood it say, "Glory be to you, Father!" "Amen."

97. 'After this dance, my beloved, the Lord went out; and we
were as men gone astray or dazed with sleep, and we fled all
ways. Even I, when I saw him suffer, did not abide at his
passion but fled to the Mount of Olives, weeping over what had
taken place. And when he was hung upon the cross on Friday,
at the sixth hour of the day, there came darkness over all the
earth. And my Lord stood in the middle of the cave and lit it up,
and said, "John, to the multitude down below in Jerusalem I
am being crucified, and pierced with lances and reeds, and gall
and vinegar is given me to drink. But to you I am speaking, and
pay attention to what I say. I put it into your mind to come up
to this mountain, so that you might hear matters needful for a
disciple to learn from his teacher, and for a man to learn from
his God."

98. 'And having said this, he showed me a cross of light set
up, and around the cross a great multitude which had no one
form; and in the cross was one form and one likeness. And the
Lord himself I beheld above the cross, not having a shape, but
only a voice, and a voice not such as was familiar to us, but a
sweet and kind voice and one truly divine, and it said to me, "It
is necessary that one man should hear these things from me, O
John, for I have need of someone who will hear. This cross of
light is sometimes called the Word by me for your sakes,
sometimes Mind, sometimes Jesus, sometimes Christ, some-
times Door, sometimes Way, sometimes Bread, sometimes
Seed, sometimes Resurrection, sometimes Son, sometimes
Father, sometimes Spirit, sometimes Life, sometimes Truth,
sometimes Faith, sometimes Grace. Thus it is called for man's
sake. But in truth, as known in itself and as spoken to us, it is
the marking off of all things and the uplifting and foundation
of those things that are fixed but had been unstable, and the
harmony of the wisdom and indeed the wisdom of the harmony. But there are on the right and on the left, powers,

principalities, dominions and demons, operations, threatenings, wrath, devils, Satan and the inferior root, from which the nature of the transient things proceeded.

99. ' "This, then, is the cross which has united all things by the Word, and marked off things transient and inferior, and then compacted all into one. But this is not the cross of wood which you will see when you go down here, neither am I he who is upon the cross, whom now you do not see, but only hear a voice. I was reckoned to be what I am not, not being what I was to many others; but they will call me something else, which is vile and not worthy of me. Therefore, just as the place of rest is neither seen nor spoken of, much less shall I, the Lord of this place, be seen or spoken of.

100. ' "Now the multitude about the cross which is the lower nature is not of one form; and those whom you see in the cross, do not have one form. That is because every member of him who came down has not yet been gathered together. But when the nature of man shall be taken up, and the race which comes to me in obedience to my voice, then he who now hears me shall be united with it and shall no longer be what it now is, but shall be above them, as I am now. For as long as you do not call yourself mine, I am not that which I was. But if you hear and hearken to me, then you shall be as I am, and shall be what I was, when I have you with myself. For from this you are. Therefore, ignore the many, and despise those who are outside the mystery! Know that I am wholly with the Father, and the Father with me.

101. ' "Therefore I have suffered none of the things which they will say of me: that suffering which I showed to you and to the rest in dance, I wish it to be called a mystery. For what you are, you see that I showed you; but what I am, that I alone know, and no one else. Let me, therefore, keep that which is my own, and that which is yours you must see through me. As for seeing me as I am in reality, I have told you this is impossible unless you are able to see me as my kinsman. You hear that I suffered, yet I suffered not; that I suffered not, yet I did suffer; that I was pierced, yet was I not wounded; hanged, and I was not hanged; that blood flowed from me, yet it did not flow; and, in a word, those things that they say of me I did not endure, and the things that they do not say those I suffered.

Now what they are I will reveal to you for I know you will understand. Perceive in me the slaying of the Logos, the piercing of the Logos, the blood of the Logos, the wounding of the Logos, the hanging of the Logos, the passion of the Logos, the nailing of the Logos, the death of the Logos. And thus I speak, discarding manhood. Therefore, in the first place think of the Logos, then you shall perceive the Lord, and thirdly the man, and what he has suffered."

102. 'When he had spoken to me these things and others which I know not how to say as he would have me, he was taken up, without any of the multitude having seen him. And when I went down, I laughed them all to scorn, inasmuch as he had told me the things which they said about him; and I held firmly this one thing in my mind, that the Lord contrived all things symbolically and as a dispensation toward men, for their conversion and salvation.'

(e) A LETTER FROM JESUS

One curiosity among New Testament apocrypha is a letter allegedly written by Jesus during his ministry in response to a request made by King Abgar of Edessa that he should visit the King to cure a malady. The letter, in Greek, is contained in Eusebius' *Church History* and represents the only example of a text written in Jesus' name: such vehicles for Jesus' direct communications were not made use of in the apocryphal tradition. The story concludes with Thomas' sending Thaddaeus to visit Edessa after Jesus' Resurrection to effect the King's cure. This second-century legend seems to have had wide currency; versions of it also exist in Latin, Syriac, and other languages.

Jesus' letter is as follows:

Copy of the things written by Jesus by the hand of Ananias the courier to Abgar the Toparch

You are blessed; you believe in me, and you have not seen me. It is written concerning me, 'Those who have seen me will not believe in me', and 'Those who have not seen me will believe and will be saved.' Regarding what you wrote to me that I should come to you, I have to complete here everything I was sent to do and, after I have accomplished it, to be taken up to him who sent me. After I have been taken up, I will send to you one of my disciples to heal your suffering and to provide life for you and those with you.

5

The Death and Resurrection of Jesus

$\diamond$

The final week in Jesus' life, from his triumphal entry into Jerusalem on Palm Sunday through to Easter Day (Holy Week or Passion Week in the church calendar), is given a disproportionate amount of space in the New Testament Gospels in comparison with the rest of his ministry. In many ways the events leading up to the crucifixion are described in a detail often lacking elsewhere in the Gospels. Such an emphasis is understandable as the early writers tried to explain the circumstances leading to the death and Resurrection of their saviour, because it was on these events that Christianity proclaimed its distinctive teaching and based its unique theological message.

The canonical Gospels relate the plots against Jesus, his arrest in the Garden of Gethsemane through the treachery of his disciple, Judas, his subsequent trials (before the Jewish Sanhedrin, before King Herod (Antipas), and before Pilate, the Roman governor), and his condemnation to death. This narrative reaches its climax in Jesus' crucifixion, death, and burial. These accounts are then followed by the Easter story, in which Jesus' Resurrection from death is proclaimed and demonstrated in a negative way with the story of his empty tomb, and in a positive way with an increasing number of post-Resurrection appearances by the risen Christ. Elaborations and other versions of the week's events are, not surprisingly, to be found in the later, non-canonical, Gospels.

The main accounts of Jesus' death in apocryphal texts occur in the Gospel of Peter and the Gospel of Nicodemus.

The Gospel of Peter is likely to have been composed in the second century. Although it was known in antiquity, this Gospel seemed to disappear without trace. Unlike many of the other apocryphal texts which have been preserved, often in multiple copies, no manuscripts of the Gospel of Peter were known until recently. Then, by chance, at the end of the nineteenth century a copy of this lost Gospel was discovered during an archaeological excavation in Egypt. Since then one or possibly two tiny fragments from this Gospel have also come to light. The main text is not complete, but what is there is given in its entirety below (1). It will be seen that this account parallels very closely the story in the four canonical Gospels, and it seems clear that the writer of the Gospel of Peter has drawn on these New Testament accounts for his version of Jesus' Passion. There are, however, some significant differences to look for. One is the cry of Jesus from the Cross ('My power, O power, you have forsaken me!'), which some commentators would interpret as an indication that the Gospel of Peter has been contaminated by unorthodox influences. A stronger heretical trait may be seen in the nearby sentence 'He held his peace as he felt no pain', which might imply that Jesus was incapable of suffering pain. If that is the correct translation, then it would indeed suggest possible Docetic influence. Nevertheless, our overall assessment of the Gospel of Peter is that the author was not self-consciously following unorthodox teaching, but that he was a typical unsophisticated and uncritical product of the second-century syncretism (or fusing of different systems of religious belief) which characterized much of the Christian world.

One particular post-Biblical characteristic found in the Gospel of Peter is the dominant anti-Jewish sentiment. Jewish malevolence is the motive here for the intention not to break Jesus' legs; and the blame for the death of Jesus is laid firmly at the door of the Jews.

Only selected extracts from the other main Passion Gospel, the Gospel of Nicodemus, are included below (2). The first half of that Gospel, the date of which is probably fifth–sixth century, is known as the Acts of Pilate and tells of Jesus' trial, death, and Resurrection. The book is concerned with Pilate's role in the sentencing of Jesus. Pilate's later career is the subject of other apocryphal works, and these are referred to in Chapter 6. The first extract under (2) tells of Jesus' meeting with Pilate. In it we note that on his first appearance, Jesus' power is shown to exceed that of the Roman state. The superiority of Christianity over earthly rule is one of the most dominant and, understandably, the most important themes throughout the whole range of apocryphal literature: it is perhaps the single most significant unifying element of teaching in a body of literature that is otherwise amorphous, heterogeneous, and widespread geographically and chronologically.

Extract (2) also contains the testimony of witnesses who speak of Jesus' good deeds. Among these witnesses is Bernice (Veronica in the Latin), identified as the woman of Mark 5: 25–9 healed of the twelve-year-long haemorrhaging. (Chapter 8 is given over to the Veronica legend.) The extract here also shows how the post-Biblical tradition was concerned to denounce and refute what was obviously a continuing charge against Christianity, namely the accusation that its founder was born of an illicit union. The New Testament's attempt in the Birth Stories to specify unambiguously the circumstances of Jesus' conception and his parents' relationship did not succeed in eliminating the kind of accusations that were resurfacing even as early as the writing of John 8: 41.

The Acts of Pilate continues for many more chapters. These cover further questioning by Pilate, the death of Jesus (which is not dealt with at length and is a straight summary of the canonical account), his burial by Joseph of Arimathaea, and a report that Jesus had been raised from the dead. The main purpose of this report about the Resurrection is to build a bridge with the second half of the Gospel of Nicodemus, which tells of Christ visiting Hades after the crucifixion—that legend is the subject of Chapter 7.

It is interesting to note that the apocryphal tradition did not seem to elaborate stories of Jesus' post-Easter appearances. To a certain extent one can see a development in the Easter stories in the New Testament from the comparatively simple account in Mark through the more detailed version in Matthew to the developed traditions in Luke and John. Comparable developments seem then to have ceased. Further elaboration is, surprisingly perhaps, not part of the apocryphal books. The apocryphal Acts do tell of several reappearances of Jesus, sometimes in different guises, to various characters, but these are not on a par with the Biblical post-Easter appearances, the main purpose of which is to convince the original followers that the crucified Jesus had left his tomb. What seems to replace stories of the Easter Jesus in the New Testament apocryphal tradition are accounts in which the risen Jesus communicates orally with believers: several apocryphal books containing discussions with the ascended Christ are recognized as a new genre, and are now classified as 'Dialogues of the Redeemer'.

The good and bad thieves crucified alongside Jesus obviously fascinated Christian writers of sermons and homilies. The penitent thief became a stock character, obviously of value in the church's preaching. His story is retold in, among other places, the Narrative of Joseph of Arimathaea, a twelfth-century legend, and part of this is given below (3).

Although Joseph of Arimathaea figures in the Gospel of Nicodemus and in the Narrative that bears his name, his principal role in these texts is as the one in whose tomb Jesus is buried. This of course is compatible with the New Testament picture, although in the apocryphal tales, especially the Gospel of Nicodemus, Joseph is given more to say and do as a result of his part in the burial. His story occurs in extract (4).

(There is nothing in the New Testament apocrypha that includes or gives rise to the Glastonbury legends or Joseph's arrival in England with the Holy Grail. All of that lies outside the apocrypha. If one seeks a literary source for those stories one must go to a thirteenth-century revision of William of Malmesbury's *De Antiquitate Glastoniensis Ecclesiae*, composed originally in *c*.1135.)

(1) *Gospel of Peter*

1. 1. . . . But of the Jews none washed their hands , neither Herod nor any of his judges. And as they would not wash Pilate stood up. 2. And then Herod the king commanded that the Lord should be taken off saying to them, 'What I have commanded you to do to him, do.'

2. 3. Now there stood there Joseph, the friend of Pilate and of the Lord, and knowing that they were about to crucify him he came to Pilate and asked for the body of the Lord for burial. 4. And Pilate sent to Herod and asked for his body. 5. And

Herod said, 'Brother Pilate, even if no one had asked for him we should bury him since the Sabbath is drawing on. For it stands written in the law: "The sun should not set on one that has been put to death." ' And he delivered him to the people before the first day of unleavened bread, their feast.

3. 6. So they took the Lord and pushed him as they ran and said, 'Let us drag the Son of God along now that we have got power over him.' 7. And they put upon him a purple robe and set him on the judgement seat and said, 'Judge righteously, O King of Israel!' 8. And one of them brought a crown of thorns and put it on the Lord's head. 9. And others who stood by spat on his eyes, and others slapped him on the cheeks, others pricked him with a reed, and some scourged him saying, 'With this honour let us honour the Son of God.'

4. 10. And they brought two malefactors and crucified the Lord between them. But he held his peace as he felt no pain. 11. And when they had set up the cross they wrote: 'This is the King of Israel.' 12. And having laid down his garments before him they divided them among themselves and cast lots for them. 13. But one of the malefactors rebuked them saying, 'We are suffering for the deeds which we have committed, but this man, who has become the saviour of men, what wrong has he done you?' 14. And they were angry with him and commanded that his legs should not be broken so that he might die in torment.

5. 15. Now it was midday and darkness covered all Judaea. And they became anxious and distressed lest the sun had already set since he was still alive. It stands written for them: 'The sun should not set on one that has been murdered.' 16. And one of them said, 'Give him to drink gall with vinegar.' And having mixed it they gave it to him to drink. 17. And they fulfilled all things and accumulated their sins on their head. 18. And many went about with lamps and as they supposed that it was night, they stumbled. 19. And the Lord called out and cried, 'My power, O power, you have forsaken me!' And having said this, he was taken up. 20. And at the same hour the veil of the temple in Jerusalem was torn in two.

6. 21. And then the Jews drew the spikes from the hands of the Lord and laid him on the earth. And the whole earth shook and there was great fear. 22. Then the sun shone and it was found to be the ninth hour. 23. And the Jews rejoiced and gave his body to Joseph that he might bury it since he had seen all the good deeds that he (Jesus) had done. 24. And he took the Lord, washed him, wrapped him in linen, and brought him into his own sepulchre, called Joseph's Garden.

7. 25. Then the Jews and the elders and the priests, perceiving what great evil they had done to themselves, began to lament and to say, 'Woe on our sins, judgement has arrived and with it the end of Jerusalem.' 26. But I mourned with my companions and, being wounded in heart, we hid ourselves for we were being sought after by them as if we were evil-doers and as persons who wanted to set fire to the temple. 27. Besides all these things we were fasting and sat mourning and weeping night and day until the Sabbath.

8. 28. But the scribes and Pharisees and elders, being assembled and hearing that the people were murmuring and beating their breasts, said, 'If at his death these exceeding great signs happened, behold how righteous he was!' 29. They were afraid and came to Pilate, entreating him and saying, (30) 'Give us soldiers that we may guard his sepulchre for three days, lest his disciples come and steal him away and the people suppose that he is risen from the dead, and do us harm.' 31. And Pilate gave them Petronius the centurion with soldiers to guard the sepulchre. And with them there came elders and scribes to the sepulchre, and all who were there together rolled a large stone (32) and laid it against the door to the sepulchre to exclude the centurion and the soldiers, and they (33) put on it seven seals, pitched a tent there and kept watch.

9. 34. Early in the morning, when the Sabbath dawned, there came a crowd from Jerusalem and the country round about to see the sealed sepulchre. 35. Now in the night in which the Lord's day dawned, when the soldiers were keeping guard, two by two in each watch, there was a loud voice in heaven, (36) and they saw the heavens open and two men come down from there in a great brightness and draw near to the sepulchre. 37. That stone which had been laid against the entrance to the sepulchre started of itself to roll and move sidewards, and the sepulchre was opened and both young men entered.

10. 38. When those soldiers saw this, they awakened the

centurion and the elders, for they also were there to mount guard. 39. And while they were narrating what they had seen, they saw three men come out from the sepulchre, two of them supporting the other and a cross following them (40) and the heads of the two reaching to heaven, but that of him who was being led reached beyond the heavens. 41. And they heard a voice out of the heavens crying, 'Have you preached to those who sleep?', 42. and from the cross there was heard the answer, 'Yes.'

11. 43. Therefore the men decided among themselves to go and report these things to Pilate. 44. And while they were still deliberating the heavens were again seen to open and a man descended and entered the tomb. 45. When those who were of the centurion's company saw this they hurried by night to Pilate, leaving the sepulchre which they were guarding, and reported everything that they had seen, being greatly agitated and saying, 'In truth he was (the) Son of God.' 46. Pilate answered and said, 'I am clean from the blood of the Son of God; it was you who desired it.' 47. Then they all came to him, beseeching him and urgently calling upon him to command the centurion and the soldiers to tell no one about the things they had seen. 48. 'For it is better for us', they said, 'to make ourselves guilty of the greatest sin before God than to fall into the hands of the people of the Jews and be stoned.' 49. Pilate therefore commanded the centurion and the soldiers to say nothing.

12. 50. At dawn on the Lord's day Mary Magdalene, a woman disciple of the Lord—for fear of the Jews, since they were inflamed with wrath—had not done at the sepulchre of the Lord what women are accustomed to do for their dead loved ones. 51. She took with her (women) friends and came to the sepulchre where he was laid. 52. And they were afraid lest the Jews should see them and said, 'Even though we could not weep and lament on that day when he was crucified, yet let us now do so at his sepulchre. 53. But who will roll away for us the stone that is across the entrance to the sepulchre, that we may go in and sit beside him and do what is due?'—(54) for the stone was great—'and we fear lest any one see us. And if we cannot do so let us at least place by the entrance what we have brought as a memorial for him, and let us weep and lament until we go home.'

13. 55. But having arrived they found the sepulchre opened. And they came near, stooped down there, and saw a young man sitting in the middle of the sepulchre, comely, and clothed with a brightly shining robe. He said to them, (56) 'Why have you come? Whom do you seek? Not the man who was crucified? He is risen and gone. But if you do not believe, stoop this way and see the place where he lay for he is not there. For he is risen and is gone to the place from which he was sent.' 57. Then the women fled frightened.

14. 58. Now it was the last day of unleavened bread and many went away and returned to their homes because the feast was at an end. 59. But we, the twelve disciples of the Lord, wept and mourned and each one, grieving for what had happened, returned to his own home. 60. But I, Simon Peter, and my brother Andrew took our nets and went to the sea. And there was with us Levi, the son of Alphaeus, whom the Lord . . .'

(2) *The Gospel of Nicodemus (Acts of Pilate)* 1. 5–9

1. 5. Now when Jesus entered, and the ensigns were holding the standards, the images on the standards bowed down and worshipped Jesus. And when the Jews saw the behaviour of the standards, how they bowed down and worshipped Jesus, they cried out loudly against the ensigns. But Pilate said to them, 'Do you not marvel how the images bowed and worshipped Jesus?' The Jews said to Pilate, 'We saw how the ensigns lowered them and worshipped him.' And the governor summoned the ensigns and asked them, 'Why did you do this?' They answered, 'We are Greeks and servers of temples: how could we worship him? We held the images; but they bowed down of their own accord and worshipped him.'

6. Then Pilate said to the rulers of the synagogue and the elders of the people, 'Choose strong men to carry the standards, and let us see whether the images bow by themselves.' So the elders of the Jews took twelve strong men and made them carry the standards by sixes, and they stood before the

judgement-seat of the governor. And Pilate said to the messenger, 'Take him out of the praetorium and bring him in again in whatever way you wish.' And Jesus left the praetorium with the messenger. And Pilate summoned those who had previously been carrying the images, and said to them, 'I have sworn by the salvation of the Caesar that, if the standards do not bow down when Jesus enters, I will cut off your heads.' And the governor commanded Jesus to enter in the second time. And the messenger did as before and begged Jesus to walk upon his scarf. He walked upon it and entered. And when he had entered, the standards bowed down again and worshipped Jesus.

2. 1. When Pilate saw this he was afraid, and tried to rise from the judgement-seat. And while he was still thinking of rising up, his wife sent to him saying, 'Have nothing to do with this righteous man. For I have suffered many things because of him by night.' And Pilate summoned all the Jews, and stood up and said to them, 'You know that my wife is pious and prefers to practice Judaism with you.' They answered him, 'Yes, we know it.' Pilate said to them, 'See, my wife sent to me saying, "Have nothing to do with this righteous man. For I have suffered many things because of him by night."' The Jews answered Pilate, 'Did we not tell you that he is a sorcerer? Behold, he has sent a dream to your wife.' 2. And Pilate called Jesus to him and said to him, 'What do these men testify against you? Do you say nothing?' Jesus answered, 'If they had no power, they would say nothing; for each man has power over his own mouth, to speak good and evil. They shall see.'

3. Then the elders of the Jews answered and said to Jesus, 'What should we see? First, that you were born of fornication; secondly, that your birth meant the death of the children in Bethlehem; thirdly, that your father Joseph and your mother Mary fled into Egypt because they had no esteem among the people.' 4. Then some of the pious among Jews stood by, who said, 'We do not say that he came of fornication, for we know that Joseph was betrothed to Mary, and he was not born of fornication.' Pilate then said to the Jews who said that he came of fornication, 'Your statement is not true; for there had been a betrothal, as your compatriots say.' Annas and Caiaphas said to Pilate, 'We, the whole multitude, cry out that he was born of fornication, and we are not believed; these are proselytes and

disciples of his.' And Pilate called to him Annas and Caiaphas
and said to them, 'What are proselytes?' They answered, 'They
are people who were born children of Greeks, and now have
become Jews.' Then those who said that he was not born of
fornication, namely Lazarus, Asterius, Antonius, Jacob,
Amnes, Zeras, Samuel, Isaac, Phineës, Crispus, Agrippa, and
Judas, said, 'We are not proselytes, but are children of Jews
and speak the truth; for we were present at the betrothal of
Joseph and Mary.'

5. And Pilate called to him these twelve men who denied
that he was born of fornication, and said to them, 'I adjure you,
by the salvation of Caesar, that your statement is true, that he
was not born of fornication.' They said to Pilate, 'We have a
law, not to swear, because it is a sin. But let *them* swear by the
salvation of Caesar that it is not as we have said, and we will be
worthy of death.' Pilate said to Annas and Caiaphas, 'Do you
not answer these things?' And Annas and Caiaphas said to
Pilate, 'These twelve men are believed who say that he was not
born of fornication. But we, the whole multitude, cry out that
he was born of fornication, and is a sorcerer, and says he is the
Son of God and a king, and we are not believed.' 6. And Pilate
ordered the whole multitude to go out, except the twelve men
who denied that he was born of fornication, and he commanded Jesus to be set apart. And he asked them, 'For what
cause do they wish to kill him?' They answered Pilate, 'They
are jealous because he heals on the Sabbath.' Pilate said, 'For
a good work do they wish to kill him?' They answered him,
'Yes.'

3. 1. And Pilate was filled with anger and went out of the
praetorium and said to them, 'I call the sun to witness that I
find no fault in this man.' The Jews answered and said to the
governor, 'If this man were not an evildoer, we would not have
handed him over to you.' And Pilate said, 'Take him yourselves
and judge him by your own law.' The Jews said to Pilate, 'It is
not lawful for us to put any man to death.' Pilate said, 'Has God
forbidden you to kill, but allowed me to do so?'

2. And Pilate entered the praetorium again and called Jesus
and asked him privately, 'Are you the king of the Jews?' Jesus
answered Pilate, 'Do you say this of your own accord, or did
others say it to you about me?' Pilate answered Jesus, 'Am I a

Jew? Your own nation and the chief priests have handed you over to me. What have you done?' Jesus answered, 'My kingship is not of this world; for if my kingship were of this world, my servants would fight, that I might not be handed over to the Jews. But now my kingship is not from here.' Pilate said to him, 'So you are a king?' Jesus answered him, 'You say that I am a king. For this cause I was born and have come, that every one who is of the truth should hear my voice.' Pilate said to him, 'What is truth?' Jesus answered him, 'Truth is from heaven.' Pilate said, 'Is there not truth upon earth?' Jesus said to Pilate, 'You see how those who speak the truth are judged by those who have authority on earth.'

4. 1. And Pilate left Jesus in the praetorium and went out to the Jews and said to them, 'I find no fault in him.' The Jews said to him, 'He said: "I am able to destroy this temple and build it in three days".' Pilate said, 'What temple?' The Jews said: 'The one which Solomon built in forty-six years. This man says he will destroy it and build it in three days.' Pilate said to them, 'I am innocent of the blood of this righteous man; you see to it.' The Jews replied, 'His blood be on us and on our children.' 2. And Pilate summoned the elders and the priests and the Levites and said to them secretly, 'Do not act in this way; for nothing of which you have accused him deserves death. For your accusation concerns healing and profanation of the Sabbath.' The elders and the priests and the Levites answered, 'If a man blasphemes against Caesar, is he worthy of death or not?' Pilate said, 'He is worthy of death.' The Jews said to Pilate, 'If a man blasphemes against Caesar, he is worthy of death, but this man has blasphemed against God.'

3. Then the governor commanded the Jews to go out from the praetorium, and he called Jesus to him and said to him, 'What shall I do with you?' Jesus answered Pilate, 'As it was given to you.' Pilate said, 'How was it given?' Jesus said, 'Moses and the prophets foretold my death and resurrection.' The Jews had made enquiries and heard, and they said to Pilate, 'What more do you need to hear than this blasphemy?' Pilate said to the Jews, 'If this word is blasphemy, take him for his blasphemy and bring him into your synagogue and judge him according to your law.' The Jews answered Pilate, 'Our law decrees that if a man sins against a man, he must receive forty

strokes save one, but he who blasphemes against God must be stoned.'

4. Pilate said to them, 'Take him yourselves and punish him as you wish.' The Jews said to Pilate, 'We wish him to be crucified.' Pilate said, 'He does not deserve to be crucified.' 5. The governor looked at the multitudes of the Jews standing around, and when he saw many of the Jews weeping, he said, 'Not all the multitude wishes him to die.' But the elders of the Jews said, 'The whole multitude of us has come, for the purpose that he should die.' Pilate said to the Jews, 'Why should he die?' The Jews said: 'Because he called himself the Son of God and a king.'

5. 1. Now Nicodemus, a Jew, stood before the governor, and said, 'I beseech you, pious one, to allow me a few words.' Pilate said, 'Speak.' Nicodemus said, 'I said to the elders and the priests and the Levites and to all the multitude in the synagogue, "What do you intend to do with this man? This man does many signs and wonders, which no other has done nor will do. Release him and wish no evil against him. If the signs which he does are from God, they will stand; if they are from men, they will come to nothing. For Moses also, when he was sent by God into Egypt, did many signs which God commanded him to do before Pharaoh, king of Egypt. And there were there physicians of Pharaoh, Jamnes and Jambres, and they also did not a few signs such as Moses did, and the Egyptians held Jamnes and Jambres as gods. And since the signs which they did were not from God, they themselves perished and those who believed them. And now let this man go, for he does not deserve death."'

2. The Jews said to Nicodemus, 'You became his disciple and speak on his behalf.' Nicodemus answered them, 'Has the governor also become his disciple, and speaks on his behalf? Did not Caesar appoint him to this high office?' Then the Jews raged and gnashed their teeth against Nicodemus. Pilate said to them, 'Why do you gnash your teeth against him, when you hear the truth?' The Jews said to Nicodemus, 'Receive his truth and his portion.' Nicodemus said, 'Amen, may it be as you have said.'

6. 1. Then one of the Jews came forward and asked the governor that he might speak a word. The governor said, 'If you wish to say anything, say it.' And the Jew said, 'For thirty-eight years I lay on a bed in anguish and pain, and when Jesus came many demoniacs and those lying sick of various diseases were healed by him. And certain young men took pity on me and carried me with my bed and brought me to him. And when Jesus saw me he had compassion, and said to me, "Take up your bed and walk." And I took up my bed and walked.' The Jews said to Pilate, 'Ask him what day it was on which he was healed.' The cured man said, 'On a Sabbath.' The Jews said, 'Did we not tell you, that he heals and casts out demons on the Sabbath?' 2. And another Jew hastened forward and said, 'I was born blind; I heard a man's voice, but did not see his face. And as Jesus passed by I cried with a loud voice, "Have mercy on me, Son of David." And he took pity on me and put his hands on my eyes and I saw immediately.' And another Jew came forward and said, 'I was bowed, and he made me straight with a word.' And another said, 'I was a leper, and he healed me with a word.'

7. 1. And a woman called Bernice crying out from a distance said, 'I had an issue of blood and I touched the hem of his garment, and the issue of blood, which had lasted twelve years, ceased.' The Jews said, 'We have a law not to permit a woman to give testimony.'

8. 1. And others, a multitude of men and women, cried out, 'This man is a prophet, and the demons are subject to him.' Pilate said to those who claimed the demons were subject to him, 'Why are your teachers also not subject to him?' They said to Pilate, 'We do not know.' Others said, 'He raised Lazarus, who was dead, out of the tomb after four days.' Then the governor began to tremble and said to all the multitude of the Jews, 'Why do you wish to shed innocent blood?'

9. 1. And he called to him Nicodemus and the twelve men who said he was not born of fornication and said to them, 'What shall I do? There is dissension among the people.' They answered him, 'We do not know. They will see to it.' Again Pilate called all the multitude of the Jews and said, 'You know the custom that at the feast of unleavened bread one prisoner is released to you. I have in the prison one condemned for murder, called Barabbas, and this Jesus who stands before you, in whom I find no fault. Whom do you wish me to release to you?' But they cried out, 'Barabbas.' Pilate said, 'Then what shall I do with Jesus who is called Christ?' The Jews cried out, 'Let him be crucified.' But some of the Jews answered, 'You are not Caesar's friend if you release this man, for he called himself the Son of God and a king. You therefore wish him and not Caesar to be king.'

2. And Pilate was angry and said to the Jews, 'Your nation is always seditious and in rebellion against your benefactors.' The Jews asked, 'What benefactors?' Pilate answered, 'I have heard that your God brought you out of Egypt out of hard slavery, and led you safely through the sea as if it had been dry land, and in the wilderness nourished you and gave you manna and quails, and gave you water to drink from a rock, and gave you the law. And in spite of all these things you provoked the anger of your God: you wanted a molten calf and angered your God, and he wished to destroy you; and Moses made supplication for you, and you were not put to death. And now you accuse me of hating the emperor.' 3. And he rose up from the judgement-seat and was on his way out when the Jews cried out, 'We know as king Caesar alone and not Jesus. Wise men brought him gifts from the east, as for a king. And when Herod heard from the wise men that a king was born, he tried to slay him. But when his father Joseph knew that, he took him and his mother, and they fled into Egypt. And when Herod heard it, he destroyed the children of the Hebrews who were born in Bethlehem.'

4. When Pilate heard these words, he was afraid. And he silenced the multitudes, because they were crying out, and said to them, 'So this is he whom Herod sought?' The Jews replied, 'Yes, this is he.' And Pilate took water and washed his hands before the sun and said, 'I am innocent of this righteous blood. You will see to it.' Again the Jews cried out, 'His blood be on us and on our children.' 5. Then Pilate commanded the curtain to be drawn before the judgement-seat on which he sat, and said to Jesus, 'Your nation has convicted you of being a king. Therefore I have decreed that you should first be scourged according to the law of the pious emperors, and then hanged on the cross in the garden where you were seized. And let Dysmas and Gestas, the two malefactors, be crucified with you.'

(3) *Narrative of Joseph of Arimathaea* 3

3. Having done many dreadful things against Jesus that night, they gave him to Pilate, the Procurator, at dawn on the day of preparation, so that he could crucify him. They all came together for this purpose. After a trial, Pilate, the Procurator, ordered him to be nailed to the cross, alongside two robbers. They were nailed up along with Jesus, Gestas on the left, and Demas on the right.

And the man on the left began to cry out and said to Jesus, 'See how many evil deeds I did on earth. If I had known you were a king I would have destroyed you too. Why do you call yourself Son of God yet cannot help yourself when you are in need? How can you help someone else with your prayer? If you are the Christ, come down from the cross, so that I may believe in you. Now I see you are perishing along with me, not like a man but like a wild beast.' And he said many other things against Jesus, blaspheming and gnashing his teeth against him. The robber was taken alive in the snare of the devil.

But the robber on his right hand, whose name was Demas, saw the godlike grace of Jesus and said, 'Jesus Christ, I know you are the Son of God. I see you, Christ, adored by countless myriads of angels . Pardon me my sins. In my trial do not let the stars come against me, or the moon, when you will judge all the world, because it was at night-time when I did my wicked deeds. Do not urge the sun, darkened now on your account, to tell the evils of my heart, for I can give you no gift for the remission of my sins. Already death is coming upon me because of my sins; but yours is the propitiation. Deliver me, O Lord of all, from your fearful judgement. Do not give the enemy power to swallow me up or to become the inheritor of my soul, as he has the soul of him hanging on the left. I see how the devil joyfully takes his soul and his flesh disappears. Do not even order me to depart to the portion of the Jews; for I see Moses and the patriarchs lamenting, and the devil rejoices over them. O Lord, before my spirit departs, order my sins to be washed away, and remember me, the sinner, in your kingdom, when upon the great throne of the Most High you shall judge the twelve tribes of Israel. For you have prepared great punishment for the world on your own account.'

And when the robber had said these things, Jesus said to him, 'Truly I say to you, Demas, that today you will be with me in paradise. And the sons of the kingdom, the children of Abraham, and Isaac, Jacob and Moses, shall be cast into outer darkness. There shall be weeping and gnashing of teeth. And you alone shall dwell in paradise until my second coming, when I am to judge those who do not confess my name.' And he said to the robber, 'Go and speak to the cherubim and the powers who wield the flaming sword, who have guarded paradise from the time that Adam, the first creation, was in paradise and sinned and did not keep my commandments and I cast him out from there. Say that none of the first shall see paradise until I come the second time to judge the living and the dead, it having been written that Jesus Christ, the Son of God, came down from the heights of heavens, and came forth from the bosom of the invisible Father without having been separated from him, and came down into the world to be made flesh and to be nailed to a cross, in order that I might save Adam, whom I fashioned. Say to my archangelic powers, the gatekeepers of paradise, to the officers of my Father: I require and order that he who has been crucified along with me should enter and receive remission of sins through me, and that, having put on an incorruptible body, he should go into paradise, and dwell where nobody has been able to dwell.'

After he had said this, Jesus gave up the ghost on the day of preparation at the ninth hour. And there was darkness over the whole earth, and there was a great earthquake. The sanctuary collapsed and the pinnacle of the temple fell.

(4) *Gospel of Nicodemus (Acts of Pilate)* 11. 3–16. 1

11. 3. But a certain man named Joseph, a member of the council, from the town of Arimathaea, who also was waiting for the kingdom of God, went to Pilate and asked for the body of Jesus. And he took it down, and wrapped it in a clean linen cloth, and placed it in a rock-hewn tomb, in which no one had ever yet been laid.

12. 1. When the Jews heard that Joseph had asked for the body, they looked for him and the twelve men who said that Jesus was not born of fornication, and for Nicodemus and for many others, who had come forward before Pilate and made known his good works. But they all hid themselves, and only Nicodemus was seen by them, because he was a ruler of the Jews. And Nicodemus said to them, 'How did you enter into the synagogue?' The Jews answered him, 'How did you enter into the synagogue? You are a sympathizer of his, and his portion shall be with you in the world to come.' Nicodemus said, 'Amen, amen.' Likewise Joseph came forth and said to them, 'Why are you angry with me, because I asked for the body of Jesus? See, I have placed it in my new tomb, having wrapped it in clean linen, and I rolled a stone in front of the door of the cave. And you have not done well with the righteous one, for you have not repented of having crucified him, but you even pierced him with a spear.'

Then the Jews seized Joseph and commanded him to be locked up until the first day of the week. They said to him, 'You know that the time prevents our doing anything against you, because the Sabbath dawns. But you also know that you will not even be counted worthy of burial, but we shall give your flesh to the birds of heaven.' Joseph said to them, 'This is the word of the boastful Goliath, who insulted the living God and the holy David. For God said through the prophet: "Vengeance is mine, I will repay, says the Lord." And now he who is uncircumcised in the flesh, but circumcised in heart, took water and washed his hands before the sun, saying, "I am innocent of this righteous blood. You will see to it." And you answered Pilate, "His blood be on us and on our children." And now I fear lest the wrath of God come upon you and your children, as you said.' When the Jews heard these words, they were embittered in their hearts, and laid hold on Joseph and seized him and shut him in a windowless house, and guards were stationed at the door. And they sealed the door of the place where Joseph was shut up.

2. And on the Sabbath the rulers of the synagogue and the priests and the Levites ordered that everybody should present himself in the synagogue on the first day of the week. And the whole multitude rose up early and took counsel in the synagogue by what death they should kill him. And when the council was in session they commanded him to be brought with great dishonour. And when they opened the door they did

not find him. And all the people were astonished and filled with
consternation because they found the seals undamaged, and
Caiaphas had the key. And they dared no longer to lay hands
on those who had spoken to Pilate on behalf of Jesus.

13. 1. And while they still sat in the synagogue wondering
about Joseph, there came some of the guard whom the Jews
had asked from Pilate to guard the tomb of Jesus, lest his
disciples should come and steal him. And they told the rulers
of the synagogue and the priests and the Levites what had
happened, 'There was a great earthquake. And we saw an angel
descend from heaven, and he rolled away the stone from the
mouth of the cave, and sat upon it, and he shone like snow and
like lightning. And we were in great fear, and lay like dead
men. And we heard the voice of the angel speaking to the
women who waited at the tomb "Do not be afraid, I know that
you seek Jesus who was crucified. He is not here. He has risen,
as he said. Come and see the place where the Lord lay. And go
quickly and tell his disciples that he has risen from the dead
and is in Galilee."'

2. The Jews asked, 'Which women did he speak to?' The
members of the guard answered, 'We do not know who they
were.' The Jews said, 'At what hour was it?' The members of
the guard answered; 'At midnight.' The Jews said, 'And why did
you not arrest the women?' The members of the guard said,
'We were like dead men through fear, and gave up hope of
seeing the light of day; how could we then have seized them?'
The Jews said, 'As the Lord lives, we do not believe you.' The
members of the guard said to the Jews, 'You saw so many signs
in that man and you did not believe; and how can you believe
us? You rightly swore, "As the Lord lives", for he *does* live.'
Again the members of the guard said, 'We have heard that you
shut up the man who asked for the body of Jesus, and sealed
the door, and that when you opened it you did not find him.
Therefore give us Joseph and we will give you Jesus.' The Jews
said, 'Joseph has gone to his own city.' And the members of the
guard said to the Jews, 'And Jesus has risen, as we heard from
the angel, and is in Galilee.' 3. And when the Jews heard these
words, they feared greatly and said, 'Take heed lest this report
be heard and all turn to Jesus.' And the Jews took counsel, and
offered a great sum of money and gave it to the soldiers of the

guard, saying, 'Say that when you were sleeping his disciples came by night and stole him. And if this is heard by the governor, we will persuade him and keep you out of trouble.'

14. 1. Now Phineës a priest and Adas a teacher and Angaeus a Levite came from Galilee to Jerusalem, and told the rulers of the synagogue and the priests and the Levites, 'We saw Jesus and his disciples sitting upon the mountain which is called Mamilch. And he said to his disciples, "Go into all the world and preach the gospel to the whole creation. He who believes and is baptized will be saved; but he who does not believe will be condemned. And these signs will accompany those who believe: in my name they will cast out demons; they will speak in new tongues; they will pick up serpents; and if they drink any deadly thing, it will not hurt them; they will lay their hands on the sick, and they will recover." And while Jesus was still speaking to his disciples, we saw him taken up into heaven.'

2. Then the elders and the priests and the Levites said, 'Give glory to the God of Israel, and confess before him if you indeed heard and saw what you have described.' Those who related them said, 'As the Lord God of our fathers Abraham, Isaac, and Jacob lives, we heard these things and saw him taken up to heaven.' The elders and the priests and the Levites said to them, 'Did you come to tell us this, or did you come to offer prayer to God?' They answered, 'To offer prayer to God.' The elders and the chief priests and the Levites said to them, 'If you came to offer prayer to God, to what purpose is this idle tale which you have babbled before all the people?' Phineës the priest and Adas the teacher and Angaeus the Levite said to the rulers of the synagogue and priests and Levites, 'If the words which we spoke about what we saw are sin, behold, we stand before you. Do with us as it seems good in your eyes.' And they took the law and adjured them to tell these words to no one. And they gave them food and drink, and sent them out of the city, after having given them money and three companions, and they ordered them to depart to Galilee. And they went away in peace.

3. But when those men had departed to Galilee, the chief priests and the rulers of the synagogue and the elders assembled in the synagogue, and shut the gate, and raised a great

lamentation, saying, 'Why has this sign happened in Israel?' But Annas and Caiaphas said, 'Why are you troubled? Why do you weep? Do you not know that his disciples gave money to the guards of the tomb and taught them to say that an angel descended from heaven and rolled away the stone from the door of the tomb?' But the priests and the elders replied, 'Let it be that his disciples stole his body. But how did the soul enter again into the body, so that Jesus now waits in Galilee?' But they, being scarcely able to give an answer, said, 'It is not lawful for us to believe the uncircumcised.'

15. 1. And Nicodemus arose and stood before the council and said, 'What you say is right. You know, people of the Lord, that the men who came from Galilee fear God and are men of honour, that they hate covetousness, and are men of peace. And they have declared on oath, "We saw Jesus on the mountain Mamilch with his disciples." He taught them what you have heard from them, namely "We saw him taken up into heaven." And no one asked them in what manner he was taken up. Just as the book of the holy scriptures tells us that Elijah also was taken up into heaven, and Elisha cried with a loud voice, and Elijah cast his sheepskin cloak upon Elisha, and Elisha cast his cloak upon the Jordan, and crossed over and went to Jericho. And the sons of the prophets met him and said, "Elisha, where is your master Elijah?" And he said that he was taken up into heaven. But they said to Elisha, "Has perhaps a spirit caught him up and cast him on one of the mountains? But let us take our servants with us and search for him." And they persuaded Elisha, and he went with them. And they searched for him for three days and did not find him, and they knew that he had been taken up. And now listen to me. Let us send to every mountain of Israel and see whether the Christ was perhaps taken up by a spirit and cast upon a mountain.' And this proposal pleased them all. And they sent to every mountain of Israel, and searched for Jesus and did not find him. But they found Joseph in Arimathaea and no one dared to seize him.

2. And they told the elders and the priests and the Levites, 'We went about to every mountain of Israel, and did not find Jesus. But Joseph we found in Arimathaea.' And when they heard about Joseph, they rejoiced and gave glory to the God of

Israel. And the rulers of the synagogue and the priests and the Levites took counsel how they should meet with Joseph, and they took a roll of papyrus and wrote to Joseph these words, 'Peace be with you. We know that we have sinned against God and against you, and we have prayed to the God of Israel that you should deign to come to your fathers and your children, because we are all troubled. For when we opened the door we did not find you. We know that we devised an evil plan against you; but the Lord helped you, and the Lord himself has brought to nothing our plan against you, honoured father Joseph.'

3. And they chose from all Israel seven men who were friends of Joseph, whom Joseph himself was acquainted with, and the rulers of the synagogue and the priests and the Levites said to them, 'See! If he receives our letter and reads it, you know that he will come with you to us. But if he does not read it, you know that he is angry with us, greet him in peace and return to us.' And they blessed the men and dismissed them. And the men came to Joseph and greeted him with reverence, and said to him, 'Peace be with you!' He replied, 'Peace be with you and all Israel!' And they gave him the letter. Joseph took the roll, read the letter and kissed it, and blessed God and said, 'Blessed be God, who has delivered the Israelites from shedding innocent blood. And blessed be the Lord, who sent his angel and sheltered me under his wings.' And he set a table before them, and they ate and drank and lay down there. 4. And they rose up early in the morning and prayed. And Joseph saddled his she-ass and went with the men, and they came to the holy city Jerusalem. And all the people met Joseph and cried, 'Peace on your arrival.' And he said to all the people, 'Peace be with you!' And all kissed him, and prayed with Joseph, and were beside themselves with joy at seeing him. And Nicodemus received him into his house and made a great feast. He invited Annas and Caiaphas and the elders and the priests and the Levites to his house, and they rejoiced, eating and drinking with Joseph. And after singing a hymn each one went to his house; but Joseph remained in the house of Nicodemus.

5. And on the next day, which was the day of preparation, the rulers of the synagogue and the priests and the Levites rose

up early and came to the house of Nicodemus. Nicodemus met
them and said, 'Peace be with you!' They answered, 'Peace be
with you and with Joseph and with all your house and with all
the house of Joseph!' And he took them into his house. And the
whole council sat down, and Joseph sat between Annas and
Caiaphas. And no one dared to speak a word to him. And
Joseph said, 'Why have you called me?' And they beckoned to
Nicodemus to speak to Joseph. Nicodemus opened his mouth
and said to Joseph, 'Father, you know that the honourable
teachers and the priests and the Levites wish to learn something from you.' Joseph answered, 'Ask me.' And Annas and
Caiaphas took the law and adjured Joseph, saying, 'Give glory
to the God of Israel and make confession to him. For Achan
also, when adjured by the prophet Joshua, did not commit
perjury, but told him everything and concealed nothing from
him. So you too must not conceal from us a single word.'
Joseph answered, 'I will not conceal anything from you.' And
they said to him, 'We were very angry because you asked for
the body of Jesus, and wrapped it in a clean linen cloth, and
placed it in a tomb. And for this reason we secured you in a
house with no window, and locked and sealed the door, and
guards watched where you were shut up. And on the first day
of the week we opened it, and did not find you, and we were
very troubled, and all the people of God were amazed until
yesterday. And now tell us what happened.'

   6. And Joseph said, 'On the day of preparation about the
tenth hour you shut me in, and I remained the whole Sabbath.
And at midnight as I stood and prayed, the house where you
shut me in was raised up by the four corners, and I saw as it
were a flash of lightning in my eyes. Full of fear I fell to the
ground. And someone took me by the hand and raised me up
from the place where I had fallen, and moisture like water
flowed from my head to my feet, and the myrrh came to my
nostrils. And he wiped my face and kissed me and said to me,
"Do not fear, Joseph. Open your eyes and see who it is who
speaks with you." I looked up and saw Jesus. Trembling, I
thought it was a phantom, and I recited the commandments.
And he said them with me. Now as you well know, a phantom
immediately flees if it meets anyone and hears the commandments. And when I saw that he said them with me, I said to

him, "Rabbi Elijah!" He said, "I am not Elijah." And I said to
him, "Who are you, Lord?" He replied, "I am Jesus, whose
body you asked for from Pilate, whom you clothed in clean
linen, on whose face you placed a cloth, and whom you placed
in your new cave, and you rolled a great stone to the door of
the cave." And I asked the one who spoke to me, "Show me the
place where I laid you." And he took me and showed me
the place where I laid him. And the linen cloth lay there, and
the cloth that was upon his face. Then I recognized that it was
Jesus. And he took me by the hand and placed me in the
middle of my house, with the doors shut, and led me to my bed
and said to me, "Peace be with you!" Then he kissed me and
said to me, "Do not go out of your house for forty days. For see,
I go to my brethren in Galilee."'

16. 1. And when the rulers of the synagogue and the priests
and the Levites heard these words from Joseph, they became
like dead men and fell to the ground and fasted until the ninth
hour. And Nicodemus and Joseph comforted Annas and
Caiaphas and the priests and Levites, saying, 'Get up and stand
on your feet, and taste bread and strengthen your souls. For
tomorrow is the Sabbath of the Lord.' And they rose up and
prayed to God, and ate and drank, and each went to his own
house.

6

Pilate

◇

Visitors to Lucerne in Switzerland may wonder why one of the nearby mountains is Mount Pilatus. The reason is that Pontius Pilate is said to be buried under it, according to an apocryphal text.

Pilate is a New Testament character whose role in the trial of Jesus and whose subsequent career figure extensively in the apocryphal literature. Reasons for this interest in the Roman governor's place in the Jesus story are not hard to find. The same motives lie behind the earlier, New Testament, interest in him.

Crucifixion was known as a distinctively Roman form of capital punishment. In any telling of Jesus' story his manner of death could not be avoided, and, as it was a death by crucifixion, Roman involvement at some stage in the judicial process had to be explained. Hence all the New Testament accounts tell how Pontius Pilate, the Procurator of Judaea, was the Roman official who passed the death sentence on Jesus. If one reads those accounts in the likeliest chronological sequence, first Mark, then Matthew, Luke, and finally John, one can discern a developing tradition regarding Pilate. The evangelists' differing emphases reflect the early church's sensitivity in handling Pilate's involvement in the trial of Jesus at a time when a growing number of converts to Christianity were coming from a non-Jewish background, when the church was spreading throughout the Empire, and when Christianity was becoming increasingly dependent on the goodwill of the Roman authorities. Basically, the evangelists were embarrassed or reluctant to blame Pilate for the death of Jesus. We thus read that Pilate's wife dreams of Jesus' innocence; that Pilate himself declares Jesus innocent three times; and that he washes the guilt for his judgement from his hands. By the time the Fourth Gospel was written, towards the end of the first century, Pilate is described as reluctantly accepting under duress his constitutional role as the only legally established figure able and qualified to pronounce a judicial death sentence.

This theme, the whitewashing or exonerating of Pilate, has as its counterpoint the blaming of the Jewish race *en bloc* for the fate of Jesus. Collectively the Jews are said to accept guilt for the death. Throughout the Gospels it is 'the Jews' who become increasingly hostile to Jesus and his message. At the trial before the Sanhedrin it is the Jewish leadership who pronounces Jesus worthy of death even before the Roman trial has begun; at the Roman trial, when Pilate offers an amnesty limited to the freeing of one prisoner, the Jews elect to have the murderer Barabbas released rather than Jesus. The Jews force Pilate to have Jesus crucified. By these means Pilate is portrayed as a mere cog in the divine drama that requires Jesus to die on a cross and be raised.

What begins in the tradition as an ambivalent attitude towards Pilate becomes fixed: Pilate is a puppet in the hands of the Jewish mob. Better and more tactful to portray the Roman governor as a weak and vacillating man than as a deicide!

This way of resolving the 'Pilate problem' by the New Testament authors did not, however, finally settle the issue. As we shall see below, the later, apocryphal, tradition reflects a continuing dilemma in judging his character. Possibly the changed attitude, especially in western European sources, was because the earlier goodwill of the Roman authorities had turned to officially inspired persecution. The ambiguous ways of treating Pilate are at their most apparent when the apocryphal legends come to the death of Pilate. When a document like the Acts of Pilate is treating the events of Jesus' Passion we can still see the influence of the canonical traditions: the picture of Pilate in these Acts is close to the New Testament's portrayal. The version in the Acts of Pilate is an elaboration of the Gospels' trial narrative. (Excerpts from that text are found in Chapter 5 on the Passion.) We again see that the apologetic tendency of the account in the Acts of Pilate is to show how Pilate tried to free himself from all responsibility for the death of Jesus by blaming it on Herod and the Jews.

But as far as Pilate's later story is concerned, where a judgement on his career is expected, he is treated variously as a saint or as an outcast. In the Eastern church, particularly in the Coptic and Ethiopic tradition, he was portrayed favourably. Those churches eventually canonized him! An apocryphal tale, taken from the text usually known as the Paradosis Pilati (that is, the 'handing over' of Pilate for chastising), is printed below (1). This shows how one Eastern legend treated Pilate and his wife, named here as Procla: although Caesar has Pilate beheaded, Pilate's destiny is a triumph. The Western church judged Pilate harshly: that tradition is represented by the second extract below (2). It comes from the text called the Mors Pilati (the Death of Pilate)—and that is the text which explains how Mount Pilatus on Lake Lucerne (Losania in the text) was so named. In that context another place-name is explained: Vienne is said to be derived from the words Via Gehenna (Hell Road). That made it an appropriate, albeit temporary, resting-place for the man who condemned Jesus to death.

In addition to these contradictory accounts of Pilate's end, I append two letters allegedly written by Pilate. The sympathetic attitude to Pilate here suggests an Eastern origin. The one addressed to the Emperor (3), named here Claudius, appears in various contexts, thereby revealing its popularity. Like so many apocryphal writings this is anti-Jewish. In it an attempt is made to see the condemnation of Jesus from Pilate's point of view. The other letter (4) is addressed to Herod Antipas. Herod's reply is also given.

(1) *Paradosis Pilati*

1. When the report reached Rome and had been read to Caesar, with not a few standing by, all were amazed that it was because of the lawlessness of Pilate that the darkness and the earthquake had come upon the whole world; and Caesar, filled with anger, sent soldiers with orders to bring Pilate a prisoner.

2. And when he had been brought to the city of the Romans and Caesar heard that Pilate was there, he sat down in the temple of the gods in the presence of the whole senate and the whole army and all the multitude of his forces. And he com-

manded Pilate to stand forward and said to him, 'How could you dare to do such a thing, you most impious one, when you had seen such great signs concerning that man? By daring to do an evil deed you have destroyed the whole world.'

3. Pilate answered, 'Almighty King, I am innocent of these things; it is the multitude of the Jews who are reckless and guilty.' Caesar asked, 'Who are they?' Pilate said, 'Herod, Archelaus, Philip, Annas and Caiaphas, and all the multitude of the Jews.' Caesar said. 'Why did you follow their advice?' Pilate said, 'This nation is rebellious and disorderly, and does not submit to your power.' Caesar said, 'As soon as they handed him over to you, you should have kept him secure and sent him to me, and not have obeyed them and crucified such a man who was righteous and did such wonderful signs as you have mentioned in your report. For it is clear from these signs that Jesus was the Christ, the king of the Jews.'

4. And when Caesar said this and named the name of Christ, all the multitude of the gods fell down, and became as dust where Caesar sat with the senate. And all the people who stood by Caesar trembled because of the utterance of the word and the fall of their gods, and gripped by fear, they all went away, each to his own house, marvelling at what had taken place. And Caesar commanded that Pilate should be guarded safely, in order that he might learn the truth about Jesus.

5. On the next day Caesar sat in the Capitol with all the senate and tried again to question Pilate. And Caesar said, 'Speak the truth, you most impious man, for through your godless behaviour against Jesus, even here the working of your evil deeds was shown in the overthrowing of the gods. Tell me now: Who is that crucified one, that his name destroyed all the gods?' Pilate answered, 'Truly, the charges made against him are true. For I myself was convinced by his deeds that he is greater than all the gods whom we worship.' Caesar said, 'Why then did you bring such audacious action against him if you were not ignorant of him, unless you wished to harm my kingdom?' Pilate answered, 'I did it because of the lawlessness and sedition of the lawless and godless Jews.'

6. Then Caesar, filled with anger, took counsel with all the senate and his forces, and ordered the following decree to be recorded against the Jews, 'To Licianus, chief governor of the

East, greeting! I have been informed that recently those Jews
who live in Jerusalem and the neighbouring Jewish towns have
had the audacity to commit a lawless crime in forcing Pilate to
crucify Jesus, who was acknowledged as God. Because of this
crime of theirs the world was darkened and dragged down to
destruction. Therefore by this decree proceed there with all
speed with a strong body of troops and take them prisoner.
Be obedient, and advance against them; by scattering them
among all the nations enslave them and expel them from
Judaea, making the nation so insignificant that it may no
longer be seen anywhere, since they are full of evil.'

7. When this decree arrived in the East, Licianus obeyed it
and destroyed the whole Jewish nation, and those who were
left in Judaea he scattered as slaves among the nations, so that
it was known to Caesar that these things had been done by
Licianus against the Jews in the East, and he was pleased.

8. And again Caesar was determined to question Pilate, and
commanded an officer called Albius to behead Pilate saying,
'As this man raised his hand against the righteous man called
Christ, so shall he fall in the same way and find no salvation.'

9. And when Pilate came to the place of execution, he
prayed silently, 'Lord, do not destroy me with the wicked
Hebrews, for had it not been because of the nation of the
lawless Jews, I would not have raised my hand against you,
because they plotted a revolt against me. You know that I acted
in ignorance. Therefore do not destroy me because of this sin,
but pardon me, Lord, and your servant Procla, who stands
with me in this hour of my death, whom you taught to prophesy that you must be nailed to the cross. Do not condemn her
also because of my sin, but pardon us and number us among
your righteous ones.'

10. And behold, when Pilate had finished his prayer, there
sounded a voice from heaven, 'All generations and families of
the Gentiles shall call you blessed, because in your governor-
ship everything was fulfilled which the prophets foretold about
me. And you yourself shall appear as my witness at my second
coming, when I shall judge the twelve tribes of Israel and those
who have not confessed my name.' And the prefect cut off
Pilate's head, and behold, an angel of the Lord received it. And
when Procla his wife saw the angel coming and receiving his

head, she was filled with joy, and immediately gave up the ghost and was buried with her husband.

(2) *Mors Pilati* (extract)

When Caesar knew of the death of Pilate, he said, 'He has justly died a most disgraceful death, seeing that his own hand has not spared him.' He was therefore bound to a great block of stone, and sunk in the river Tiber. However, malignant and filthy spirits, rejoicing in his malignant and filthy body, kept moving in the waters, and in a terrible manner caused lightning and tempests, thunder and hail, so that everyone was in constant fear. Therefore the Romans pulled him out of the river Tiber and carried him off in derision to Vienne, and sunk him in the river Rhône. Vienne means the Way of Gehenna, because it became a place of cursing. But evil spirits were at work and did the same things there too, so the people, unwilling to endure a plague of demons, removed that vessel of malediction and sent him to be buried in the territory of Losania. The inhabitants there were also troubled by the same visitations, so they removed him and sunk him in a lake, surrounded by mountains, where to this day, according to the tales of some, sundry diabolical machinations occur.

(3) *Gospel of Nicodemus* (*Christ's Descent*) 29 (Latin A)

Pontius Pilate to Claudius, his King, greeting.

There happened recently something which I myself brought to light. The Jews through envy have punished themselves and their posterity with a cruel punishment. For their fathers had a promise that God would send them from heaven his holy one, who would rightly be called their king and whom God had promised to send to earth by a virgin. Yet when he came to Judaea when I was governor, and they saw that he restored sight to the blind, cleansed lepers, healed paralytics, expelled evil spirits from men, and even raised the dead, and commanded the winds, and walked dry-shod upon the waves of the sea, and did many other miracles, and all the people of the

Jews acknowledged him to be the Son of God, the chief priests were moved by envy against him and they seized him and delivered him to me, and telling one lie after another they said he was a sorcerer and acting contrary to their law. And I believed this was so and ordered him to be scourged, and handed him over to their will. And they crucified him and set guards over him after he was buried. But he rose again on the third day, while my soldiers kept watch. But the Jews were so carried away by their wickedness that they gave money to my soldiers saying, 'Say that his disciples stole his body.' But after receiving the money they were unable to keep silent about what had happened. For they testified that he had arisen and that they had seen it, and that they had received money from the Jews. I have reported this lest anyone should lie about it and lest you should think that the lies of the Jews should be believed.

(4) *Letters of Pilate and Herod* (summaries)

The Letter of Pilate to Herod

It was no good thing which I did at your persuasion when I crucified Jesus. I ascertained from the centurion and the soldiers that he rose again, and I sent to Galilee and learned that he was preaching there to above five hundred believers.

My wife Procla took Longinus, the believing centurion, and ten soldiers who had kept the sepulchre, and went forth and found him sitting in a tilled field teaching a multitude. He saw them, addressed them, and spoke of his victory over death and hell. Procla and the rest returned and told me. I was in great distress, and put on a mourning garment and went with her and fifty soldiers to Galilee. We found Jesus: and as we approached him there was a sound in heaven and thunder, and the earth trembled and gave forth a sweet odour. We fell on our faces and the Lord came and raised us up, and I saw on him the scars of the passion, and he laid his hands on my shoulders, saying, 'All generations and families shall call you blessed, because in your days the Son of Man died and rose again.'

The Letter of Herod to Pilate

It is in no small sorrow that I write to you.

My dear daughter Herodias was playing upon the ice and fell in up to her neck. And her mother caught at her head to save her, and it was cut off, and the water swept her body away. My wife is sitting with the head on her knees, weeping, and all the house is full of sorrow.

I am in great distress of mind at the death of Jesus, and reflecting on my sins in killing John Baptist and massacring the Innocents. 'Since, then, you are able to see the man Jesus again, strive for me and intercede for me: for to you Gentiles the kingdom is given, according to the prophets and Christ.'

Lesbonax my son is in the last stages of a decline. I am afflicted with dropsy, and worms are coming out of my mouth. My wife's left eye is blinded through weeping. Righteous are the judgements of God, because we mocked at the eye of the righteous. Vengeance will come on the Jews and the priests, and the Gentiles will inherit the kingdom, and the children of light be cast out.

And, Pilate, since we are of one age, bury my family honourably: it is better for us to be buried by you than by the priests, who are doomed to speedy destruction. Farewell. I have sent you my wife's earrings and my own signet ring. I am already beginning to receive judgement in this world, but I fear the judgement hereafter much more. This is temporary, that is everlasting.

7

Jesus in the Underworld

The Christian affirmation of belief in Jesus' descent to Hades is in the Apostles' Creed and in the so-called Athanasian Creed, as well as being article III in the Anglican Thirty-Nine Articles. The Biblical origin for this belief, which is a major and normative part of Christian tradition, seems to be based on a particular interpretation of I Peter 3: 19 ('In the spirit he (Christ) went and preached to the imprisoned spirits'). Not surprisingly, that statement encouraged later generations of Christians to elaborate what was meant by Jesus' appearance before imprisoned spirits. The apocryphal stories of Jesus' descent to the underworld reflect those elaborations.

The main text describing these events is the fifth–sixth-century Descensus ad Inferos (the Descent of Jesus to Hades), found in several manuscripts as the second half of the Gospel of Nicodemus, the first half being the Acts of Pilate. Extracts from this text are printed under (1) below.

In this tradition Jesus' arrival in Hades after his death by crucifixion spells the end of death as a permanent state. 'Hades' by transference is the domain of the character, Hades (known elsewhere in mythology as Pluto). He rules over the world of departed spirits. This realm seems close to the idea of the Hebrew Sheol. (In the creeds the word 'hell' is erroneous and confusing.) Hades is not hell or Tartarus—those are names for the place of eternal punishment, and the opposite of heaven, the place of the eternally blessed. We read of heaven and hell in Chapter 15.

The age-old cycle of death and decay inaugurated by Adam's sin is now said to have been reversed by Christ's inability to be bound by death. This orthodox belief, so strongly present in the New Testament Gospels and in Paul's writings, is in effect dramatized in the Descensus. Another orthodox belief dramatized in this apocryphon is that the faithful will be raised from death because Christ is the first-fruits of those raised. This belief is graphically illustrated by Christ leading Adam and all others out of Hades and into paradise. Among those appearing in this Gospel is a favourite character in the apocryphal writings, the repentant thief crucified alongside Jesus: he is on his way to paradise direct, just as Jesus had promised, when he encounters the newly raised procession.

The first extract from this text shows the two characters, Satan (that supreme embodiment of evil, the devil, the adversary of God) and Hades, aware of Jesus' imminent arrival in their midst. They are powerless to stop his descent. Other extracts tell of Jesus' arrival and his triumph over Satan. The faithful are then released. The whole narrative is presented as a written account commissioned by the chief priests of the Jerusalem Temple from the newly resurrected sons of Simeon: the men tell their story as eyewitnesses of the events in Hades.

Another text which parallels in part the Descensus is the Questions of Bartholomew, dated perhaps as early as the second century. In that book Bartholomew confronts Jesus in the period before his Ascension. Extracts adapted from the Greek text appear under (2) below: among them is Bartholomew's question concerning Jesus' whereabouts after his crucifixion (when he is said to have 'vanished' from the cross). Jesus' reply is remarkably consistent with the story in the Descensus. Other questions are posed by Bartholomew and a further extract below includes his request to meet the adversary of men—called here Beliar. (Beliar is usually known as Belial in the Bible, in the Dead Sea Scrolls, and also in Milton's *Paradise Lost*, where he is the fallen angel who represents impurity.)

The scene when Christ releases the faithful from Hades (often called the Harrowing of Hell) was a popular episode in the Middle Ages. The saddlers' performance of this scene in the York cycle of mystery plays is the climax of the conflict between God and the devil for possession of the souls of men.

(1) *The Gospel of Nicodemus (Christ's Descent)* 4(20)–10(26)

4(20). 1. Satan the heir of darkness came and said to Hades, 'All devouring and insatiable one, listen to my words. There is one of the race of the Jews, Jesus by name, who calls himself the Son of God. But he is a man, and at our instigation the Jews crucified him. And now that he is dead, be prepared that we may secure him here. For I know that he is a man, and I heard him saying, "My soul is very sorrowful, even to death." He caused me much trouble in the world above while he lived among mortals. For wherever he found my servants, he cast them out, and all those whom I had made to be crippled or blind or lame, leprous and the like, he healed with only a word, and many whom I had made ready for burial he also made alive again with only a word.' 2. Hades said, 'Is he so powerful that he does such things with only a word? And if he is of such power, are you able to withstand him? It seems to me that no one will be able to withstand such as he is. But if you say that you heard how he feared death, he said this to mock and laugh at you, wishing to seize you with a strong hand. And woe, woe to you for all eternity.' Satan answered, 'O all-devouring and insatiable Hades, did you fear so greatly when you heard about our common foe? I did not fear him, but worked upon the Jews, and they crucified him and gave him gall and vinegar to drink. Therefore prepare yourself to get him firmly into your power when he comes.'

3. Hades answered, 'O heir of darkness, son of perdition, devil, you have just told me that many whom you made ready for burial he made alive again with only a word. If then he freed others from the grave, how and with what power will he be held by us? A short time ago I devoured a certain dead man called Lazarus, and soon afterwards one of the living drew him up forcibly from my entrails with only a word. And I think it is the one of whom you speak. If, therefore, we receive him here, I fear lest we run the risk of losing the others also. For, behold, I see that all those whom I have devoured from the beginning of the world are disquieted. My belly is in pain. Lazarus who was snatched from me before seems to me no good sign. For not like a dead man, but like an eagle he flew away from me, so

quickly did the earth cast him out. Therefore I adjure you by
your gifts and mine, do not bring him here. For I believe that
he comes here to raise all the dead. And I tell you this: By the
darkness which surrounds us, if you bring him here, none of
the dead will be left for me.'

5(21). 1. While Satan and Hades were speaking thus to one
another, a loud voice like thunder sounded, 'Lift up your gates,
O rulers, and be lifted up, O everlasting doors, and the King of
Glory shall come in.' When Hades heard this, he said to Satan,
'Go out, if you can, and withstand him.' So Satan went out.
Then Hades said to his demons, 'Secure strongly and firmly the
gates of brass and the bars of iron, and hold my bolts, and
stand upright and keep watch on everything. For if he comes
in, woe will seize us. 2. When the forefathers heard that, they
all began to mock him, saying, 'O all-devouring and insatiable
one, open, that the King of Glory may come in.' The prophet
David said, 'Do you not know, blind one, that when I lived in
the world, I prophesied that word: "Lift up your gates, O
rulers"?' Isaiah said, 'I foresaw this by the Holy Spirit and
wrote, "The dead shall arise, and those who are in the tombs
shall be raised up, and those who are under the earth shall
rejoice. O death, where is your sting? O Hades, where is your
victory?"' 3. Again the voice sounded, 'Lift up the gates.' When
Hades heard the voice the second time, he answered as if he
did not know it and said, 'Who is this King of Glory?' The
angels of the Lord said, 'The Lord strong and mighty, the Lord
mighty in battle.' And immediately at this answer the gates of
brass were broken in pieces and the bars of iron were crushed
and all the dead who were bound were loosed from their
chains, and we with them. And the King of Glory entered as a
man, and all the dark places of Hades were illuminated.

6(22). 1. Hades at once cried out, 'We are defeated, woe to
us. But who are you, who have such authority and power? And
who are you, who without sin have come here, you who appear
small and can do great things, who are humble and exalted,
slave and master, soldier and king, and have authority over
both the dead and the living? You were nailed to the cross, and
laid in the sepulchre, and now you have become free and
have destroyed all our power. Are you Jesus, of whom the chief
ruler Satan said to us that through the cross and death you

would inherit the whole world?' 2. Then the King of Glory seized the chief ruler Satan by the head and handed him over to the angels, saying, 'Bind with irons his hands and his feet and his neck and his mouth.' Then he gave him to Hades and said, 'Take him and hold him fast until my second coming.'

7(23). 1. And Hades took Satan and said to him, 'O Beelzebub, heir of fire and torment, enemy of the saints, through what necessity did you contrive that the King of Glory should be crucified, so that he should come here and strip us naked? Turn and see that not one dead man is left in me, but all that you gained through the tree of knowledge you have lost through the tree of the cross. All your joy is changed into sorrow. You wished to kill the King of Glory, but have killed yourself. For since I have received you to hold you fast, you shall learn by experience what evils I shall do to you. O arch-devil, the beginning of death, the root of sin, the end of all evil, what evil did you find in Jesus to procure his destruction? How did you dare to commit such great wickedness? How did you study to bring down such a man into this darkness, through whom you have been deprived of all who have died since the beginning?'

8(24). 1. While Hades was thus speaking with Satan, the King of Glory stretched out his right hand, and took hold of our forefather Adam and raised him up. Then he turned to the rest and said, 'Come with me, all you who have died through the tree which this man touched. For behold, I raise you all up again through the tree of the cross.' With that he sent them all out. And our forefather Adam was seen to be full of joy, and said, 'I give thanks to your majesty, O Lord, because you have brought me up from the lowest Hades.' Likewise all the prophets and the saints said, 'We give you thanks, O Christ, Saviour of the world, because you have brought up our life from destruction'. 2. When they had said this, the Saviour blessed Adam with the sign of the cross on his forehead. And he did this also to the patriarchs and prophets and martyrs and forefathers, and he took them and sprang up out of Hades. And as he went the holy fathers sang praises, following him and saying, 'Blessed be he who comes in the name of the Lord. Alleluia. To him be the glory of all the saints.'

9(25). 1. Thus he went into paradise holding our forefather Adam by the hand, and he handed him and all the righteous to Michael the archangel. And as they were entering the gate of paradise, two old men met them. The holy fathers asked them, 'Who are you, who have not seen death nor gone down into Hades, but dwell in paradise with your bodies and souls?' One of them answered, 'I am Enoch, who pleased God and was removed here by him. And this is Elijah the Tishbite. We are to live until the end of the world. But then we are to be sent by God to withstand Antichrist and to be killed by him. And after three days we shall rise again and be caught up in clouds to meet the Lord.'

10(26). 1. While they were saying this there came another, a humble man, carrying a cross on his shoulder. The holy fathers asked him, 'Who are you, who have the appearance of a robber, and what is the cross you carry on your shoulder?' He answered, 'I was, as you say, a robber and a thief in the world, and therefore the Jews took me and delivered me to the death of the cross together with our Lord Jesus Christ. When he hung on the cross, I saw the wonders which happened and believed in him. And I appealed to him and said, "Lord, when you reign as king, do not forget me." And immediately he said to me, "Truly, truly, today, I say to you, you shall be with me in paradise." So I came into paradise carrying my cross, and found Michael the archangel, and said to him, "Our Lord Jesus Christ, who was crucified, has sent me here. Lead me, therefore, to the gate of Eden." And when the flaming sword saw the sign of the cross, it opened to me and I went in. Then the archangel said to me, "Wait a short while. For Adam also, the forefather of the race of men, comes with the righteous, that they also may enter in." And now that I have seen you, I have come to meet you.' When the saints heard this, they all cried with a loud voice, 'Great is our Lord, and great is his power.'

(2) *The Questions of Bartholomew* I. 1–11, 21–34; IV. 7–44

I. 1. After the resurrection from the dead of our Lord Jesus Christ, Bartholomew came to the Lord and questioned him, saying, 'Lord, reveal to me the mysteries of the heavens.'

2. Jesus answered and said to him, 'If I put not off the body of the flesh, I shall not be able to tell them to you.'

4. Bartholomew therefore drew near to the Lord and said, 'I have a word to speak to you, Lord.'

5. And Jesus said to him, 'I know what you are about to say; say then what you will and I will answer you.'

6. And Bartholomew said, 'Lord, when you went to be hanged upon the cross, I followed you afar off and saw you hung upon the cross, and the angels coming down from heaven and worshipping you. And when there came darkness, (7) I looked and I saw that you vanished away from the cross, and I heard only a voice in the parts under the earth, and great wailing and gnashing of teeth all of a sudden. Tell me, Lord, where did you go to from the cross?'

8. And Jesus answered and said, 'Blessed are you, Bartholomew, my beloved, because you saw this mystery; and now I will tell you all things whatsoever you ask me. 9. For when I vanished from the cross, then I went down into Hades that I might bring up Adam and all those who were with him, according to the supplication of Michael the archangel.

10. Then Bartholomew said, 'Lord, what was the voice which was heard?'

11. Jesus said to him, 'Hades said to Beliar, "As I perceive, a God comes hither."'

21. Bartholomew said to him, 'Tell me, Lord, who was he whom the angels carried up in their hands, that man who was very great of stature?'

22. Jesus answered and said to him, 'It was Adam the first-formed, for whose sake I came down from heaven upon earth. And I said to him, "I was hung upon the cross for you and for your children's sake." And he, when he heard it, groaned and said, "Such was your good pleasure, O Lord."'

23. Again Bartholomew said, 'Lord, I saw the angels ascending before Adam and singing praises. 24. But one of the angels who was very great, above the rest, would not ascend with them; and there was in his hand a sword of fire, and he was looking steadfastly upon you only.'

25. 'And all the angels besought him that he would go up with them, but he would not. But when you commanded him to go up, I beheld a flame of fire issuing out of his hands and going even to the city of Jerusalem.' 26. And Jesus said to him, 'Blessed are you, Bartholomew my beloved, because you saw these mysteries. This was one of the angels of vengeance which stand before my Father's throne: and this angel he sent to me. 27. And for this cause he would not ascend, because he desired to destroy all the powers of the world. But when I commanded him to ascend, there went a flame out of his hand and rent asunder the veil of the temple, and parted it in two pieces for a witness to the children of Israel for my passion because they crucified me.'

28. And when he had spoken he said to the apostles, 'Tarry for me in this place, for today a sacrifice is offered in paradise.' 29. And Bartholomew answered and said to Jesus, 'Lord, what is the sacrifice which is offered in paradise?' And Jesus said, 'There are souls of the righteous which today have departed out of the body and go to paradise, and unless I be present they cannot enter into paradise.'

30. And Bartholomew said, 'Lord, how many souls depart out of the world daily?' Jesus said to him, 'Thirty thousand.'

31. Bartholomew said to him, 'Lord, when you were with us teaching the word, did you receive the sacrifices in paradise?' Jesus answered and said to him, 'Verily I say unto you, my beloved, that I both taught the word with you and continually sat with my Father and received the sacrifices in paradise every day.' 32. Bartholomew answered and said to him, 'Lord, if thirty thousand souls depart out of the world every day , how many souls out of them are found righteous?' Jesus said to him, 'Hardly fifty-three, my beloved.' 33. Again Bartholomew said, 'And how do three only enter into paradise?' Jesus said to him, 'The fifty-three enter into paradise or are laid up in Abraham's bosom: but the others go into the place of the resurrection, for the three are not like the fifty.'

34. Bartholomew said to him, 'Lord, how many souls above the number are born into the world daily?' Jesus said to him, 'One soul only is born above the number of those who depart.'

IV. 7. When Jesus appeared again, Bartholomew said to him, 'Lord, show us the adversary of men that we may behold him, of what fashion he is, and what is his work, and whence he comes forth, and what power he has that he spared not even you but caused you to be hanged upon the tree.' 8. But Jesus looked upon him and said, 'You bold heart! You ask for that which you are not able to look upon.' 9. But Bartholomew was troubled and fell at Jesus' feet and began to speak thus, 'O lamp that cannot be quenched, Lord Jesu Christ, maker of the eternal light, who have given to those who love you the grace that beautifies all, and have given us the eternal light by your coming into the world, who have . . . the heavenly essence by a word . . . have accomplished the work of the Father, have turned the shamefacedness of Adam into mirth, have done away the sorrow of Eve with a cheerful countenance by your birth from a virgin: remember not evil against me but grant me the work of my asking.'

10. And as he spoke, Jesus raised him up and said to him, 'Bartholomew, will you see the adversary of men? I tell you that when you behold him not only you but the rest of the apostles and Mary will fall on your faces and become as dead corpses.'

11. But they all said unto him, 'Lord, let us behold him.'

12. And he led them down from the Mount of Olives and looked wrathfully upon the angels that keep hell, and beckoned to Michael to sound the trumpet in the height of the heavens. And Michael sounded, and the earth shook, and Beliar came up, being held by six hundred and sixty angels and bound with fiery chains. 13. And the length of him was one thousand six hundred cubits and his breadth forty cubits and his face was like a lightning of fire and his eyes full of darkness. And out of his nostrils came a stinking smoke; and his mouth was as the gulf of a precipice, and one of his wings was fourscore cubits. 14. And straightway when the apostles saw him, they fell to the earth on their faces and became as dead. 15. But Jesus came near and raised the apostles and gave them a spirit of power, and he said to Bartholomew, 'Come near, Bartholomew, and trample your feet on his neck, and he will tell you his work, what it is, and how he deceives men.' 16. And Jesus stood afar off with the rest of the apostles. 17. And Bartholomew was afraid and raised his voice and said, 'Blessed be the name of your immortal Kingdom from henceforth even for ever.' And when he had spoken, Jesus ordered

him, saying, 'Go and tread upon the neck of Beliar.' And
Bartholomew ran quickly upon him and trod upon his neck,
and Beliar trembled.

18. And Bartholomew was afraid and fled, and said to Jesus,
'Lord, give me a hem of your garments that I may have courage
to draw near to him.' 19. But Jesus said to him, 'You cannot
take a hem of my garments, for these are not my garments
which I wore before I was crucified.' 20. And Bartholomew
said, 'Lord, I fear because, just as he did not spare your angels,
he will swallow me up also.' 21. Jesus said to him, 'Were not all
things made by my word, and by the will of my Father the
spirits were made subject to Solomon? You, therefore, being
commanded by my word, go in my name and ask him what
you will.' 22. And Bartholomew made the sign of the cross and
prayed to Jesus and went behind him. And Jesus said to him,
'Draw near.' And as Bartholomew drew near, the fire was
kindled on every side, so that his garments appeared fiery.
Jesus said to Bartholomew, 'As I said to you, tread upon his
neck and ask him what is his power.' And Bartholomew went
and trod upon his neck, and pressed down his face into the
earth as far as his ears. 23. And Bartholomew said to him, 'Tell
me who you are and what is your name.' And he said to him,
'Lighten me a little, and I will tell you who I am and how I
came hither, and what my work is and what my power is.'
24. And he eased him and said to him, 'Say all that you have
done and all that you will do.' 25. And Beliar answered and
said, 'If you will know my name, at the first I was called
Satanael, which is interpreted a messenger of God, but when I
rejected the image of God my name was called Satanas, that is,
an angel that keeps hell.' 26. And again Bartholomew said to
him, 'Reveal to me all things and hide nothing from me.'
27. And he said to him, 'I swear to you by the power of the
glory of God that even if I would hide anything I cannot, for he
who would convict me is near. For if I were able I would have
destroyed you like one of those who were before you. 28. For
indeed I was formed the first angel; for when God made the
heavens, he took a handful of fire and formed me first, Michael
second, Gabriel third, Uriel fourth, Raphael fifth, Nathanael
sixth, and other angels of whom I cannot tell the names. For
they are the rod-bearers of God, and they smite me with their

rods and pursue me seven times in the night and seven times in the day, and leave me not at all and break in pieces all my power. These are the angels of vengeance who stand before the throne of God: these are the angels that were first formed. 30. And after them were formed all the angels. In the first heaven are a hundred myriads, and in the second a hundred myriads, and in the third a hundred myriads, and in the fourth a hundred myriads, and in the fifth a hundred myriads, and in the sixth a hundred myriads, and in the seventh is the first firmament wherein are the powers which work upon men. 31. For there are four other angels set over the winds. The first angel is over the north, and he is called Chairoum, and has in his hand a rod of fire and restrains the superfluity of moisture that the earth be not too wet. 32. And the angel that is over the north is called Oertha: he has a torch of fire and puts it to his sides, and they warm his great coldness so that he may not freeze the world. 33. And the angel that is over the south is called Kerkoutha, and they break his fierceness so that he may not shake the earth. 34. And the angel that is over the south-west is called Naoutha, and he has a rod of snow in his hand and puts it into his mouth, and quenches the fire that comes out of his mouth. And if the angel did not quench it at his mouth it would set all the world on fire. 35. And there is another angel over the sea which makes it rough with the waves. 36. But the rest I will not tell you, for he who stands by does not permit it.'

37. Bartholomew said to him, 'How do you chastise the souls of men?' 38. Beliar said to him, 'Do you wish me to describe the punishment of the hypocrites, of the backbiters, of the jesters, of the idolaters, and the covetous, and the adulterers, and the wizards, and the diviners, and of those who believe in us, and of all whom I look upon?' 39. Bartholomew said to him, 'I wish you to be brief.' 40. And he smote his teeth together, gnashing them, and there came up out of the bottomless pit a wheel having a sword flashing with fire, and in the sword were pipes. 41. And he asked him, saying, 'What is this sword?' 42. And he said, 'This sword is the sword of the gluttonous, for into this pipe are sent those who through their gluttony devise all manner of sin; into the second pipe are sent the backbiters who slander their neighbours secretly; into the

third pipe are sent the hypocrites and the rest whom I overthrow by my contrivance.' 43. And Bartholomew said, 'Do you
then do these things by yourself alone?' 44. And Satan said, 'If
I were able to go forth by myself I would have destroyed the
whole world in three days, but neither I nor any of the six
hundred go forth. For we have other swift ministers whom we
command, and we furnish them with a hook of many points
and send them forth to hunt, and they catch for us souls of
men, enticing them with various tempting baits, that is, by
drunkenness and laughter, by backbiting, hypocrisy, pleasures, fornication, and the rest of the trifles that come out of
their treasures.'

8

Veronica

$\diamond$

Veronica in the Latin tradition, and Bernice or Berenice in the Greek, is the woman who is identified in apocryphal texts (such as the Acts of Pilate and the Book of the Resurrection of Jesus Christ by Bartholomew the Apostle) as the unnamed woman cured by Jesus of her issue of blood in Mark 5: 25.

The later apocryphal tradition in the medieval text known as the Vindicta Salvatoris (or the Avenging of the Saviour) names Veronica as the woman who wiped Christ's face with a cloth. According to the legend, the image of his face was preserved on the cloth. The story in the Vindicta Salvatoris, from which the extract below is taken, tells how Titus, a convert to Christianity, came with Vespasian in order to destroy the enemies of Christ by overthrowing Jerusalem. The Emperor, Tiberius, then sent his kinsman, Velosian, to Jerusalem to locate Veronica and her cloth, so that through it he (the Emperor) could be cured of an illness. The tone throughout much of this book is anti-Jewish.

(The medieval Latin text known as the Mors Pilati also tells of Veronica and her wonder-working kerchief.)

From the eighth century a 'veil of Veronica' has been preserved in Rome, from the end of the thirteenth century in St Peter's. In the fourteenth and fifteenth centuries it was the object of much veneration, as it was believed to effect cures. But Veronica has been given a place of continuing devotion in Christian practice because of the Stations of the Cross. Once the fourteen Stations became a standard pictorial means of encouraging meditation on the Passion of Christ, Station six, depicting the wiping of Jesus' face by Veronica, helped perpetuate the fame of this woman.

Popular etymology explains that 'Veronica' means 'true

image' (*vera icon*)—as opposed to spurious images of Christ. The name is applied to the cloth and to the woman whose headcloth it was. (A sudarium with the image of Christ imprinted on it is known in English as a vernicle. Even one of the torero's movements with his cape is called a veronica!)

Vindicta Salvatoris 32–5

32. Then they made a search with great diligence to seek the portrait of the Lord; and they found a woman named Veronica who had the portrait of the Lord. 33. Then the Emperor Tiberius said to Velosian, 'How have you kept it?' And he answered, 'I have it in clean cloth of gold, rolled up in a shawl.' And the Emperor Tiberius said, 'Bring it to me, and spread it before my face, that I may fall to the ground and bending my knees, may adore it on the ground.' Then Velosian spread out his shawl with the cloth of gold on which the portrait of the Lord had been imprinted; and the Emperor Tiberius saw it. And he immediately adored the image of the Lord with a pure heart, and his flesh was cleansed and became as the flesh of a little child. And all the blind, the lepers, the lame, the dumb, the deaf, and those possessed by various diseases, who were there present, were healed, and cured, and cleansed. 34. And the Emperor Tiberius bowed his head and bent his knees, and pondered the words, 'Blessed is the womb which bore you, and the breasts which you sucked', and he groaned to the Lord, saying with tears, 'God of heaven and earth, do not permit me to sin, but confirm my soul and my body, and place me in your kingdom, because in your name do I always trust: free me from all evils, as you freed the three children from the furnace of blazing fire.'

35. Then the Emperor Tiberius said to Velosian, 'Velosian, have you seen any of those men who saw Christ?' Velosian answered, 'I have.' He said, 'Did you ask how they baptize those who believed in Christ?' Velosian said, 'Here, my lord, we have one of the disciples of Christ himself.' Then he ordered Nathan to be summoned to come to him. Nathan therefore came and baptized him in the name of the Father, and of the Son, and of the Holy Ghost. Amen. Immediately the Emperor Tiberius, made whole from all his diseases, ascended upon his throne,

and said, 'Blessed are you, O Lord God Almighty, and worthy
to be praised, who have freed me from the snare of death, and
cleansed me from all my iniquities; because I have greatly
sinned before you, O Lord my God, and I am not worthy to see
your face.' And then the Emperor Tiberius was instructed in all
the articles of the faith, fully, and with strong faith.

9

Zacharias

———————————— ✧ ————————————

Zacharias (or Zechariah or Zachariah), a Jewish priest, appears in Luke 1 and receives a vision promising him and his aged wife, Elizabeth, a son. That son is John the Baptist. Zacharias celebrates the child's birth with the hymn known to Christianity as the Benedictus. So much for the New Testament references to Zacharias. But, like many such figures in the New Testament, Zacharias became the subject of later tradition. At the end of the Protevangelium of James, a book largely given over to the birth and childhood of the Virgin Mary and to the birth of Jesus, the story changes from the escape of the infant John and his mother at the time of Herod's Massacre of the Innocents to a scene in which John's priestly father, Zacharias, is murdered in the Jerusalem Temple by command of Herod. It is likely that the story was a late appendix to the Protevangelium and is an elaboration of Jesus' prophecy to the Jews in Matthew 23: 35: 'On you will fall the guilt of all the innocent blood spilt on the ground, from the blood of innocent Abel to the blood of Zechariah, son of Berachiah, whom you murdered between the sanctuary and the altar.' Whoever that Zechariah was, the apocryphal tradition obviously identified him with the Baptist's father and thus created the story below which would be seen as a fulfilment of the prophecy. It is interesting to note that after Zacharias' murder his successor as priest is said to be Simeon, another character taken from Luke's infancy narrative.

Protevangelium of James 23–4

23. 1. Herod was searching for John, and sent officers to Zacharias saying, 'Where have you hidden your son?' And he answered and said to them, 'I am a minister of God and serve in the temple of the Lord. I do not know where my son is.' 2. And the officers departed and told all this to Herod. Then Herod was angry and said, 'His son is to be king over Israel!' And he sent to him again saying, 'Tell the truth. Where is your son? You know that you are at my mercy.' And the officers departed and told him these things. 3. And Zacharias said, 'I am a witness of God. Pour out blood! But the Lord will receive my spirit, for you shed innocent blood at the threshold of the temple of the Lord.' And about daybreak Zacharias was slain. And the children of Israel did not know that he had been slain.

24. 1. But at the hour of the salutation the priests were departing, and the customary blessing of Zacharias did not take place. And the priests stood waiting for Zacharias, to greet him with prayer and to glorify the Most High. 2. But when he failed to come they were all afraid. But one of them took courage and went in and he saw beside the altar congealed blood; and a voice said, 'Zacharias has been slain, and his blood shall not be wiped away until his avenger comes.' And when he heard these words, he was afraid and went out and told the priests what he had seen. 3. And they took courage and entered and saw what had happened. And the ceiling panels of the temple wailed, and they split their clothes from the top to the bottom. And they did not find his body, but they found his blood turned into stone. And they were afraid, and went out and told all the people that Zacharias had been slain. And all the tribes of the people heard and they mourned him and lamented three days and three nights. 4. And after the three days the priests took counsel whom they should appoint in his stead and the lot fell upon Simeon. Now it was he to whom it had been revealed by the Holy Spirit that he should not see death until he had seen the Christ in the flesh.

B

Stories relating to the Growth
of the Church

✧

In the New Testament the Acts of the Apostles, written towards
the end of the first century, tells of the travels of several of the
earliest followers of Jesus in the period after his death. The
miracles effected by these apostles, principally Peter and Paul,
their speeches, their travels, and their successes in converting
others to the Christian cause dominate canonical Acts. From
the second century onwards this style of writing continued.
Several apocryphal Acts were composed, usually with one particular apostle, although occasionally two, centre stage. Not
surprisingly, books of Acts were written recounting the travels
and deeds of some of the founders of the church. Those Acts
telling of Peter and Paul and of John and of Thomas and of
Andrew, written in the second century, were particularly influential. (The Manichaean sect, a radical ascetic offshoot of
Persian Gnosticism, popular in Egypt and Rome in the second
and fourth centuries, gathered these five Acts into a corpus to
which they, falsely, attributed a common authorship and
which they substituted for the canonical Acts of the Apostles.)
It is extracts from each of these major Acts that occur in the
following five chapters.

The eponymous hero of all these Acts is, to a large extent, a
stock character. He is a fearless champion for Christ, display-
ing prodigious deeds of courage, performing spectacular miracles, delivering himself of effective speeches, defending in
public his faith, withstanding hardship and suffering depri-
vation (including imprisonments and torture), and dying typi-
cally as a martyr. Paul in the Acts of Paul is not the historic
figure discerned in the New Testament letters. Peter is not the

disciple recognized in the canonical Gospels. They and the other apostles, John, Thomas, Andrew, who figure in the different Acts are each merely a personification of the obedient apostle venerated as an ideal figure in the areas where the stories originated. The places where the stories are located are also largely conventional. Other characters, Jewish, Christian, and pagan are also two-dimensional. One may wish to argue for the historical value of parts of the canonical Acts of the Apostles. Few would defend the historicity of these apocryphal Acts. The stories are pious fiction. The yarns were, however, the inspirational reading matter of many generations of Christians from East to West. The apocryphal Acts were best-sellers, copied over several centuries, translated into different languages, and spawning many imitations. Apart from their entertainment value, they may be seen as 'historical' in the sense that they show the interests, beliefs, and attitudes of those second-century Christians who produced and first read them. At a time when the intellectual leaders of the churches were hammering out doctrines and creeds, literature like these Acts was the popular reading matter of the average person in the pew. As a consequence, it is interesting to balance this literature with the sermons, homilies, and apologetics written by the illustrious church fathers.

10

Peter

◆

In the New Testament Peter, the Galilean fisherman, is the most prominent of Jesus' followers. He is among the first of the disciples called by Jesus; he is frequently the spokesman and leader of the twelve disciples; he is prominent throughout Jesus' ministry and an active participant in many of the most significant and well-known events. His confession at Caesarea Philippi in Matthew 16: 16 that Jesus is the Messiah earns him the promise that he is the rock on whom Jesus will found his church. (The claim of the Papacy rests on an interpretation of these words.) Peter's threefold denial of Christ at the time of the trial is also famous. In the Resurrection stories Peter is said in the Gospels to have been granted a personal appearance of the risen Christ. In the Acts of the Apostles Peter is the leader of the Jerusalem church; the first half of that book is largely devoted to the travels, teachings, and miracles of Peter. His prominence as a pillar of the church is also clear in Paul's writings. Two New Testament letters bear his name. Several second-century works also attribute their authorship to Peter, including the apocryphal Preaching of Peter.

It is not surprising to find that many legends and traditions gathered around the name of Peter, the largest collection of them outside the Bible being in the second-century Acts of Peter. This apocryphal work is not available in its entirety but sufficient from it survives to enable scholars to reconstruct at least part of the original.

The extracts below come from the portions of the ancient Acts now extant in different sources. First (1) are included the strange tale of Peter and his daughter, and the episode with the gardener's daughter. The anti-sex teaching of those stories is a recurrent theme in much of the apocryphal tradition. These are followed by a somewhat typical miracle—the reviving of a dead tunny fish.

A longer section then follows; this concerns Peter and Simon Magus. The confrontation of the two Simons, the apostle Peter and the magician, is the conflict of Good versus Bad. The church historian Eusebius described Simon Magus as the first heretic, so it is not surprising that Simon, pre-eminently, was to be seen as the embodiment of evil. In the Acts of the Apostles 8 the story of the meeting of the two men is related in a mere fifteen verses. In the Acts of Peter several chapters are devoted to the stories about Simon Magus and Peter. The extracts below (2) concern the public trial of strength between the two when Peter successfully raises to life a lad whom Simon Magus has killed, the ability of the two men to raise a senator, and the grand finale when Simon attempts to fly.

The well-known *Quo Vadis?* scene ('Whither goest thou, O Lord?') occurs in the Acts of Paul and the Acts of Peter. The latter seems to have been the original, and is thus included in the present chapter (3). The episode has Peter, fleeing Rome, being met by Jesus, who regards the impending death of his apostle as the re-enacting of his own crucifixion; Peter is thereby encouraged to face his own execution. The episode and its supposed location is commemorated by the church of Sta Maria delle Piante on the Appian Way.

An extract from Peter's martyrdom follows (4). In many of the apocryphal Acts it is the death of the apostle which was the episode that survived, even if many of the preceding stories were excised or censored. In Peter's case his crucifixion is said to have been upside down to avoid mimicking Jesus' death. The inverse crucifixion is an unusual feature, but the preceding speech by the apostle is typical. Like a grand opera singer expiring after a lengthy death-bed aria, the apostles in these apocryphal Acts usually deliver themselves of a lengthy farewell—in Andrew's case in a speech lasting over three days. Peter's speech, given below, is a highly complex and mystical meditation on the significance of the Cross. The speech is a good representative of the more enigmatic writing that characterizes some apocryphal texts.

Later tradition located Peter's crucifixion and his burial on the site of St Peter's, Rome.

(1a) *Berlin Codex 8502.4*

But on the first day of the week, which is the Lord's Day, a multitude gathered together, and they brought many sick people to Peter for him to cure them. And one of the multitude was bold enough to say to Peter, 'Peter, behold, before our eyes you made many blind see and deaf hear and the lame walk, and you have helped the weak and given them strength; why have you not helped your virgin daughter, who has grown up beautiful and believed in the name of God? For behold, one of her sides is completely paralysed, and there she is helpless in the corner. We can see those whom you have cured, but you have neglected your own daughter.'

But Peter smiled and said to him, 'My son, God alone knows why her body is sick. Know that God is not unable or powerless to give his gift to my daughter. But in order that your soul may be convinced and those present believe the more'—he looked at his daughter and said to her, 'Arise from your place with the help of none except Jesus, and walk naturally before those present and come to me.' And she arose and came to him. The multitude rejoiced at what had taken place. And Peter said to them, 'Behold, your hearts are convinced that God is not powerless concerning the things which we ask of him.' They rejoiced the more and glorified God. Then Peter said to his daughter, 'Return to your place, sit down there and be helpless again, for it is good for me and you.' And the girl went back, lay down in her place and became as before. The whole multitude wept and besought Peter to make her well.

Peter said to them, 'As the Lord lives, this is good for her and for me. For on the day on which she was born to me I saw a vision and the Lord said to me, "Peter, this day has been born for you a great affliction, for this daughter will harm many souls, if her body remains well!" I, however, thought that the vision mocked me.

'When the girl was ten years old she became a stumbling-block to many. And a very rich man, Ptolemy by name, when he saw the girl bathing with her mother, sent for her to take her for his wife, but her mother did not consent. He often sent for her, for he could not wait ... [*Two-page gap in the manuscript*] . . . 'Ptolemy brought the girl, and leaving her before the door of the house went away.

'When I saw this, I and her mother went downstairs and found the girl with one side of her body paralysed from head to foot and dried up. We carried her away, praising the Lord that he had kept his servant from defilement and violation. This is the reason why the girl remains thus to this day. But now you shall hear what happened to Ptolemy. He repented and lamented night and day over that which had happened to him, and because of the many tears which he shed he became blind. Having decided to hang himself, behold, about the ninth hour of that day, whilst alone in his bedroom, he saw a great light which illuminated the whole house, and he heard a voice saying to him, "Ptolemy, God has not given the vessels for corruption and shame; it is not right for you, as a believer in me, to violate my virgin, whom you are to know as your sister, as if I had become one spirit to both of you—but arise, and speedily go to the house of the apostle Peter and you shall see my glory. He will explain the matter to you." And Ptolemy did not delay, but ordered his servants to show him the way and bring him to me. When he had come to me, he told all that had happened to him in the power of Jesus Christ, our Lord. And he saw with the eyes of his flesh and with the eyes of his soul, and many people set their hope on Christ; he did good to them and gave them the gift of God.

'After this Ptolemy died; he departed and went to his Lord. When he made his will, he left a piece of land in the name of my daughter because through her he became a believer in God and was made whole. I, however, who was appointed trustee, have acted carefully. I sold the acre, and God alone knows that neither I nor my daughter have kept anything from the money of the acre, but I sent the whole sum to the poor. Know, therefore, O servant of Christ Jesus, that God cares for his people and prepares for each what is good—even when we think that God has forgotten us. Now then, brethren, let us mourn, be watchful, and pray, and God's goodness will look upon us, and we hope for it.'

And Peter delivered other speeches before them, and glorifying the name of the Lord Christ he gave of the bread to all of them, and after distributing it he rose and went into the house.

(1*b*) Pseudo-Titus, *de dispositione Sanctimonii* (extract)

Consider and take note of the event about which the following account informs us:

A peasant had a girl who was a virgin. She was also his only daughter, and therefore he besought Peter to offer a prayer for her. After he had prayed, the apostle said to the father that the Lord would bestow upon her what was expedient for her soul. Immediately the girl fell down dead.

O reward worthy and ever pleasing to God, to escape the shamelessness of the flesh and to destroy the pride of the blood!

But this distrustful old man, failing to recognize the worth of the heavenly grace, the divine blessing, besought Peter again that his only daughter be raised from the dead. And some days later, after she had been raised, a man who passed himself off as a believer came into the house of the old man to stay with him and seduced the girl, and the two of them never appeared again.

(1*c*) *Acts of Peter* 13

13. And Peter turning around saw a smoked tunny fish hanging in a window. He took it, saying to the people, 'When you see this swimming in the water like a fish, will you be able to believe in him whom I preach?' And all said with one voice, 'Indeed we shall believe you.' So he went to the pond near by, saying, 'In your name, O Jesus Christ, in whom they do not yet believe, I say, "Tunny, in the presence of all these, live and swim like a fish."' And he cast the tunny into the pond, and it became alive and began to swim. The multitude saw the swimming fish and he made it swim not only for that hour but, lest they said that it was a deception, he made it swim longer, thereby attracting crowds from all parts and showing that the smoked tunny had again become a living fish. The success was such that many, seeing that the fish was alive, threw pieces of bread into the water. Very many who had witnessed this followed Peter and believed in the Lord, and met day and night in the house of Narcissus the presbyter. And Peter spoke to them of the prophetical writings and of the things done by our Lord Jesus Christ in word and deed.

(2) *Acts of Peter* 25–6, 28, 31–2

25. The prefect wished to show his impartiality to both Peter and Simon, so that he might not appear to be acting unjustly. And he summoned one of his slaves and spoke to Simon, 'Take him and kill him.' To Peter he said, 'And you revive him.' And to the people the prefect said, 'It is for you to decide which of these is accepted before God, he who kills, or he who revives.' And Simon whispered something into the ear of the slave and made him speechless, and he died. . . . 26. The prefect in the forum looked at Peter and said, 'What do you say, Peter? Behold, the lad is dead; the emperor liked him, and I spared him not. I had indeed many other young men; but I trusted in you and in your Lord whom you proclaim, if indeed you are sure and truthful: therefore I allowed him to die.' And Peter said, 'God is neither tempted nor weighed in the balance. But he is to be worshipped with the whole heart by those whom he loves and he will hear those who are worthy. Since, however, my God and Lord Jesus Christ is now tempted among you, he is doing many signs and miracles through me to turn you from your sins. In your power, revive now through my voice, O Lord, in the presence of all, him whom Simon killed by his touch.' And Peter said to the master of the lad, 'Come, take hold of him by the right hand and you shall have him alive and walking with you.' And the prefect Agrippa ran and came to the lad, took his hand, and restored him to life. And when the multitude saw this they cried, 'There is only one God, the God of Peter.'

28. When the news had spread through the entire city, the mother of a senator came, and making her way through the multitude she threw herself at Peter's feet and said, 'I heard many people say that you are a minister of the merciful God and that you impart his mercy to all who desire this light. Bestow, therefore, also to my son this light, since I have learned that you are not ungenerous towards any one; do not turn away from a lady, who entreats you.' Peter said to her, 'Do you believe in my God through whom your son shall rise?' And the mother, weeping, said with a loud voice, 'I believe, Peter, I believe.' The whole multitude cried out, 'Give the mother her

son.' And Peter said, 'Let him be brought here into the presence of all.' And Peter, turning to the people, said, 'Men of Rome, I, too, am one of you! I have human flesh and I am a sinner, but I have obtained mercy. Do not imagine that what I do, I do in my own power; I do it in the power of my Lord Jesus Christ who is the judge of the living and the dead. I believe in him, I have been sent by him, and I dare to call upon him to raise the dead. Go, therefore, woman, and have your son brought here and have him raised.' And the woman made her way through the multitude, ran into the street with great joy, and believed with her heart; coming to the house she made her slaves carry him and came back to the forum. And she told the young men to cover their heads and go before the bier and carry everything that she intended to spend on the body of her son in front of the bier, so that Peter, seeing this, might have pity on the body and on her. With them all as mourners she came to the assembly, followed by a multitude of senators and ladies who came to see God's wonderful deeds. And Nicostratus (the man who had died) was very noble and respected in the senate. They brought him and placed him before Peter. And Peter asked them to be silent and said with a very loud voice, 'Romans, let a righteous judgement now take place between me and Simon, and judge which of us believes in the living God, he or I. Let him revive the body which is before us, and believe in him as an angel of God. If he is not able I will call upon my God. I will restore the son alive to his mother and then you shall believe that he is a sorcerer and deceiver, this man who enjoys your hospitality.' When they heard this, it seemed right to them what Peter had said. They encouraged Simon saying, 'Show yourself publicly what you can do; either you convince us or you shall be convicted. Why do you stand still? Commence.'

When Simon perceived that they all pushed him, he stood in silence. When the people had become quiet and were looking at him, Simon cried out and said, 'Romans, when you see that the dead man is raised, will you cast Peter out of the city?' And the whole multitude said, 'We shall not only cast him out but also burn him at once.' Simon came to the head of the dead man, bowed three times, and he showed the people how the dead man had lifted up his head and moved it, and opened his

eyes and lightly bowed to Simon. And immediately they began
to gather wood to burn Peter. But Peter, having received the
power of Christ, lifted up his voice and said to those who were
shouting against him, 'Now I see, Romans, that I must not call
you foolish and silly so long as your eyes and your ears and
your senses are blinded. So long as your mind is darkened you
do not perceive that you are bewitched, since you seemingly
believe that a dead man rose who has not risen. I would have
been content, Romans, to keep silent and to die in silence and
to leave you among the illusions of this world. But the punishment of the unquenchable fire is before my eyes. If you agree,
let the dead man speak, let him rise; if he is alive, let him untie
the band from his chin, let him call his mother and say to you,
"Bawlers, why are you crying?" Let him beckon to you with his
hand. If, therefore, you wish to see that he is dead and you are
spellbound, let this man step back from the bier, this one who
persuaded you to withdraw from Christ, and you shall see the
dead man as you saw him when you brought him in.' And the
prefect Agrippa could no longer restrain himself but rose and
with his own hand pushed Simon away. And the dead man
looked as he had before. And the people were enraged and,
converted from the magical spell of Simon, began to cry, 'Hear,
O Caesar, should the dead not rise let Simon be burned instead
of Peter, because he has really deceived us.' But Peter stretched
forth his hand and said, 'Romans, be patient. I do not say that
Simon should be burned if the boy is restored; it is only when
I tell you to do it, that you will.' And the people cried, 'Even if
you should not wish it, Peter, we shall do it.' Peter said to them,
'If you continue, the boy shall not rise. We have learned not to
recompense evil for evil, but we have learned to love our
enemies and to pray for those who persecute us. For should
even he repent, it is better. For God will not remember the evil.
Let him, therefore, come to the light of Christ. But if he cannot,
let him inherit the portion of his father, the devil. But do not let
your hands be contaminated.' Having thus spoken to the
people he came to the boy, and before raising him he said to
his mother, 'These young men, whom you set free in honour of
your son, can as free men obey their living master. For I know
that the souls of some among them will be wounded when they
see your risen son and serve again as slaves. But let them all be

free and receive their subsistence as before—for your son shall
rise again—and let them be with him.' And Peter looked at her
for some time awaiting the answer. And the mother of the boy
said, 'How can I do otherwise? Therefore I declare before the
prefect that they should possess all that which I had to spend
on the corpse of my son.' Peter said to her, 'Let the rest be
divided among the widows.' And Peter rejoiced in his soul and
said in the spirit, 'O Lord, who are merciful, Jesus Christ,
manifest yourself to your servant Peter who calls upon you, as
you always show mercy and goodness. In the presence of all
these who have been set free, that they may be able to serve, let
Nicostratus now arise.' And Peter touched the side of the lad
and said, 'Arise.' And the lad arose, took up his garment and sat
and untied his chin, asked for other garments, came down
from the bier, and said to Peter, 'I beg you, man, let us go to
our Lord Christ, whom I heard speak to you; he said to you,
pointing at me, "Bring him here, for he belongs to me."' When
Peter heard this he was still more strengthened in the spirit by
the help of the Lord and said to the people, 'Romans, thus the
dead are awakened, thus they speak, thus they walk when they
are raised; they live for so long as it pleases God. But now I
turn to you who came to see the spectacle. If you repent now
from your sins and from all your man-made gods and from all
uncleanness and lust, you shall receive the communion of
Christ in faith so that you may obtain life for eternity.'

29. From that hour on they worshipped him like a god, and
the sick, whom they had at home, they brought to his feet to be
cured by him.

31. And they also brought the sick to him on the Sabbath and
asked him to treat them. And many paralytics and podagrous
people were healed, and those who had two- and four-day
fevers and other diseases, and believed in the name of Jesus
Christ, and very many were added every day to the grace of the
Lord. When some days had passed Simon the magician promised the people that he could persuade Peter not to believe in
the true God but in a fallacious one. As he performed many
tricks those among the disciples who were steadfast laughed
him to scorn. In the dining halls he made some spirits appear
which had the semblance of life, but in reality did not exist.

And what more shall I say? Having spoken a great deal about
magic he seemingly cured the lame and blind for a time, and
many dead persons, too, he made alive and made them move
about, as well as Stratonicus. In all this Peter followed him and
refuted him before those who saw it. And as he was always out
of favour, and was ridiculed by the Romans and lost their
confidence since he promised to do something which he could
not do, it came about that he said to them, 'Romans, you now
think that Peter has overcome me as if he were mightier than
I, and you now pay more attention to him. You are mistaken.
For tomorrow I shall leave you godless and impious ones and
take refuge with God above, whose power I am, though en-
feebled. If, therefore, you have fallen, behold I stand. I ascend
to the father, and shall say to him, "Me, your son who stands,
they desired to bring low; however, I had no deal with them,
but returned to myself."'

32. And on the following day a still larger multitude gathered on the *via sacra* to see him fly. And Peter also went to the
place to see the spectacle and to refute him. For when he came
to Rome he astonished the people by his flying. But Peter, who
rebuked him, was not yet at Rome, which he so misled and
deceived that some were driven out of their senses. And standing on an elevated place, upon seeing Peter he began to speak.
'Peter, now as I am about to ascend in the presence of all the
onlookers, I say to you, if your God is almighty (he whom the
Jews killed, and they stoned you who were chosen by him), let
him show that faith in him is of God; let it be manifested by
this event, whether it is worthy of God. For I ascend and will
show myself to this people what kind of being I am.' And,
behold, he was lifted up and they saw him ascending over
Rome and over its temples and hills. And the believers looked
at Peter. And beholding the incredible spectacle Peter cried to
the Lord Jesus Christ, 'If you allow him to do what he has
undertaken, all who believed in you shall be overthrown, and
the signs and wonders, which you have shown to them through
me, will not be believed. Make haste, O Lord, show your mercy
and let him fall down and become crippled but not die; let him
be disabled and break his leg in three places.' And he fell down
and broke his leg in three places. And they cast stones upon
him, and each went to his home having faith in Peter. And one

of Simon's friends, Gemellus by name, from whom Simon had received much money and who had a Greek wife, quickly ran along the street, and seeing him with his leg broken said, 'Simon, if God's power is broken, shall not that God, whose power you are, be darkened?' And Gemellus ran and followed Peter and said to him, 'I also wish to be one of those who believe in Christ.' And Peter said, 'How could I object, my brother? Come and stay with us.' And Simon, being in misery, found some helpers who carried him by night on a stretcher from Rome to Aricia. There he remained and stayed with a man named Castor who on account of sorcery had been driven from Rome to Terracina. Following an operation Simon, the messenger of the devil, ended his life.

(3) *Acts of Peter* 35

35. When he went out of the gate he saw the Lord come into Rome. And when he saw him he said, 'Lord, where are you going?' And the Lord said to him, 'I go to Rome to be crucified.' And Peter said to him, 'Lord, are you being crucified again?' And he said, 'Yes, Peter, again I shall be crucified.' And Peter came to himself; and he saw the Lord ascending to heaven. Then he returned to Rome, rejoicing and praising the Lord because he had said, 'I am being crucified.' This was to happen to Peter.

(4) *Acts of Peter* 37–40

37. And when he had come to the cross he began to say, 'O name of the cross, hidden mystery; O unspeakable mercy, which is expressed in the name of the cross; O nature of man, which cannot be separated from God; O ineffable and inseparable love, which cannot be shown by impure lips; I seize you now I am standing at the end of my earthly career. I will make known what you are. I will not conceal the mystery of the cross once closed and hidden to my soul. You who hope in Christ, think not this to be a cross which is visible; for my passion, like that of Christ, is entirely different from that which is visible. And now especially, since you who can hear can hear it from me who am in the last and parting hour of life, listen. Keep

your souls from everything which you can perceive with the senses, from all that seems to be, and is not truly real. Close these your eyes, shut these your ears; withdraw from actions which are seen outwardly and you shall perceive the facts about Christ and the whole mystery of your salvation. But the hour has come for you, Peter, to deliver your body to those who are taking it. Take it, whose business it is. Of you, executioners, I ask to crucify me with head downwards, and not otherwise. And the reason I shall explain to those who listen.'

38. After they had hanged him up as he wished he began to speak again, 'Men, whose calling it is to hear, listen to what I, being hanged, am about to tell you now. Understand the mystery of the whole creation and the beginning of all things, how it was. For the first man, whose image I bear, in falling head downward showed a manner of birth which did not formerly exist, for it was dead, having no motion. He, having been drawn down, he who cast his origin upon the earth, established the whole of the cosmic system, suspended after the manner of his calling, whereby he showed the right as the left and the left as the right and changed all signs of nature, to behold the ugly as beautiful and the really evil as good. Concerning this the Lord says in a mystery, "Unless you make the right as the left and the left as the right, and the top as the bottom and the front as the back, you shall not know the Kingdom." I explain this information to you, and the manner of my suspension is symbolic of that man who was first made. You, my beloved, who now hear, and those who shall hear it, must renounce the first error and turn again. For you ought to come to the cross of Christ, who is the extended Word, the one and only, concerning whom the Spirit says, "For what else is Christ than the Word, the sound of God?" The Word is this upright tree on which I am crucified; the sound, however, is the crossbeam, namely the nature of man; and the nail which holds the crossbeam to the upright in the middle is the conversion and repentance of man.

39. 'Since you have made this known and revealed these things to me, O Word of life, which is now called tree, I thank you, not with these lips which are nailed, neither with this tongue, through which comes forth truth and falsehood, nor with this word, which is produced by the skill of earthly na-

ture, but I thank you, O King, with that voice which is heard through silence, which is not heard by all, which does not come through the organs of the body, which does not enter the ears of flesh nor is heard by corruptible substance, which is not in the world or sounds upon earth, which is also not written in books, nor belongs to one, nor to another, but with this voice, Jesus Christ, I thank you: with the silence of the voice with which the Spirit within me intercedes, who loves you, speaks with you, and sees you. You are known only to the Spirit. You are to me, father, mother, brother, friend, servant, steward. You are all, and all is in you; and you are Being, and there is nothing that is except you. To him, brethren, you also take refuge and learn that your existence is in him alone, and you shall then obtain that of which he said to you, "Eye has not seen, nor ear heard, neither has it entered into the heart of man." We now ask undefiled Jesus for that which you promised to give us; we praise you, we thank you, we confess you in glorifying you, though we are weak, because you alone are God and no other, to whom be glory now and for ever, Amen.'

40. When the multitude surrounding him cried Amen, Peter, during this Amen, gave up his spirit to the Lord. When Marcellus saw that the blessed Peter had given up the ghost, without communicating with anyone, since it was not allowed, he took him down from the cross with his own hands and bathed him in milk and wine. And he ground seven pounds of mastic and also fifty pounds of myrrh and aloes and spice and anointed his body, and filled a very costly marble coffin with Attic honey and buried him in his own tomb. And Peter came to Marcellus by night and said, 'Marcellus did you not hear the Lord say, "Let the dead be buried by their own dead"?' When Marcellus said, 'Yes', Peter said to him, 'What you spent on the dead is lost. For though alive you were like a dead man caring for the dead.' When Marcellus awoke he told of the appearance of Peter to the brethren, and he remained with those who had been strengthened by Peter in the faith of Christ, strengthening himself even more till the arrival of Paul at Rome.

11
Paul

--- ✧ ---

Of the twenty-seven books in the New Testament close to half are letters attributed to Paul's authorship. The Acts of the Apostles tells of Paul's conversion to Christianity on the road to Damascus, and his subsequent missionary journeys, teachings, miracles, and trials. The canonical Acts ends with Paul under house arrest in Rome awaiting death. The New Testament, however, does not record the end of Paul's life.

It is left to the second-century apocryphal book, the Acts of Paul, to attempt a fuller picture of Paul's career. This Acts is independent of the Acts of the Apostles; it parallels but does not duplicate our knowledge of Paul's ministry in the canonical Acts and Pauline letters.

This chapter is divided into two parts, (a) and (b).

(a) PAUL'S MISSIONARY JOURNEY

The first extract (1), from the Acts of Paul, is a famous passage describing Paul's physical appearance taken from the section dealing with Paul and Thecla. This is followed by another part of this extensive story (2). Thecla is a rare example of a woman apostle. The full story begins with her listening to Paul preach. She is captivated by him and his message, and resolves to follow him. She renounces her fiancé and angers her mother by this action. Her mother orders her to be burned. The story tells of her miraculous escape from that fate, and a subsequent ordeal when she is exposed to the wild beasts in the arena. Following this escape she performs an auto-baptism (itself a peculiar rite) and sets out as an apostle. Thecla was venerated as a saint until 1969, when her cult was suppressed.

The next extract (3) comes from an unpublished Coptic fragment which tells of Paul and the lion at Ephesus. There is a sequel to it, also given, which comes from the Acts of Paul. The section in the Acts of Paul, from which the extract is excerpted, is fragmentary and the account of Paul's baptizing the lion has not survived here except as a reminiscence. Nevertheless, the story continues beyond the point reached in the Coptic text. Such an incident is famous in various contexts, and it obviously has interesting parallels with the Daniel story in the Old Testament and even closer links with the story of Androcles in secular literature.

Paul's martyrdom at the end of the Acts is also reproduced below (4). It is followed by an episode showing that Paul, like his Lord before him, is not bound by death. The Trappist monastery of Tre Fontane three miles south of Rome is the traditional site of Paul's martyrdom. According to a legend—not from the apocryphal New Testament—Paul's head, on severance from his body, bounced three times on the ground in three places, from which issued the three springs that gave the site its name. This late tradition shows that the apocryphal texts do not exhaust the stock of legendary material about Biblical worthies. Yet another late legend locates the place of Paul's burial to the site of the basilica of S. Paoli fuori le Mura in Rome.

(1) *Acts of Paul* 3

3. Paul, a man small in size, bald-headed, bandy-legged, of noble mien, with eyebrows meeting, rather hook-nosed, full of grace. Sometimes he seemed like a man, and sometimes he had the face of an angel.

(2) *Acts of Paul: Acts of Paul and Thecla* 7–43

7. And while Paul was speaking in the midst of the church in the house of Onesiphorus a certain virgin named Thecla, the daughter of Theoclia, betrothed to a man named Thamyris, was sitting at the window close by and listened day and night to the discourse of virginity, as proclaimed by Paul. And she did not look away from the window, but was led on by faith,

rejoicing exceedingly. And when she saw many women and virgins going in to Paul she also had an eager desire to be deemed worthy to stand in Paul's presence and hear the word of Christ. For she had not yet seen Paul in person, but only heard his word.

8. As she did not move from the window her mother sent to Thamyris. And he came gladly as if already receiving her in marriage. And Thamyris said to Theoclia, 'Where, then, is my Thecla that I may see her?' And Theoclia answered, 'I have a strange story to tell you, Thamyris. For three days and three nights Thecla does not rise from the window either to eat or to drink; but looking earnestly as if upon some pleasant sight she is devoted to a foreigner teaching deceitful and artful discourses, so that I wonder how a virgin of her great modesty exposes herself to such extreme discomfort.

9. 'Thamyris, this man will overturn the city of the Iconians and your Thecla too; for all the women and the young men go in to him to be taught by him. He says one must fear only one God and live in chastity. Moreover, my daughter, clinging to the window like a spider, lays hold of what is said by him with a strange eagerness and fearful emotion. For the virgin looks eagerly at what is said by him and has been captivated. But go near and speak to her, for she is betrothed to you.'

10. And Thamyris greeted her with a kiss, but at the same time being afraid of her overpowering emotion said, 'Thecla, my betrothed, why do you sit thus? And what sort of feeling holds you distracted? Come back to your Thamyris and be ashamed.' Moreover, her mother said the same, 'Why do you sit thus looking down, my child, and answering nothing, like a sick woman?' And those who were in the house wept bitterly, Thamyris for the loss of a wife, Theoclia for that of a child, and the maidservants for that of a mistress. And there was a great outpouring of lamentation in the house. And while these things were going on Thecla did not turn away but kept attending to the word of Paul.

11. And Thamyris, jumping up, went into the street, and watched all who went in to Paul and came out. And he saw two men bitterly quarrelling with each other and he said to them, 'Men, who are you and tell me who is this man among you, leading astray the souls of young men and deceiving virgins so

that they should not marry but remain as they are? I promise you money enough if you tell me about him, for I am the chief man of this city.'

12. And Demas and Hermogenes said to him, 'Who he is we do not know. But he deprives the husbands of wives and maidens of husbands, saying, "There is for you no resurrection unless you remain chaste and do not pollute the flesh."'

13. And Thamyris said to them, 'Come into my house and refresh yourselves.' And they went to a sumptuous supper and much wine and great wealth and a splendid table. And Thamyris made them drink, for he loved Thecla and wished to take her as wife. And during the supper Thamyris said, 'Men, tell me what is his teaching that I also may know it, for I am greatly distressed about Thecla, because she so loves the stranger and I am prevented from marrying.'

14. And Demas and Hermogenes said, 'Bring him before the Governor Castellius because he persuades the multitude to embrace the new teaching of the Christians, and he will destroy him and you shall have Thecla as your wife. And we shall teach you about the resurrection which he says is to come, that it has already taken place in the children and that we rise again, after having come to the knowledge of the true God.'

15. And when Thamyris heard these things he rose up early in the morning and, filled with jealousy and anger, went into the house of Onesiphorus with rulers and officers and a great crowd with batons and said to Paul, 'You have deceived the city of the Iconians and especially my betrothed bride so that she will not have me! Let us go to the governor Castellius!' And the whole crowd cried, 'Away with the sorcerer for he has misled all our wives!', and the multitude was also incited.

16. And Thamyris standing before the tribunal said with a great shout, 'O proconsul, this man—we do not know where he comes from—makes virgins averse to marriage. Let him say before you why he teaches thus.' But Demas and Hermogenes said to Thamyris, 'Say that he is a Christian and he will die at once.' But the governor kept his resolve and called Paul, saying, 'Who are you and what do you teach? For they bring no small accusation against you.'

17. And Paul, lifting up his voice, said, 'If I today must tell any of my teachings then listen, O proconsul. The living God,

the God of vengeance, the jealous God, the God who has need of nothing, who seeks the salvation of men, has sent me that I may rescue them from corruption and uncleanness and from all pleasure, and from death, that they may sin no more. On this account God sent his Son whose gospel I preach and teach, that in him men have hope, who alone has had compassion upon a world led astray, that men may be no longer under judgement but may have faith and fear of God and knowledge of honesty and love of truth. If then I teach the things revealed to me by God what harm do I do, O proconsul?' When the governor heard this he ordered Paul to be bound and sent to prison until he had time to hear him more attentively.

18. And Thecla, by night, took off her bracelets and gave them to the gatekeeper; and when the door was opened to her she went into the prison. To the jailer she gave a silver mirror and was thus enabled to go in to Paul and, sitting at his feet, she heard the great deeds of God. And Paul was afraid of nothing, but trusted in God. And her faith also increased and she kissed his bonds.

19. And when Thecla was sought for by her family and Thamyris they were hunting through the streets as if she had been lost. One of the gatekeeper's fellow slaves informed them that she had gone out by night. And they examined the gatekeeper who said to them, 'She has gone to the foreigner in the prison.' And they went and found her, so to say, chained to him by affection. And having gone out from there they incited the people and informed the governor what had happened.

20. And he ordered Paul to be brought before the tribunal, but Thecla was riveted to the place where Paul had sat whilst in prison. And the governor ordered her also to be brought to the tribunal, and she came with an exceedingly great joy. And when Paul had been led forth the crowd vehemently cried out, 'He is a sorcerer. Away with him!' But the governor gladly heard Paul speak about the holy works of Christ. And having taken counsel, he summoned Thecla and said, 'Why do you not marry Thamyris, according to the law of the Iconians?' But she stood looking earnestly at Paul. And when she gave no answer Theoclia, her mother, cried out saying, 'Burn the wicked one; burn her who will not marry in the midst of the theatre, that all the women who have been taught by this man may be afraid.'

21. And the governor was greatly moved, and after scourging Paul he cast him out of the city. But Thecla he condemned to be burned. And immediately the governor arose and went away to the theatre. And the whole multitude went out to witness the spectacle. But as a lamb in the wilderness looks around for the shepherd, so Thecla kept searching for Paul. And having looked into the crowd she saw the Lord sitting in the likeness of Paul and said, 'As if I were unable to endure, Paul has come to look after me.' And she gazed upon him with great earnestness, but he went up into heaven.

22. And the boys and girls brought wood and straw in order that Thecla might be burned. And when she came in naked the governor wept and admired the power that was in her. And the executioners arranged the wood and told her to go up on the pile. And having made the sign of the cross she went up on the pile. And they lighted the fire. And though a great fire was blazing it did not touch her. For God, having compassion upon her, made an underground rumbling, and a cloud full of water and hail overshadowed the theatre from above, and all its contents were poured out so that many were in danger of death. And the fire was put out and Thecla saved.

23. And Paul was fasting with Onesiphorus and his wife and his children in a new tomb on the way which led from Iconium to Daphne. And after many days had been spent in fasting the children said to Paul, 'We are hungry.' And they had nothing with which to buy bread, for Onesiphorus had left the things of this world and followed Paul with all his house. And Paul, having taken off his cloak, said, 'Go, my child, sell this and buy some loaves and bring them.' And when the child was buying them he saw Thecla their neighbour and was astonished and said, 'Thecla, where are you going?' And she said, 'I have been saved from the fire and am following Paul.' And the child said, 'Come, I shall take you to him; for he has been mourning for you and praying and fasting six days already.'

24. And when she had come to the tomb Paul was kneeling and praying, 'Father of Christ, let not the fire touch Thecla but stand by her, for she is yours'; she, standing behind him, cried out, 'O Father who made the heaven and the earth, the Father of your beloved Son Jesus Christ, I praise you that you have saved me from the fire that I may see Paul again.' And Paul,

rising up, saw her and said, 'O God, who knows the heart, Father of our Lord Jesus Christ, I praise you because you have speedily heard my prayer.'

25. And there was great love in the tomb as Paul and Onesiphorus and the others all rejoiced. And they had five loaves and vegetables and water, and they rejoiced in the holy works of Christ. And Thecla said to Paul, 'I will cut my hair off and I shall follow you wherever you go.' But he said, 'Times are evil and you are beautiful. I am afraid lest another temptation come upon you worse than the first and that you do not withstand it but become mad after men.' And Thecla said, 'Only give me the seal in Christ, and no temptation shall touch me.' And Paul said, 'Thecla, be patient; you shall receive the water.'

26. And Paul sent away Onesiphorus and all his family to Iconium and went into Antioch, taking Thecla with him. And as soon as they had arrived a certain Syrian, Alexander by name, an influential citizen of Antioch, seeing Thecla, became enamoured of her and tried to bribe Paul with gifts and presents. But Paul said, 'I know not the woman of whom you speak, nor is she mine.' But he, being of great power, embraced her in the street. But she would not endure it and looked about for Paul. And she cried out bitterly, saying, 'Do not force the stranger; do not force the servant of God. I am one of the chief persons of the Iconians and because I would not marry Thamyris I have been cast out of the city.' And taking hold of Alexander, she tore his cloak and pulled off his crown and made him a laughing-stock.

27. And he, although loving her, nevertheless felt ashamed of what had happened and led her before the governor; and as she confessed that she had done these things he condemned her to the wild beasts. The women of the city cried out before the tribunal, 'Evil judgement! impious judgement!' And Thecla asked the governor that she might remain pure until she was to fight with the wild beasts. And a rich woman named Queen Tryphaena, whose daughter was dead, took her under her protection and had her for a consolation.

28. And when the beasts were exhibited they bound her to a fierce lioness, and Queen Tryphaena followed her. And the

lioness, with Thecla sitting upon her, licked her feet; and all the multitude was astonished. And the charge on her inscription was 'Sacrilegious.' And the women and children cried out again and again, 'O God, outrageous things take place in this city.' And after the exhibition Tryphaena received her again. For her dead daughter Falconilla had said to her in a dream, 'Mother, receive this stranger, the forsaken Thecla, in my place, that she may pray for me and I may come to the place of the just.'

29. And when, after the exhibition, Tryphaena had received her she was grieved because Thecla had to fight on the following day with the wild beasts, but on the other hand she loved her dearly like her daughter Falconilla and said, 'Thecla, my second child, come, pray for my child that she may live in eternity, for this I saw in my sleep.' And without hesitation she lifted up her voice and said, 'My God, Son of the Most High, who are in heaven, grant her wish that her daughter Falconilla may live in eternity.' And when Thecla had spoken Tryphaena grieved very much, considering that such beauty was to be thrown to the wild beasts.

30. And when it was dawn Alexander came to her, for it was he who arranged the exhibition of wild beasts, and said, 'The governor has taken his seat and the crowd is clamouring for us; get ready, I will take her to fight with the wild beasts.' And Tryphaena put him to flight with a loud cry, saying, 'A second mourning for my Falconilla has come upon my house, and there is no one to help, neither child for she is dead, nor kinsman for I am a widow. God of Thecla, my child, help Thecla.'

31. And the governor sent soldiers to bring Thecla. Tryphaena did not leave her but took her by the hand and led her away saying, 'My daughter Falconilla I took away to the tomb, but you, Thecla, I take to fight the wild beasts.' And Thecla wept bitterly and sighed to the Lord, 'O Lord God, in whom I trust, to whom I have fled for refuge, who did deliver me from the fire, reward Tryphaena who has had compassion on your servant and because she kept me pure.'

32. And there arose a tumult: the wild beasts roared, the people and the women sitting together were crying, some

saying, 'Away with the sacrilegious person!', others saying, 'O
that the city would be destroyed on account of this iniquity!'
Kill us all, proconsul; miserable spectacle, evil judgement!'

33. And Thecla, having been taken from the hands of
Tryphaena, was stripped and received a girdle and was thrown
into the arena. And lions and bears were let loose upon her.
And a fierce lioness ran up and lay down at her feet. And the
multitude of the women cried aloud. And a bear ran upon her,
but the lioness went to meet it and tore the bear to pieces. And
again a lion that had been trained to fight against men, which
belonged to Alexander, ran upon her. And the lioness, encoun-
tering the lion, was killed along with it. And the women cried
the more since the lioness, her protector, was dead.

34. Then they sent in many beasts as she was standing and
stretching forth her hands and praying. And when she had
finished her prayer she turned around and saw a large pit full
of water and said, 'Now it is time to wash myself.' And she
threw herself in saying, 'In the name of Jesus Christ I baptize
myself on my last day.' When the women and the multitude
saw it they wept and said, 'Do not throw yourself into the
water!'; even the governor shed tears because the seals were to
devour such beauty. She then threw herself into the water in
the name of Jesus Christ, but the seals, having seen a flash of
lightning, floated dead on the surface. And there was round her
a cloud of fire so that the beasts could neither touch her nor
could she be seen naked.

35. But the women lamented when other and fiercer animals were let loose; some threw petals, others nard, others
cassia, others amomum, so that there was an abundance of
perfumes. And all the wild beasts were hypnotized and did not
touch her. And Alexander said to the governor, 'I have some
terrible bulls to which we will bind her.' And the governor
consented grudgingly, 'Do what you will.' And they bound her
by the feet between the bulls and put red-hot irons under their
genitals so that they, being rendered more furious, might kill
her. They rushed forward but the burning flame around her
consumed the ropes, and she was as if she had not been bound.

36. And Tryphaena fainted standing beside the arena, so
that the servants said, 'Queen Tryphaena is dead.' And the
governor put a stop to the games and the whole city was in

dismay. And Alexander fell down at the feet of the governor and cried, 'Have mercy upon me and upon the city and set the woman free, lest the city also be destroyed. For if Caesar hear of these things he will possibly destroy the city along with us because his kinswoman, Queen Tryphaena, has died at the theatre gate.'

37. And the governor summoned Thecla out of the midst of the beasts and said to her, 'Who are you? And what is there about you that not one of the wild beasts touched you?' She answered, 'I am a servant of the living God and, as to what there is about me, I have believed in the son of God in whom he is well pleased; that is why not one of the beasts touched me. For he alone is the goal of salvation and the basis of immortal life. For he is a refuge to the tempest-tossed, a solace to the afflicted, a shelter to the despairing; in brief, whoever does not believe in him shall not live but be dead forever.'

38. When the governor heard these things he ordered garments to be brought and to be put on her. And she said, 'He who clothed me when I was naked among the beasts will in the day of judgement clothe me with salvation.' And taking the garments she put them on.

And the governor immediately issued an edict saying, 'I release to you the pious Thecla, the servant of God.' And the women shouted aloud and with one voice praised God, 'One is the God, who saved Thecla', so that the whole city was shaken by their voices.

39. And Tryphaena, having received the good news, went with the multitude to meet Thecla. After embracing her she said, 'Now I believe that the dead are raised! Now I believe that my child lives. Come inside and all that is mine I shall assign to you.' And Thecla went in with her and rested eight days, instructing her in the word of God, so that many of the maid-servants believed. And there was great joy in the house.

40. And Thecla longed for Paul and sought him, looking in every direction. And she was told that he was in Myra. And wearing a mantle that she had altered so as to make a man's cloak, she came with a band of young men and maidens to Myra, where she found Paul speaking the word of God and went to him. And he was astonished at seeing her and her companions, thinking that some new temptation was coming

upon her. And perceiving this, she said to him, 'I have received baptism, O Paul; for he who worked with you for the gospel has worked with me also for baptism.'

41. And Paul, taking her, led her to the house of Hermias and heard everything from her, so that he greatly wondered and those who heard were strengthened and prayed for Tryphaena. And Thecla rose up and said to Paul, 'I am going to Iconium.' Paul answered, 'Go, and teach the word of God.' And Tryphaena sent her much clothing and gold so that she could leave many things to Paul for the service of the poor.

42. And coming to Iconium she went into the house of Onesiphorus and fell upon the place where Paul had sat and taught the word of God, and she cried and said, 'My God and God of this house where the light shone upon me, Jesus Christ, Son of God, my help in prison, my help before the governors, my help in the fire, my help among the wild beasts, you alone are God and to you be glory for ever. Amen.'

43. And she found Thamyris dead but her mother alive. And calling her mother she said, 'Theoclia, my mother, can you believe that the Lord lives in heaven? For if you desire wealth the Lord will give it to you through me; or if you desire your child, behold, I am standing beside you.'

And having thus testified, she went to Seleucia and enlightened many by the word of God; then she rested in a glorious sleep.

(3a) *Unpublished Coptic Fragment* (part)

There came a great and terrible lion out of the valley of the burial ground . . . But when I (= Paul) finished praying, the beast cast himself at my feet. I was filled with the Spirit and looked at him, and said, 'Lion, what do you want?' He said, 'I wish to be baptized.' I glorified God, who had given speech to the beast and salvation to his servants.

Now there was a great river in that place; I went down into it and he followed me. As doves in terror before eagles fly into a house in order to escape, so it was with Lemma and Amnia, who did not cease to pray humbly, until I had praised and glorified God. I myself was in fear and wonderment, in that I was about to lead the lion like an ox and baptize him in the

water. But I stood on the bank, men and brethren, and cried
out, saying, 'You who dwell in the heights, who looked upon
the humble, who gave rest to the afflicted, who with Daniel
shut the mouths of the lions, who sent to me our Lord Jesus
Christ, grant that we escape the beast, and accomplish the
plan, which you appointed.'

When I had prayed thus, I took the lion by the mane and in
the name of Jesus Christ immersed him three times. When he
came up out of the water he shook out his mane and said to
me, 'Grace be with you!' And I said to him, 'And likewise with
you.'

The lion ran off to the country rejoicing (for this was revealed to me in my heart). A lioness met him, but he did not
yield to her and ran off.

(3b) *Acts of Paul: Ephesus* (part)

At dawn there was a cry from the citizens, 'Let us go to the
spectacle! Come, let us see the man who possesses God fighting
with the beasts!' Hieronymus himself joined them; he commanded Diophantes and the other slaves to bring Paul into the
stadium. He was dragged in, saying nothing but bowed down
and groaning because he was led in triumph by the city. And
when he was brought out he was immediately flung into the
stadium. Everybody was angry at Paul's dignified bearing.
Hieronymus ordered a very fierce lion, which had but recently
been captured, to be set loose against him ... But the lion
looked at Paul, and Paul at the lion. Then Paul recognized that
this was the lion which had come and been baptized. And
borne along by faith Paul said, 'Lion, was it you whom I
baptized?' And the lion in answer said to Paul, 'Yes.' Paul spoke
to it again and said, 'And how were you captured?' The lion
said with its own voice, 'Just as you were, Paul.' After
Hieronymus had sent many beasts so that Paul might be slain,
and archers that the lion too might be killed, a violent and
exceedingly heavy hail-storm fell from heaven, although the
sky was clear: many died and all the rest took to flight. But it
did not touch Paul or the lion although the other beasts perished under the weight of the hail, which was so heavy that
Hieronymus' ear was hit and torn off, and the people cried out

as they fled, 'Save us, O God, save us, O God of the man who fought with the beasts!' And Paul took leave of the lion, which spoke no more, and went out of the stadium and down to the harbour and embarked on the ship which was sailing for Macedonia, for there were many who were sailing as if the city were about to perish. So he embarked too like one of the fugitives, but the lion went away into the mountains as was natural for it.

(4) *Acts of Paul: Martyrdom* 5–7

5. And turning toward the east, Paul lifted up his hands to heaven and prayed at length; and after having conversed in Hebrew with the fathers during prayer he bent his neck, without speaking any more. When the executioner cut off his head milk splashed on the tunic of the soldier. And the soldier and all who stood near by were astonished at this sight and glorified God who had thus honoured Paul. And they went away and reported everything to Caesar.

6. When he heard of it he was amazed and did not know what to say. While many philosophers and the centurion were assembled with the emperor Paul came about the ninth hour, and in the presence of all he said, 'Caesar, behold, here is Paul, the soldier of God; I am not dead but live in my God. But upon you, unhappy one, many evils and great punishment will come because you have unjustly shed the blood of the righteous not many days ago.' And having spoken this Paul departed from him. When Nero had heard he commanded that the prisoners be released, Patroclus as well as Barsabas with his friends.

7. And, as Paul had told them, Longus and Cestus, the centurion, came in fear very early to the grave of Paul. And when they drew near they found two men in prayer and Paul with them, and they became frightened when they saw the unexpected miracle, but Titus and Luke, being afraid at the sight of Longus and Cestus, turned to run away.

But they followed and said to them, 'We follow you not in order to kill you, blessed men of God, as you imagine, but in order to live, that you may do to us as Paul promised us. We have just seen him in prayer beside you.' Upon hearing this Titus and Luke gave them joyfully the seal in the Lord, glorifying God and the Father of our Lord Jesus Christ to whom be glory for ever and ever. Amen.

(b) PAUL'S LETTERS

Perhaps it is not surprising to learn that Paul's reputation as a prolific letter-writer encouraged the creation of apocryphal letters composed in his name. Two examples are given here.

The first is the Letter to the Laodiceans. Colossians 4: 16 refers to a letter Paul claims to have written to the church in Laodicea. That letter did not survive. Predictably, a letter was concocted which purported to be that missing text. This spurious epistle to the Laodiceans is certainly not from Paul's hand, but its forger made use of Pauline phrases taken from his genuine letters, principally Philippians and Galatians. It dates from the second–fourth century. Several Latin Biblical manuscripts include this letter even though it was never included in the canon of authorized scripture.

The second apocryphal correspondence is the so-called 3 Corinthians located in the Acts of Paul in the context of Paul's visit to Philippi. 3 Corinthians may well have had an independent existence prior to its having been incorporated in the Acts of Paul. The extract below (2) contains the Corinthians' letter to Paul and his reply.

(1) *Epistle to the Laodiceans*

1. Paul, an apostle not of men and not through man, but through Jesus Christ, to the brethren who are in Laodicea: 2. Grace to you and peace from God the Father and the Lord Jesus Christ.

3. I thank Christ in all my prayer that you continue in him and persevere in his works, in expectation of the promise at the day of judgement. 4. And may you not be deceived by the vain talk of some people who tell tales that they may lead you away from the truth of the gospel which is proclaimed by me. 5. And now may God grant that those who come from me for the furtherance of the truth of the gospel may be able to serve and to do good works for the well-being of eternal life.

6. And now my bonds are manifest, which I suffer in Christ, on account of which I am glad and rejoice. 7. This to me leads to eternal salvation, which itself is brought about through your prayers and by the help of the Holy Spirit, whether it be through life or through death. 8. For my life is in Christ and to die is joy.

9. And his mercy will work in you, that you may have the same love and be of one mind. 10. Therefore, beloved, as you have heard in my presence, so hold fast and work in the fear of God, and eternal life will be yours. 11. For it is God who works in you. 12. And do without hesitation what you do. 13. And for the rest, beloved, rejoice in Christ and beware of those who are out for sordid gain. 14. May all your requests be manifest before God, and be steadfast in the mind of Christ. 15. And do what is pure, true, proper, just and lovely. 16. And what you have heard and received, hold in your heart, and peace will be with you.

17. Salute all the brethren with the holy kiss. 18. The saints salute you. 19. The grace of the Lord Jesus Christ be with your spirit. 20. And see that (this epistle) is read to the Colossians and that of the Colossians to you.

(2) *Acts of Paul: Philippi* (part)

Letter of the Corinthians to the Apostle Paul

I. 1. Stephanus and his fellow-presbyters Daphnus and Eubulus and Theophilus and Zeno to Paul, the brother in the Lord—greeting! 2. Two individuals have come to Corinth, named Simon and Cleobius, who overthrow the faith of some through pernicious words. 3. These you shall examine yourself. 4. For we never heard such things either from you or from the other apostles. 5. But we keep what we have received from you and from the others. 6. Since the Lord has shown us mercy, while you are still in the flesh we should hear this from you once more. 7. Come to us or write to us. 8. For we believe, as it has been revealed to Theonoe, that the Lord has delivered you from the hands of the godless. 9. What they say and teach is as follows: 10. They assert that one must not appeal to the prophets (11) and that God is not almighty, (12) there is no resurrection of the body, (13) man has not been made by God, (14) Christ has neither come in the flesh, nor was he born of Mary, (15) and the world is not the work of God but of angels. 16. Wherefore we beseech you, brother, be diligent to come to us that the Corinthian church may remain without stumbling and the foolishness of these men be confounded. Farewell in the Lord!

II. 1. The deacons, Threptus and Eutychus, took the letter to Philippi (2) and Paul received it, being himself in prison because of Stratonike, the wife of Apollophanes; and he became very sad, (3) and exclaimed saying, 'It would have been better had I died and were with the Lord than to abide in the flesh and to hear such words so that sorrow comes upon sorrow, (4) and to be in prison in the face of such great distress and behold such mischief where the wiles of Satan are busy!' 5. And in great affliction Paul wrote the answer to the letter.

Paul's Epistle to the Corinthians

III. 1. Paul, the prisoner of Jesus Christ, to the brethren at Corinth—greeting! 2. Being in many afflictions, I marvel not that the teachings of the evil one had such rapid success. 3. For my Lord Jesus Christ will quickly come, since he is rejected by those who falsify his teaching. 4. For I delivered to you first of all what I received from the apostles before me who were always with Jesus Christ, (5) that our Lord Jesus Christ was born of Mary of the seed of David, the Father having sent the spirit from heaven into her (6) that he might come into this world and save all flesh by his own flesh and that he might raise us in the flesh from the dead as he has presented himself to us as our example. 7. And since man is created by his Father, (8) for this reason was he sought by him when he was lost, to become alive by adoption. 9. For the almighty God, maker of heaven and earth, sent the prophets first to the Jews to deliver them from their sins, (10) for he wished to save the house of Israel; therefore he took from the spirit of Christ and poured it out upon the prophets who proclaimed the true worship of God for a long period of time. 11. For the wicked prince who wished to be God himself laid his hands on them and killed them and bound all flesh of man to his pleasure. 12. But the almighty God, being just, and not wishing to repudiate his creation had mercy (13) and sent his Spirit into Mary the Galilean, (15) that the evil one might be conquered by the same flesh by which he held sway, and be convinced that he is not God. 16. For by his own body Jesus Christ saved all flesh, (17) presenting in his own body a temple of righteousness (18) through which we are saved. 19. They who follow them are not children of righteousness but of wrath, who despise the wisdom of God and in their disbelief assert that heaven and earth and all that is in them are not a work of God. 20. They have the accursed belief of the serpent. 21. Turn away from them and keep aloof from their teaching. 24. And those who say that there is no resurrection of the flesh shall have no resurrection, (25) for they do not believe him who had thus risen. 26. For they do not know, O Corinthians, about the sowing of wheat or some other grain that it is cast naked into the ground and having perished rises up again by the will of God in a body and clothed. 27. And he not only raises the body which is sown, but blesses it manifold. 28. And if one will not take the parable of the seeds (29) let him look at Jonah, the son of Amathios who, being unwilling to preach to the Ninevites, was swallowed up by the whale. 30. And after three days and three nights God heard the prayer of Jonah out of deepest hell, and nothing was corrupted, not even a hair nor an eyelid. 31. How much more will he raise you up, who have believed in Christ Jesus, as he himself was raised up. 32. When a corpse was thrown on the bones of the prophet Elisha by one of the children of Israel the corpse rose from death; how much more shall you rise up on that day with a whole body, after you have been thrown upon the body and bones and Spirit of the Lord. 34. If, however, you receive anything else let no man trouble me, (35) for I have these bonds on me that I may win Christ, and I bear his marks that I may attain to the resurrection of the dead. 36. And whoever accepts this rule which we have received by the blessed prophets and the holy gospel, shall receive a reward, (37) but for whomsoever deviates from this rule fire shall be for him and for those who preceded him therein (38) since they are Godless men, a generation of vipers. 39. Resist them in the power of the Lord. 40. Peace be with you.

12

John

$\diamond$

The John of the stories in this chapter is the son of Zebedee, one of the inner core of Jesus' twelve disciples, the other two being John's brother, James, and Simon Peter. The New Testament has John present at some of the most poignant moments in Jesus' ministry, the raising of Jairus' daughter (Mark 5: 37), the Transfiguration (Mark 9: 2–8), and the agony in the Garden of Gethsemane (Mark 14: 33). From the second century onwards he has been commonly accepted as the author of the Fourth Gospel (the Gospel of John) and identified as the anonymous 'beloved disciple' who appears several times in that Gospel. If this is a correct identification, then it is John to whom Jesus entrusts his mother at his death. For that reason, the figures at the foot of Jesus' cross on rood screens in churches, and in other representations of the death of Jesus, are named as John, and the Virgin Mary.

Some modern scholars accept that this John is the author of the first, if not all three, of the letters of John in the New Testament. Tradition also has this same John the author of the Book of Revelation—the John of Patmos—but many critical problems make such an identification unlikely.

In the rest of the New Testament John appears in the Acts of the Apostles as a companion of Peter in Jerusalem; and Paul in his Epistle to the Galatians 2 knows John as one of the pillars of the church.

Beyond the New Testament it is to the Acts of John that we turn for many of the later traditions about this apostle. The remains of the ancient Acts of John, which dates from the second century, have had to be reconstructed from several later sources, as is the case with most of the other apocryphal Acts. It is of interest to note that John is one of the few apostles in the apocryphal tales whose life does not end in martyrdom. At the end of the Acts of John he utters a long prayer and then merely lies down in a grave and 'peacefully yielded up the ghost'.

Among the elements now recognized as having belonged to the original Acts is the humorous story about the obedient bedbugs. This is reproduced below (1). That extract is followed by a story in which the apostle survives the drinking of poison (2). The story, also possibly part of the ancient Acts, may have been created to dramatize Jesus' statement found in the longer ending to Mark's Gospel (Mark 16: 18) that believers will come to no harm even if they drink 'any deadly poison'.

Another extract (3), possibly from the ancient Acts, is the story of John and the Partridge. This legend was known to Herder and included in his poem 'Saint John'.

The long extract (4), given at the end of this chapter, is part of the strange tale of Drusiana. This racy narrative with its attempted necrophiliac rape scene gives an insight into the inspirational reading matter of early Christians. The story, like many others, may strike modern readers as crudely sensational or superstitious but it is none the less orthodox in its underlying piety and in its teaching of the power and effectiveness of belief in God and faith in Christ. It is the framework in which such orthodoxy is expressed that has caused this, and comparable stories in these Acts, to be branded as 'apocryphal' in the popular definition of the word.

The influence of the apocryphal legends about John is to be seen in the windows of Chartres and Bourges, which portray many scenes from his life. In painting it was conventional to depict John holding a chalice with a viper coming out of it. El Greco's Saint John in the Prado is a well-known example. This image is a clear reference to the story of the poison cup, a legend which gained wide currency through its having been included in Jacob de Voragine's *Golden Legend*.

(1) *Acts of John* 60–1

60. On the first day we came to a lonely inn, and when we were trying to find a bed for John we experienced a strange event. There was one bedstead without covers over which we spread

our cloaks which we had brought and requested him to lie down and to rest, whilst we slept on the floor. He had hardly lain down, when he was molested by bugs. But as they became more and more troublesome, and as it was midnight already, we all heard him say to them, 'I say to you, you bugs, be considerate; leave your home for this night and go to rest in a place which is far away from the servants of God!' And while we laughed and talked, John fell asleep. And we conversed quietly, and thanks to him we remained undisturbed.

61. When it was day, I rose first, and with me Verus and Andronicus. And in the door of the room which we had taken was a mass of bugs. And having called all the brethren, we went outside to have a full view of them. John was still asleep. When he woke up we showed him what we had seen. And sitting up in bed and seeing them, he said, 'Since you have been wise to heed my warning, go back to your place!' When he had spoken and had risen from the bed, the bugs hastened from the door to the bed, ran up the legs into the joints and disappeared. And John said again, 'This creature heard the voice of a man and kept quiet and was obedient. We, however, hear God's voice, and yet irresponsibly transgress his commandments. And how long will this go on?'

(2) Pseudo-Abdias, *Virtutes Iohannis* VIII

VIII. Now when Aristodemus, who was chief priest of all those idols, saw this he was filled with a wicked spirit, and stirred up sedition among the people, so that one group of people prepared themselves to fight against the other. And John turned to him and said, 'Tell me, Aristodemus, what can I do to take away the anger from your soul?' And Aristodemus said, 'If you want me to believe in your God, I will give you poison to drink, and if you drink it, and do not die, it will appear that your God is true.' The apostle answered, 'If you give me poison to drink, when I call on the name of my Lord it will not be able to harm me.' Aristodemus said again, 'First I wish you to see others drink it and die straightway, so that your heart may recoil from that cup.' And the blessed John said, 'I have told you already that I am prepared to drink it, that you may believe in the Lord Jesus Christ when you see me whole after drinking the cup of poison.' Aristodemus therefore went to the proconsul and asked of him two men who were to undergo the sentence of death. And when he had set them in the midst of the market-place before all the people, in the sight of the apostle he made them drink the poison; and as soon as they had drunk it, they gave up the ghost. Then Aristodemus turned to John and said, 'Hearken to me and depart from your teaching with which you call away the people from the worship of the gods; or take and drink this, that you may show that your God is almighty if, after you have drunk, you can remain whole.' Then the blessed John, with those who had drunk the poison lying dead, like a fearless and brave man took the cup and, making the sign of the cross, said, 'My God, and the Father of our Lord Jesus Christ, by whose word the heavens were established, unto whom all things are subject, whom all creation serves, whom all power obeys, fears, and trembles, when we call on you for succour; upon hearing whose name the serpent is still, the dragon flees, the viper is quiet, the frog is still and strengthless, the scorpion is quenched, the serpent vanquished, and the spider does no harm; in a word, all venomous things, and the fiercest reptiles and troublesome beasts are covered with darkness, and all roots hurtful to the health of men dry up. I say, quench the venom of this poison, put out its deadly work-ings, void it of the strength which it has in it, and grant in your sight to all these whom you have created eyes that they may see and ears that they may hear and a heart that they may understand your greatness.' And when he had said this, he armed his mouth and all his body with the sign of the cross and drank all that was in the cup. And after he had drunk, he said, 'I ask that those for whose sake I have drunk be turned to you, O Lord, and by your enlightening receive the salvation which is in you.' And when for the space of three hours the people saw that John was of a cheerful countenance, and that there was no sign at all of paleness or fear in him, they began to cry out with a loud voice, 'He whom John worships is the one true God.'

But even so Aristodemus did not believe, though the people reproached him. But he turned to John and said, 'This one thing I lack: if you in the name of your God raise up these who have died by this poison, my mind will be cleansed of all doubt.' When he said that, the people rose against Aristodemus, saying, 'We will burn you and your house if you go on to trouble the apostle further with your words.' John, therefore, seeing that there was a fierce sedition asked for silence, and said in the hearing of all, 'The first of the virtues of God which we ought to imitate is patience, by which we are able to bear with the foolishness of unbelievers. Wherefore if Aristodemus is still held by unbelief, let us loose the knots of his unbelief. He shall be compelled, even though late, to acknowledge his creator; for I will not cease from this work until a remedy shall bring help to his wounds, and like physicians who have in their hands a sick man needing medicine, so also, if Aristodemus be not yet cured by that which has already been done, he shall be cured by that which I will now do.' And he called Aristodemus to him, and gave him his coat, and he himself stood clad only in his mantle. And Aristodemus said to him, 'Why have you given me your coat?' John said to him, 'That you may even so be put to shame and depart from your unbelief.' And Aristodemus said, 'And how shall your coat make me depart from unbelief?' The apostle answered, 'Go and cast it upon the bodies of the dead, and say: "The apostle of our Lord Jesus Christ has sent me that in his name you may rise again, that all may know that life and death are servants of my Lord Jesus Christ."' When Aristodemus had done this, and had seen them rise, he worshipped John, and ran quickly to the proconsul and began to say with a loud voice, 'Hear me, hear me, proconsul; I think you remember that I have often stirred up your wrath against John and devised many things against him daily, and so I fear that I may feel his wrath; for he is a god hidden in the form of a man, and has drunk poison, and not only continues whole, but those who died by the poison he has recalled to life by my means, by the touch of his coat, and they have no mark of death upon them.' When the proconsul heard this he said, 'And what will you have me do?' Aristodemus answered, 'Let us go and fall at his feet and ask pardon, and whatever he commands us let us do.' Then they came together and cast themselves down and besought forgiveness. And he received them and offered prayer and thanksgiving to God, and he ordained them a fast of a week and when it was fulfilled he baptized them.

(3) *Acts of John* 56–7

56. One day John was seated and a partridge flew through the
air and was playing in the sand before him. John looked at this
with amazement. And a priest, one of the hearers, came to
John and saw the partridge playing before him. He was offended and said to himself, 'Such a great man rejoices over a
partridge playing in the sand!' But John perceived his thoughts
and said to him, 'It would be better if you, too, my son, would
look at a partridge playing in the sand, and not contaminate
yourself with disgraceful and impure acts. He who expects the
repentance and conversion of all has brought you here for this
purpose. For I have no need of a partridge playing in the sand.
The partridge is your soul.'

57. When the old man heard this and perceived that he was
not unknown, but that Christ's apostle had said everything
which was in his heart, he fell to the ground and said, 'Now I
know that God dwells in you, blessed John. And blessed is he
who has not tempted God in you! He who tempts you, tempts
him who cannot be tempted.' And he asked him to pray for
him. And he instructed him, gave him commandments, dismissed him and praised God who is over all.

(4) *Acts of John* 63–86

63. And while great love and endless joy prevailed among the
brethren, one, a servant of Satan, coveted Drusiana, although
he saw and knew that she was the wife of Andronicus. Very
many people remonstrated with him, 'It is impossible for you
to obtain this woman, especially since she has separated even
from her husband out of piety. Or do you alone not know that
Andronicus, who was not the godly man he now is, had locked
her up in a tomb, saying, "Either I'll have you as a wife, as I had
you before, or you must die!" And she preferred to die rather
than to commit the repugnant act. Now, if out of piety she
withheld her consent to sexual intercourse with her husband
and master, but persuaded him to become like-minded, should
she consent to you, who wish to commit adultery with her?
Desist from your passion, which gives you no rest! Desist from
your scheme, which you cannot accomplish!'

64. Though his intimate friends remonstrated with him, they could not persuade him. He was even so impudent as to send word to her. When Drusiana heard of his disgraceful passion and shameless demands, she became very despondent, and after two days she was feverish. She said, 'Oh, if I only had not come back to my native city where I have become a stumbling-block to a man who believes not in the worship of God! For if he were filled with God's word, he would not fall into such a passion. Therefore, O Lord, since I have become accessory to a blow which struck an ignorant soul, deliver me from this prison and take me soon to you!' And without being understood by anyone Drusiana departed this life in the presence of John, not rejoicing but sorrowing over the physical trouble of that man.

65. And Andronicus was sad and carried a hidden sorrow in his heart, and wept bitterly, so that John could only silence him by saying to him, 'Drusiana has departed this unjust life for a better hope.' To this answered Andronicus, 'Of this I am certain, John, and I have no doubt in the belief in my God. My hopes are grounded on the fact, that she departed this life pure.'

66. After she was interred, John took Andronicus aside, and having learned of the cause he sorrowed more than Andronicus. And he kept silence, considering the threats of the enemy, and sat still a little. When the brethren were assembled to hear which words he would say concerning the departed, he began to speak:

67. 'When the helmsman who crosses the ocean has landed with the ship and passengers in a quiet haven free from storms, he feels secure. The husbandman who sowed the seed-grains in the ground and cared for them with great pains is only then to enjoy a rest from his labours when he has harvested abundant corn in his barns. Whoever promises to take part in a race should rejoice only when he has obtained the prize. He whose name is entered on the list of prize-fighting should triumph only after he receives the crowns. And thus it is with all races and skills, when they do not fail at the end, but are carried out, as they were intended.

68. 'So I think it is with the faith which every one of us practises, and which can be decided as having been the true

one only when it remains the same to the end of life. For there are many obstacles which cause unrest to human reasoning: cares, children, parents, glory, poverty, flattery, youth, beauty, boasting, desire for riches, anger, pride, frivolity, envy, passion, carelessness, violence, lust, slaves, money, pretence, and all the other similar obstacles which exist in life; it is the same for the helmsman who takes his course for a quiet journey and is opposed by the adverse winds and a great tempest and a mighty wave, when the heaven is serene; it is the same for the husbandman who is opposed by untimely weather and blight and creeping worms appearing from the ground; for the athletes, the near miss, and for the craftsman the obstacles to their skills.

69. 'The believer must above all things consider the end and carefully examine how it will come, whether energetic and sober and without impediment, or in confusion and flattering worldly things and bound by passions. Thus one can praise the beauty of the body only when it is completely naked; and the greatness of the general when he has happily finished the whole campaign as he promised; and the excellence of the physician when he has succeeded in every cure; and so one praises a soul filled with faith and worthy of God if it has happily accomplished that which it promised, not one which made a good beginning, and gradually descended into the errors of life and became weak, nor the numb soul which made an effort to attain higher things and was afterwards reduced to perishable, nor that which loved the temporal more than the eternal, nor that which exchanged the perishable for the lasting, nor that which honoured what was not to be honoured and loved works of dishonour, nor that which accepted pledges from Satan and received the serpent into its house, nor one which was reviled for God's sake and afterwards was ashamed, nor one which consented with the mouth but did not show it by the deed; but we praise one which refused to be inflamed by filthy lust, to succumb to levity, to be ensnared by thirst after money, or to be betrayed by the strength of the body and anger.'

70. While John continued to preach to the brethren that they despise earthly goods for the sake of the eternal ones, the lover of Drusiana, inflamed by the influence of the

polymorphous Satan to the most ardent passions, bribed the greedy steward of Andronicus with money. And he opened the tomb of Drusiana and left him to accomplish on the body that which was once denied to him. Since he had not procured her during her lifetime, he continually thought of her body after she was dead, and exclaimed, 'Although when living you refused to unite with me in love, after your death I will dishonour your corpse.' Being in such a frame of mind he obtained the opportunity to execute his impious plan through the accursed steward, and both went to the tomb. Having opened the door, they began to take the graveclothes from the corpse, and said, 'What have you gained, unhappy Drusiana? Could you not have done this while you were alive? It need not have grieved you if you had done it willingly.'

71. Whilst they spoke and only the shift remained, there appeared something wonderful, which people that do such things deserve to experience. A serpent appeared from somewhere, bit the steward, and killed him. And the serpent did not bite the young man, but encircled his feet, hissing fearfully, and when he fell down, the serpent sat on him.

72. On the following day John and Andronicus and the brethren went at the break of day to the tomb in which Drusiana had been for three days, so that we might break bread there. And when we were about to start, the keys were not to be found. And John said to Andronicus, 'It is right that they are lost, for Drusiana is not in the tomb. Nevertheless, let us go, that you do not appear neglectful, and the doors will open of themselves, since the Lord has already given us many other things.'

73. When we came to the place, the doors opened at the master's behest, and at the tomb of Drusiana we saw a beautiful youth smiling. When John saw him, he exclaimed and said, 'Do you come before us here also, noble one? And why?' And he heard a voice saying to him, 'For the sake of Drusiana, whom you are to raise up. I found her almost defiled on account of the dead man lying near the tomb.' And when the noble one had thus spoken to John he ascended to heaven before the eyes of all. And John turned to the other side of the tomb and saw a young man, the very prominent Ephesian Callimachus—for this is what he was called—and on him a huge snake sleeping,

also the steward of Andronicus, named Fortunatus, dead. On seeing both, he stood helpless and said to the brethren, 'What does all this mean? Or why did the Lord not reveal to me what took place here, for he was always concernd for me?'

74. When Andronicus saw these bodies, he jumped up and went to the tomb of Drusiana. And when he saw her in her shift, he said to John, 'I understand what took place, blessed servant of God. This Callimachus loved my sister. And as he could not get her, although he tried it often, he no doubt bribed this accursed steward of mine with a great sum of money with the intention—as one can now see—to accomplish his purpose through him. For this Callimachus said to many, "If she will not yield to me alive, rape shall be committed on her death." This, O master, the noble one saw and did not allow her earthly remains to be violated. That is why those who engineered this are dead. And the voice which came to you "Raise Drusiana!" foretold this. For she departed this life through sorrow. And I believe him who said that this is one of the men who was led astray. For you were asked to raise him. As for the other I know that he does not deserve salvation. But one thing I ask of you. Raise Callimachus first, and he shall confess what took place.'

75. And John looked at the corpse and said to the poisonous snake, 'Depart from him who is to serve Jesus Christ!' Then he rose and prayed, 'God, whose name is rightly praised by us; God, who overcomes each harmful work; God, whose will is done, who always hears us, make your grace now efficacious on this youth! And if through him some dispensation is to take place, make it known to us, when he is raised!' And the young man immediately arose and kept silence for a whole hour.

76. When the man had regained his senses, John asked what his intrusion into the tomb meant. And having learned from him what Andronicus had already told him, how he passionately loved Drusiana, John asked further whether he had accomplished his wicked design to commit rape on the holy earthly remains. And he replied, 'How could I have accomplished this when this fearful beast killed Fortunatus with one bite before my eyes? And this deservedly so, for he encouraged me to such madness, after I had already desisted from the illtimed and dreadful frenzy—but he frightened me and put me in the state in which you saw me, before I arose. But I will tell

you another greater miracle, which nearly slew me and almost killed me. When my soul was seized with mad passion and the incurable disease was troubling me, when I had already robbed her of the grave-clothes with which she was dressed, and went from the grave to put them down as you see, I turned back to perpetrate the abominable deed. And I saw a beautiful youth covering her with this cloak. Rays of light fell from his face upon hers, and he turned to me also and said, "Callimachus, die, that you may live." Who it was, I knew not, servant of God. Since you have come here, I know that it was an angel of God. And this I truly know, that the true God is preached by you; and I am sure of it. But I pray you, see to it that I may be delivered from this fate and dreadful crime, and bring me to your God as a man who had gone astray in scandalous, abominable, deceit. On my knees I ask for your help. I will become one of those who hope in Christ so that the voice may also prove true, which spoke here to me, "Die to live!" And it is already fulfilled. For that unbeliever, godless, lawless man, is dead; I am raised by you as a believer, faithful and godly, that I may know the truth, which I ask of you to reveal to me.'

77. And John, rejoicing, contemplated the whole spectacle of the salvation of men and said, 'O Lord Jesus Christ, I do not know what your power is. I am amazed at your great mercy and endless forbearance. Oh, what greatness descended to servitude! O unspeakable freedom, which was enslaved by us! O inconceivable glory, which has come upon us! You have kept the grave from shame, and redeemed that man who contaminated himself with blood, and taught him to be chaste who meant to violate dead bodies. Father, full of mercy and compassion toward him who disregarded you, we praise, glorify, and honour you and thank you for your great goodness and long-suffering, holy Jesus, for you alone are God and none else; you, against whose power all devices can do nothing now and in all eternity! Amen!'

78. After these words, John took Callimachus, kissed him, and said, 'Glory be to our God, who had mercy upon you, child, and deemed me worthy to praise his power, and delivered you by a wise method from that madness and intoxication and called you to rest and renewal of life.'

79. When Andronicus saw that Callimachus had been raised from the dead, he and the brethren besought John to raise Drusiana also, and said, 'John, let her be raised and happily complete life's short space, which she gave up out of sorrow for Callimachus, because she thought she was a temptation to him! And when it pleases the Lord, he will take her to himself.' And without delay John went to the grave, seized her hand and said, 'You who alone are God, I call upon you, the immense, the unspeakable, the incomprehensible, to whom all worldly power is subject, before whom every authority bows, before whom every pride falls down and is silent, before whose voice the demons are confounded, at whose contemplation the whole creation surrenders in quiet meditation. Your name will be hallowed by us. Raise Drusiana that Callimachus be still further strengthened in you who alone can do what is wholly impossible with man, and have given salvation and resurrection, and let Drusiana come out comforted because, in consequence of the conversion of the youth, she no more has the least impediment to long for you!'

80. Having spoken thus John said, 'Drusiana, arise!' And she arose and came from the tomb. And when she saw that she wore nothing but her shirt, she was perplexed how to explain what had happened. Having learned everything from Andronicus, while John was upon his face and Callimachus with tears praised God, she also rejoiced and praised God.

81. Having dressed herself and looked around, she saw Fortunatus. And she said to John, 'Father, he too shall rise, though he tried so much to become my betrayer.' When Callimachus heard her speaking thus, he said, 'No, I beg you, Drusiana. For the voice which I heard did not mention him, but only concerned you, and when I saw I believed. If he were good, God out of mercy would have certainly raised him through the blessed John. He knew that the man should have a bad death.' And John answered him, 'My son, we have not learnt to recompense evil with evil. For God has not recompensed the evil which we have done to him, but has given us repentance. And although we did not know his name, he did not forget us, but had mercy upon us. And when we reviled him, he forsook us not, but was merciful. And when we were disbelieving, he remembered not the evil. And when we perse-

cuted his brethren, he did not requite us, but made us repent, turn away from sin, and called us to himself, as he called you also, child Callimachus, and, without remembering your former sins, made you his servant through his long-suffering mercy. If you do not wish me to raise Fortunatus, let Drusiana do it.'

82. Without wavering, but in the joy of her spirit and soul, she went to the body of Fortunatus and said, 'God of the ages, Jesus Christ, God of truth, you allowed me to see signs and wonders and granted me to partake of your name. You breathed into me your spirit with your polymorphous face, and showed much compassion. With your rich goodness, you protected me when my former husband, Andronicus, did violence to me, and gave me your servant Andronicus as a brother. Until now you have kept me, your maiden, pure. You raised me when I was dead through your servant John. To me, risen and freed from offence, you showed me him who was offended at me. You gave me perfect rest in you, and delivered me from the secret madness. I love you with all my heart. I beseech you, Christ, not to dismiss Drusiana's petition, who asks of you the resurrection of Fortunatus, though he tried so much to become my betrayer.'

83. And she took the hand of the dead man and said, 'Rise, Fortunatus, in the name of our Lord Jesus Christ!' And Fortunatus rose up. And seeing John in the tomb and Andronicus and Drusiana risen from the dead and Callimachus now a believer, he said, 'O how far the power of these awful people has spread! I wish I were not raised, but remained dead, so as not to see them.' And with these words he ran from the tomb.

84. And when John perceived the unchangeable soul of Fortunatus, he said, 'O nature, unchanged for the better! O source of the soul, remaining in the filth! O essence of corruption, full of darkness! O death, dancing among those belonging to you! O fruitless tree, full of fire! O wood, producing coal as fruit! O forest, with trees full of unhealthy shoots, neighbour of unbelief! You showed us who you are, and you will always be convicted with your children. And the power of praising higher things is unknown to you, for you do not have it. Therefore as your issue is, so is your root and nature. Vanish away from

those who hope in the Lord—from their thoughts, from their mind, from their souls, from their bodies, from their action, from their life, from their conversation, from their activity, from their deeds, from their counsel, from their resurrection to God, from their fragrance which you will share, from their fastings, from their prayers, from their holy baptism, from their eucharist, from the nourishment of their flesh, from their drink, from their dress, from their agape, from their acts of mourning, from their continence, and from their righteousness. From all these, most unholy and abominable Satan, shall Jesus Christ, our God and judge of those who are like you and your nature, remove you.'

85. After these words John prayed, fetched a loaf of bread to the tomb to break it, and said, 'We praise your name, who have converted us from error and unmerciful lusts. We praise you who have brought before our eyes that which we saw. We bear witness to your goodness manifested to us in various ways. We hallow your gracious name, Lord, and thank you who have convicted those who are convicted by you. We thank you, Lord Jesus Christ, that we believe in your unchangeable mercy. We thank you that you are in need of a saved human nature. We thank you that you gave this sure faith, that you alone are God, now and for ever. We, your servants, thank you, O holy One, we who are assembled with good reason and risen from the dead.'

86. Having thus prayed and praised God, he made all the brethren partake of the eucharist of the Lord and then left the tomb. And when he had come into the house of Andronicus, he said to the brethren, 'Dear brethren, a spirit within me has prophesied that, in consequence of the bite of the serpent, Fortunatus would die of blood-poisoning. Let someone make haste and inquire whether it is so!' And one of the young men ran and found him dead already, the poison having spread and reached his heart. And he returned to John, reporting that he had been dead three hours already. And John said, 'You have your child, devil!'

Thus John rejoiced with the brethren in the Lord.

13

Thomas

✧

In the New Testament Thomas is included among the twelve disciples in all four Gospels. In John's Gospel the name Thomas is translated Didymus meaning 'twin', and it is because of this interpretation that his name is associated with several apocryphal works. For example, as the twin of Christ, Thomas is said to have been the author of the Gospel of Thomas.

He is Doubting Thomas of John's Gospel, but the apparent faithlessness in doubting the report of Jesus' Resurrection is overtaken by his recognition of Jesus' divinity in the confession 'My Lord and my God' of John 20: 28. His subsequent career as an apostle is not to be found in the New Testament. For legends about his later life we need to turn to the apocryphal tradition.

The Acts of Thomas, which is likely to have originated in the second century like the other major Acts, has, unlike them, survived in its entirety. It is a Pilgrim's Progress of 170 chapters divided into thirteen acts and the Martyrdom. The story tells of Thomas' election to evangelize India, and his adventures there.

The Malabar Christians of South India today claim Thomas as their founder, although there is nothing whatsoever of historical value in these Acts to justify the claim. The Indian setting for the stories is arbitrary. As with other apocryphal Acts, local colour is absent, names of characters of little importance, and events fictional. Even the apostle is a stock character representing Good during his breathless round of travels, with their often conventional miracles, preaching, and conversions.

Among the episodes is the story of Thomas' meeting with

King Gundaphorus and the building of what turns out to be not the earthly palace the king commissions but a heavenly mansion such as Jesus promised. That story is given below (1). The popularity of the legend increased by its being included in the *Golden Legend*, that medieval best-seller drawn up by Jacob of Voragine in the thirteenth century. The *Golden Legend* contains a series of lives of the saints and anecdotes about Christian festivals. It was translated into several languages and maintained its popularity for at least two centuries. Because of its publication many of our apocryphal stories had a further lease of life. In the case of the Gundaphorus episode, its inclusion in the *Golden Legend* might account for Thomas being made the patron saint of architects, and for artistic representations of Thomas carrying a builder's T-square.

Among other extracts from the Acts of Thomas are three splendid poems (2 below). The first (2*a*) occurs at the end of the Gundaphorus story and is a hymn spoken by the apostle at the anointing of the newly converted king and his brother. The second (2*b*) occurs during a eucharist. Both poems may well represent a tradition independent of the book in which they are now to be read. In other words, these could be examples of early Christian hymns, somewhat tinged with Gnosticism, taken over by the author of the Acts of Thomas. The third poem here (2*c*) is the famous Hymn of the Pearl, or Hymn of the Soul. That too is likely to have been adopted by the author and given its present somewhat artificial context of Thomas preaching in prison. The hymn is a vivid oriental poem which is plainly an allegory, although the precise identification of the events and characters is controversial, making it difficult to be confident what the allegory is. Possibly it can be seen as the story of Christ's incarnation. Or it is, perhaps, the story of Everyman, who seeks and eventually finds his divine origins. It might even be a Gnostic allegory. But whatever its original interpretation, it reads well despite some tantalizing textual problems, and it merits a place in any library of religious literature.

This chapter concludes (3) with part of Thomas' farewell speech, his death, and a miracle following the death. This last item is of particular interest as it seems to be one of the earliest stories involving a Christian martyr's relics. The veneration of relics is found in the New Testament in the story in the Acts of the Apostles 19: 12 where cures are effected by handkerchiefs that had been touched by Paul. The cult of relics, in particular the honouring of the material remains of a dead saint, spread rapidly throughout the church from the mid-second century onwards. This veneration was approved by the church and the practices associated with the worship of relics have remained a popular element in many branches of Christianity.

(1) *Acts of Thomas* 17–26

17. When the apostle came into the cities of India with Abban the merchant, Abban went away to greet King Gundaphorus and told him about the carpenter whom he had brought with him. And the king was glad and ordered him to appear before him. When he had come in the king said to him, 'What trade do you know?' The apostle said to him, 'That of the carpenter and the house-builder.' The king said to him, 'What work in wood do you know and what in stone?' The apostle said, 'In wood, ploughs, yokes, balances, pulleys, and ships and oars and masts; in stone, monuments, temples, and royal palaces.' And the king said, 'Will you build me a palace?' And he answered, 'Yes, I shall build it and finish it; for because of this I have come, to build and to do carpenter's work.'

18. And the king, having accepted him, took him out of the gates of the city, and on the way began to discuss with him the building of the palace, and how the foundations should be laid, till they came to the place where the work was to be carried out. And he said, 'Here is where I wish the building to be!' And the apostle said, 'Yes, this place is suitable for the building.' For the place was wooded and there was water there. And the king said, 'Begin at once!' And he answered, 'I cannot commence now.' The king said, 'When can you?' He said, 'I shall begin in November and finish in April.' And the king was surprised, and said, 'Every building is built in the summer, but can you build and finish a palace in the winter?' And the apostle replied 'Thus it must be done; it is impossible any other way.' And the king said, 'If you have resolved upon this, draw a plan for me how the work is to be done, since I shall come here after some time.' And the apostle took a reed, measured

the place, and marked it out: the doors to be set towards the rising of the sun, to face the light; the windows toward the west, to the winds; the bakehouse he made toward the south; and the water-pipes necessary for the supply toward the north. When the king saw this, he said to the apostle, 'You are truly a craftsman, and it is fitting that you should serve kings.' And having left a lot of money with him, he went away.

19. And at the appointed times the king sent coined silver and the necessities for his and the workmen's living. And the apostle took everything and divided it, going about in the cities and surrounding villages, distributing to the poor and needy, and bestowing alms, and gave them relief, saying, 'The king knows that he will receive royal recompense, but the poor must be refreshed, as their condition requires it.' After this the king sent a messenger to the apostle, having written the following: 'Let me know what you have done or what I should send to you or what you need.' The apostle sent word to him saying, 'The palace is built, and only the roof remains to be done.' Upon hearing this the king sent him again gold and uncoined silver and wrote, 'If the palace is built, let it be roofed.' And the apostle said to the Lord, 'I thank you, Lord, in every respect, that you died for a short time, that I may live in you for ever, and that you have sold me, to deliver many through me.' And he did not cease to teach and refresh the afflicted, saying, 'The Lord has dispensed this to you and he gives to each his food. For he is the support of the orphans and the nourisher of the widows, and rest and repose to all who are afflicted.'

20. When the king came to the city he inquired of his friends concerning the palace which Judas, surnamed Thomas, had built for him. And they said to him, 'He has neither built a palace, nor did he do anything of that which he promised to do, but he goes about in the cities and villages, and if he has anything he gives it to the poor, and teaches a new God, heals the sick, drives out demons, and performs many miracles. And we believe that he is a magician. But his acts of compassion and the cures done by him as a free gift, still more his simplicity and gentleness and fidelity, show that he is a just man, or an apostle of the new God, whom he preaches. For he continually fasts and prays and eats only bread with salt, and his drink is water, and he wears one coat, whether in warm

weather or in cold, and he takes nothing from anyone but gives to others what he has.' Upon hearing this the king hit his face with his hands, shaking his head for a long time.

21. And he sent for the merchant who had brought him, and for the apostle, and said to him, 'Have you built the palace?' And he said, 'Yes, I have built it.' The king said, 'When shall we go to inspect it?' And he answered and said, 'Now you cannot see it, but you shall see it when you depart this life.' And the king was very angry and ordered both the merchant and Judas Thomas to be bound and cast into prison, until he should find out to whom the property of the king had been given, and so destroy him and the merchant. And the apostle went to prison rejoicing and said to the merchant, 'Fear nothing, believe only in the God who is preached by me, and you shall be freed from this world, and obtain life in the world to come.'

And the king considered by what death he should kill them. He decided to flog them and burn them with fire. On that very night Gad, the king's brother, fell ill; and through the grief and disappointment which the king had suffered he was grievously depressed. And having sent for the king he said to him, 'Brother and king, I commend to you my house and my children. For I have been grieved on account of the insult that has befallen you, and lo, I am dying, and if you do not proceed against the life of that magician you will give my soul no rest in Hades.' And the king said to his brother, 'I considered the whole night by what death I should kill him, and I have decided to flog him and burn him with fire, together with the merchant who brought him.'

22. While they were talking, the soul of Gad, his brother, departed, and the king mourned for Gad exceedingly, because he loved him, and ordered him to be prepared for burial in a royal and costly robe. While this was going on, angels received the soul of Gad, the king's brother, and took it up into heaven, showing him the places and mansions there, asking him, 'In what place do you wish to dwell?' And when they came near the edifice of the apostle Thomas, which he had erected for the king, Gad, upon beholding it, said to the angels, 'I entreat you, my lords, let me dwell in one of these lower chambers.' But they said to him, 'In this building you cannot dwell.' And he said, 'Why not?' They answered, 'This palace is the one which

that Christian has built for your brother.' But he said, 'I entreat you, my lords, allow me to go to my brother to buy this palace from him. For my brother does not know what it is like, and he will sell it to me.'

23. And the angels let the soul of Gad go. And as they were putting on him the burial robe his soul came into him. And he said to those standing round him, 'Call my brother to me, that I may beg of him a request.' Straightway they sent the good news to their king, saying, 'Your brother has become alive again!' And the king arose and with a great multitude went to his brother. And coming in he went to the bed as if stupefied, unable to speak to him. And his brother said, 'I know and I am convinced, brother, that if anyone had asked of you the half of your kingdom, you would give it for my sake. Wherefore I entreat you to grant one favour, which I beg of you to do: that you sell to me that which I ask from you.' And the king answered and said, 'And what is it that you wish me to sell to you?' And he said, 'Assure me by an oath that you will grant it to me.' And the king swore to him, 'Whatever of my possession you ask, I will give you.' And he said to him, 'Sell me the palace which you have in heaven.' And the king said, 'A palace in heaven—where does this come to me from?' And he said, 'It is the one that Christian built for you, the man who is now in prison, whom the merchant brought, having bought him from a certain Jesus. I mean that Hebrew slave whom you wished to punish, having suffered some deception from him, on account of whom I also was grieved and died, and now have come alive again.'

24. Then the king heard and understood his words about the eternal benefits that were conferred upon him and destined for him, and said, 'That palace I cannot sell you, but I pray to be permitted to enter into it and to dwell there, being deemed worthy to belong to its inhabitants. And if you really wish to buy such a palace, behold, the man is alive, and will build you a better one than that.' And immediately he sent and brought the apostle out of prison, and the merchant who had been shut up along with him, saying, 'I entreat you, as a man entreating the servant of God, pray for me, and ask him, whose servant you are, to pardon me and to overlook what I have done to you or intended to do, and that I may become worthy to be an

inhabitant of that house for which indeed I have done nothing, but which you, labouring alone, have built for me with the help of the grace of your God, and that I may also become a servant and serve this God, whom you preach.' His brother also fell down before the apostle and said, 'I entreat you and supplicate before your God that I may become worthy of this service and become partaker of that which was shown to me by his angels.'

25. And the apostle, seized with joy, said, 'I give thanks to you, Lord Jesus, that you have revealed your truth in these men. For you alone are the God of truth and not another; and you are he who knows all things that are unknown to many; you, O Lord, are he who in all things shows mercy and compassion to men. For men, through the error that is in them, have overlooked you, but you have not forsaken them. And now, because I entreat you and supplicate you, accept the king and his brother and unite them with your flock, cleanse them by your baptism and anoint them with your oil from the error which encompasses them. Protect them also from the wolves and bring them into your meadows. Give them to drink of your ambrosial fountain, which is never fouled and never dries up. For they entreat and supplicate you and wish to become your servants, and on this account they have also resolved to be persecuted by your enemies and to endure for your sake hatred, insult, and death, as you also have suffered all this for our sakes, in order to gain us. You are Lord and truly a good shepherd. Grant to them that they put their trust in you alone, and obtain the help coming from you and hope of their salvation, which they expect from you alone, and that they may be confirmed in your mysteries and receive the perfect benefits of your graces and gifts, and flourish in your service and bear fruit to perfection in your Father.'

26. Being well disposed now toward the apostle, King Gundaphorus and his brother Gad followed him, never leaving him, providing for the poor, giving to all, and relieving all.

(2) *Acts of Thomas* 27, 50, 108–13

(*a*) And the apostle took the oil, poured it over their heads, anointed and chrismed them, and began to say:

'Come, holy name of Christ, which is above every name;
Come, power of the Most High, and perfect compassion;
Come, gift most high;
Come, compassionate mother;
Come, fellowship of the male;
Come, revealer of secret mysteries;
Come, mother of the seven houses, that there may be rest
    for you in the eighth house.
Come, elder of the five members: intelligence, thought,
    prudence, reflection, reasoning,
Communicate with these young men!
Come, Holy Spirit, and purify their loins and their hearts,
And seal them in the name of the Father and of the Son
    and of the Holy Ghost.'

(*b*) And Thomas said,

'Come, perfect compassion;
Come, fellowship with the male;
Come, you who know the mysteries of the Chosen One;
Come, you who have partaken in all the combats of the
    noble combatant;
Come, rest, that reveals the great deeds of the whole
    greatness;
Come, you who disclose secrets
And make manifest the mysteries;
Come, holy dove,
Who bear the twin young;
Come, secret mother;
Come, you who are manifest in your deeds;
Come, giver of joy
And of rest to those who are united to you;
Come and commune with us in this eucharist,
Which we celebrate in your name,
And in the agape
In which we are united at your calling.'

And having thus spoken he made the sign of the cross upon the
bread, broke it, and began to distribute it.

(*c*)

1 When I was a little child, in my father's palace, **108**.
2 And enjoyed the wealth and luxury of those who nurtured me,
3 My parents equipped me with provisions and sent me out from the East, our homeland.
4 From the wealth of our treasury they gave me a great burden,
5 Which was light so that I could carry it by myself:
6 Gold from the land above, silver from great treasuries,
7 And stones, chalcedonies of India and agates from Kushan.
8 And they girded me with steel,
9 And they took away from me the garment set with gems and spangled with gold
   Which they had made out of love for me
10 And the yellow robe which was made for my size,
11 And they made a covenant with me
   And wrote it in my mind that I might not forget:
12 'If you go down to Egypt and bring the one pearl
13 Which is in the land of the devouring serpent,
14 You shall put on again that garment set with stones and the robe which lies over it,
15 And with your brother, our next in command, you shall be a herald for our kingdom.'
16 So I departed from the East on a difficult and frightening **109**.
   road led by two guides,
17 And I was very young to travel on it.
18 I passed over the borders of the Mosani, where there is the meeting-place of the merchants of the East,
19 And reached the land of the Babylonians.
20 I went down to Egypt, and my companions parted from me.
21 I went straight to the serpent and stayed near his den
22 Until he should slumber and sleep, so that I might take the pearl from him.
23 Being alone I altered my appearance and seemed an alien even to my own people,

24 But I saw one of my kinsmen there, a free-born man from the East,

25 A youth fair and beautiful, the son of courtiers.

26 He came and kept me company.

27 And I made him my intimate friend, a comrade with whom I communicated my business.

28 Being exhorted to guard against the Egyptians and against partaking of unclean things,

29 I clothed myself in garments like theirs, so that I would not be seen as a stranger

30 And as one who had come from abroad to take the pearl, Lest the Egyptians might arouse the serpent against me.

31 But somehow they learned that I was not their countryman.

32 They dealt with me treacherously, and I tasted their food.

33 I no longer recognized that I was a king's son, and I served their king.

34 I forgot the pearl for which my parents had sent me.

35 And I fell into a deep sleep because of the heaviness of their food.

110.   36 While I was suffering these things my parents were aware of it and grieved over me.

37 And a proclamation was heralded in our kingdom that all should present themselves at our doors.

38 The kings of Parthia and those in office, and the great men of the East

39 Resolved that I should not be left in Egypt.

40 So the courtiers wrote me a letter:

41 'From your father the king of kings and your mother, the mistress of the East

42 And their brothers, who are second to us, To our son in Egypt, greetings!

43 Awake, and rise from your sleep.

44 Listen to the words in this letter, Remember you are the son of kings, You have fallen beneath the yoke of slavery.

45 Remember your gold-spangled garment,

46 Recall the pearl for which you were sent to Egypt,

47 Your name has been called to the book of life,

48 Together with that of your brother whom you have received in our kingdom.'

49 And the king sealed it to make it an ambassador, **111.**

50 Because of the wicked Babylonian children and the tyrannical demons of the Labyrinth.[1]

53 I rose from sleep when I recognized its voice,

54 I took it up and kissed it and I read.

55 And what was written concerned that which was engraved on my heart.

56 And I immediately remembered that I was a son of kings and that my freedom demanded my people.

57 I remembered the pearl for which I had been sent to Egypt,

58 And the fact that I had come to snatch it from the terrifying serpent.

59 I subdued it by calling out my father's name,[2]

61 And I snatched the pearl and turned about to go to my parents.

62 And I took off the dirty clothing and left it behind in their land.

63 And directed my way forthwith to the light of our Eastern home.

64 And on the road I found a female who lifted me up.

65 She awakened me, giving me an oracle with her voice, and guided me to the light.

66 The Royal silken garment shone before my eyes.[3]

68 And with familial love leading me and drawing me on

69 I passed by the Labyrinth,
   And leaving Babylon behind on the left,

70 I reached Meson which is a great coast.[4]

75 But I could not recall my splendour, **112.**

---

[1] In Syriac are found vv. 51–2: (51) 'It flew in the form of an eagle, the king of birds, (52) It flew and alighted beside me and became all speech.'

[2] Syriac adds v. 60: 'And the name of our second in rank and of my mother, the Queen of the East'.

[3] Syriac adds v. 67: 'And with its voice and its guidance encouraging me to speed'.

[4] Syriac adds vv. 71–4: 'And my splendid robe which I had taken off | And my toga with which it was wrapped about | From the heights of Hyrcania | My parents sent there | By the hand of their treasurers, | Who for their faithfulness were so entrusted.'

For it had been when I was still a child and quite young
that I had left it behind in my father's palace.

76 But, when suddenly I saw my garment reflected as in a
mirror,

77 I perceived in it my whole self as well
And through it I knew and saw myself.

78 For though we originated from the one and the same we
were partially divided,
Then again we were one, with a single form.

79 The treasurers too who had brought the garment

80 I saw as two beings, but there existed a single form in
both,
One royal symbol consisting of two halves.

81 And they had my money and wealth in their hands and
gave me my reward:

82 The fine garment of glorious colours,

83 Which was embroidered with gold, precious stones, and
pearls to give a good appearance.

84 It was fastened at the collar[5]

86 And the image of the King of Kings was all over it.

87 Stones of lapis lazuli had been skilfully fixed to the
collar,

113.   88 And I saw in turn that motions of knowledge were stirring
throughout it,

89 And that it was prepared to speak.

90 Then I heard it speak:

91 'It is I who belong to the one who is stronger than all men
and for whose sake I was written about by the father
himself.'

92 And I took note of my stature,

93 And all the royal feelings rested on me as its energy increased.

94 Thrust out by his hand the garment hastened to me as I
went to receive it,

95 And a longing aroused me to rush and meet it and to
receive it.

96 And I stretched out and took it and adorned myself with
the beauty of its colours.

---

[5] Syriac adds v. 85: 'And with stones of adamant all its seams were fastened.'

97 And I covered myself completely with my royal robe over it.

98 When I had put it on I ascended to the land of peace and homage.

99 And I lowered my head and prostrated myself before the splendour of the father who had sent it to me.

100 For it was I who had obeyed his commands
And it was I who had also kept the promise,

101 And I mingled at the doors of his ancient royal building.

102 He took delight in me and received me in his palace.

103 All his subjects were singing hymns with harmonious voices.

104 He allowed me also to be admitted to the doors of the king himself,

105 So that with my gifts and the pearl I might appear before the king himself.

(3) *Acts of Thomas* 164–6, 168, 170

164. When the apostle had said these things, Misdaeus considered how he should put him to death; he was afraid because of the many people who were subject to him, for many of the nobles and of those in authority believed in him. He therefore took him and went out of the city, and armed soldiers also went with him. And the people supposed that the king desired to learn something from him, and they stood still and gave heed. And when they had walked one mile, he delivered him to four soldiers and an officer, and commanded them to take him into the mountain and there pierce him with spears and put an end to him, and return again to the city. And having said this to the soldiers he himself returned to the city.

165. But the onlookers ran after Thomas, desiring to deliver him from death. And two soldiers went at the right hand of the apostle and two on his left, holding spears, and the officer held his hand and supported him. And the apostle Thomas said, 'O the hidden mysteries which even until our departure are accomplished in us! O riches of his glory, who will not suffer us to be swallowed up in this passion of the body! Four are they that cast me down, for of four am I made; and one is he who draws me, for of one I am, and to him I go. And this I now

understand, that my Lord and God Jesus Christ, being of one, was pierced by one, but I, who am of four, am pierced by four.'

166. And having come up into the mountain to the place where he was to be slain, he said to those who held him and to the rest, 'Brethren, hearken to me now at the last; for I am come to my departure out of the body. Let not then the eyes of your heart be blinded nor your ears be made deaf. Believe in the God whom I preach, and be not guides to yourselves in the hardness of your heart, but walk in all your liberty, and in the glory that is toward men and the life that is toward God.'

168. And when he had thus prayed he said to the soldiers, 'Come here and accomplish the commandments of him who sent you.' And the four came and pierced him with their spears, and he fell down and died.

And all the brethren wept; and they brought beautiful robes and much fair linen, and buried him in a royal sepulchre wherein the earlier kings were laid.

170. Now it came to pass after a long time that one of the children of Misdaeus the king was a demoniac and no one could cure him, for the devil was extremely fierce. And Misdaeus the king took thought and said, 'I will go and open the sepulchre, and take a bone of the apostle of God and hang it upon my son, and he shall be healed.' But while Misdaeus thought about this, the apostle Thomas appeared to him and said to him, 'You did not believe in a living man, and will you believe in the dead? Yet fear not, for my Lord Jesus Christ has compassion on you and pities you of his goodness.'

And he went and opened the sepulchre, but did not find the apostle there, for one of the brethren had stolen him away and taken him to Mesopotamia; but from that place where the bones of the apostle had lain Misdaeus took dust and put it about his son's neck, saying, 'I believe in you, Jesu Christ, now that he has left me who troubles men and opposes them lest they should see you.' And when he had hung it upon his son, the boy was cured.

14

Andrew

Andrew, the brother of Simon Peter and one of Jesus' twelve disciples, is named as a participant in a couple of New Testament narratives. He is a spokesman in the Feeding of the Five Thousand (John 6: 8) and in the episode in John 12: 20–2 when some Greeks wish to meet Jesus. But he is not one of the prominent disciples, nor does he figure in the stories in the Acts of the Apostles. But in the Christian literature of the following centuries legends about his exploits became popular.

Of the five major apocryphal Acts the Acts of Andrew is the one whose original contents are most widely dispersed in later documents. Much of the original story has, however, been lost. The famous sixth-century bishop and historian, Gregory of Tours, produced an abstract of the Acts of Andrew from which he claims to have eliminated tedious speeches. Gregory's Epitome, concentrating on the miracles of Andrew, has survived and it gives a useful guide to the scale and contents of the original Acts of Andrew. We are, however, not dependent entirely on Gregory's later, censored, version of the second-century original. Some manuscripts, of varying dates, have enabled scholars to reconstruct at least parts of the earlier, original, Acts.

The first extract below (1), which comes from the original Acts of Andrew, concerns a case of impersonation in the marital bed. Parallels to this may be found in other literatures, often in comic contexts. In the case of the story of Maximilla and the maid, Euclia, who represents her mistress in bed, the motive is that Maximilla, having converted to Christianity, wishes to maintain a chaste life. Extreme asceticism and chastity within marriage are recurrent themes in apocryphal literature. The rejection of conjugal rights in this, as in many other comparable stories in the apocryphal Acts, is often the reason why the apostle responsible for the conversion of the wives is arrested and ultimately killed. That is certainly the reason why Andrew is martyred; Maximilla's husband Aegeates is a prominent pagan citizen and, as he is proconsul, he is able to have Andrew punished. The episode with Euclia occurs quite early in the book, but the antagonism of Aegeates for Andrew continues throughout the Acts and reaches its climax in the death of Andrew at the end.

The extracts under (2) below come from Gregory's Epitome, and these give the flavour of Andrew's miracles.

A section of Andrew's farewell speech, which is said to have lasted over three days, and the story of his crucifixion are given (3).

In later literature we find a legend associating Andrew with Ethiopia in the Old English poem, *Andreas*, attributed to Cynewulf. Another late legend claims that Andrew's relics were removed from Patras to Scotland, hence the choice of Andrew as its patron saint.

There is nothing in the apocryphal tradition to indicate that Andrew's crucifixion was unusual. Whereas the Acts of Peter puts great emphasis on the story of Peter's inverse crucifixion, there is nothing in the Acts of Andrew to indicate that Andrew's cross was special. Early depictions of Andrew's crucifixion show him on an upright cross. It was only from the fourteenth century onwards that he became normally associated with a decussate cross, known in heraldry as the saltire cross and more generally as St Andrew's cross.

(1) *Acts of Andrew* 17–22

17. Maximilla then planned the following. She summoned a shapely exceedingly wanton servant-girl named Euclia and told her something that delighted her and met her desires. 'You will have me as a benefactor of all your needs, providing you scheme with me and carry out what I advise.' Because she wanted to live chastely from that time on, Maximilla told Euclia what she wanted and got her word agreeing to it, and so for some time she employed the following subterfuge. Just as a woman customarily adorns herself to look like her rival,

Maximilla groomed Euclia in just such finery and put her
forward to sleep with Aegeates in her stead. Having used her as
his lover, he let her get up and go to her own bedroom, just as
Maximilla used to. By so doing, Maximilla escaped detection
for some time, and thereby got relief, rejoiced in the Lord, and
never left Andrew.

18. When eight months had elapsed, Euclia demanded that
her lady procure her freedom. That same day, Maximilla
granted her whatever she asked. A few days later she made
more demands, this time a large sum of money, and Maximilla
gave it to her without hesitation. When Euclia demanded some
of her jewellery, Maximilla did not object. In a word, even
though Euclia regularly took clothing, fine linen, and head-
bands from Maximilla, she was not content but flaunted the
affair before the other servants, boasting and vaunting herself.

The slaves, though indignant at Euclia's bragging, at first
curbed themselves from injuring her. But she would laugh at
them when showing them the gifts her mistress had given her.
Euclia's fellow servants recognized them but were at a loss
about what to do. Wishing to provide even greater proof of
what she was saying, Euclia stationed two of them at the head
of her master's bed when he was drunk, in order to convince
them that she was indeed sleeping with him as though she
were Maximilla. When she woke him from a deep sleep, she
and the fellow servants observing the situation heard:
'Maximilla, my queen, why do you come so late?' Euclia said
nothing, and the attending servants left the bedroom without a
sound.

19. But Maximilla, supposing that Euclia was true to her
word and reliable because of the gifts given her, spent her
nights resting with Andrew along with Stratocles and all the
other brethren. Andrew saw a vision, and as Maximilla listened, he told the brethren, 'Today at the home of Aegeates
some new contrivance is brewing, brimming with trouble and
wrath.' Maximilla begged him to disclose what this might be,
but he said, 'Do not be eager to learn from me what you are to
recognize soon enough.'

20. She altered her customary attire and entered the
praetorium gate in full view. The household servants who had
known about the affair—how it was that every day she and

Stratocles went to Andrew, and at what hour she returned to her own bedroom—took her to be a visitor. She entered the proconsul's praetorium at that hour trying to escape detection. When they had forcibly exposed her they noticed she was their mistress. Some of them wanted to divulge the ruse and to tell Aegeates, while the others, motivated by hypocrisy toward their mistress, feigned fondness for her and silenced the others, assaulted them as though they were insane, and drove them out. While the slaves were fighting each other Maximilla burst into her bedroom and prayed that the Lord would fend her from every evil.

21. One hour later, those who had fought on Maximilla's behalf against their fellow servants set upon her, fawning, expecting to receive some reward, as though they were servants of Aegeates. The blessed lady considered them deserving of their request and summoned Iphidama: 'Give them their due.' She ordered that those who had hypocritically simulated affection for her be given one thousand denarii and commanded them to disclose the matter to no one.

Even though they solemnly swore themselves to silence about what they had seen, at the instigation of their father the devil they went to their master immediately, money in hand, and told him the whole story, including how their own fellow servant submitted to the plan Maximilla devised because she no longer wanted to sleep with Aegeates, repulsed by sexual intercourse with him as a heinous and despicable act.

22. The proconsul learned everything in detail, how Euclia had shared his bed as though she were his spouse, and how she confessed to having done so to her fellow slaves. Through interrogation he also discovered her motivation, for under torture she confessed to all the payments she received from her lady for keeping quiet.

The proconsul, furious at her for boasting to her fellow servants and for saying these things in order to defame her mistress—he wanted the matter to be kept secret since he was still fond of his spouse—cut out Euclia's tongue, mutilated her, and ordered her thrown outside. She stayed there without food for several days before she became food for the dogs. The rest of the servants who had told their story to him—there were three of them—he crucified.

(2) Gregory of Tours, *Epitome* 11–14 (summary)

11. At Philippi were two brothers, one of whom had two sons, the other two daughters. They were rich and noble, and said, 'There is no family as good as ours in the place: let us marry our sons to our daughters.' It was agreed and the earnest paid by the father of the sons. On the wedding-day a word from God came to them, 'Wait till my servant Andrew comes: he will tell you what you should do.' All preparations had been made, and guests bidden, but they waited. On the third day Andrew came: they went out to meet him with wreaths and told him how they had been charged to wait for him, and how things stood. His face was shining so that they marvelled at him. He said, 'Do not, my children, be deceived: rather repent, for you have sinned in thinking to join together those who are near of kin. We do not forbid or shun marriage. It is a divine institution: but we condemn incestuous unions.' The parents were troubled and prayed for pardon. The young people saw Andrew's face like that of an angel, and said, 'We are sure that your teaching is true.' The apostle blessed them and departed.

12. At Thessalonica was a rich noble youth, Exuos, who came without his parents' knowledge and asked to be shown the way of truth. He was taught, and believed, and followed Andrew, taking no care of his worldly estate. The parents heard that he was at Philippi and tried to bribe him with gifts to leave Andrew. He said, 'Would that you had not these riches, then you would know the true God, and escape his wrath.' Andrew, too, came down from the third storey and preached to them, but in vain: he retired and shut the doors of the house. They gathered a band and came to burn the house, saying, 'Death to the son who has forsaken his parents', and brought torches, reeds, and faggots, and set the house on fire. It blazed up. Exuos took a bottle of water and prayed, 'Lord Jesus Christ, in whose hand is the nature of all the elements, who moisten the dry and dry the moist, cool the hot and kindle the quenched, put out this fire that your servants may not grow evil, but be more enkindled unto faith.' He sprinkled the flames and they died. 'He is become a sorcerer', said the parents, and got ladders, to climb up and kill them, but God blinded them. They remained obstinate, but one Lysimachus, a citizen, said, 'Why

persevere? God is fighting for these. Desist, lest heavenly fire consume you.' They were touched, and said, 'This is the true God.' It was now night, but a light shone out, and they received sight. They went up and fell before Andrew and asked pardon, and their repentance made Lysimachus say, 'Truly Christ whom Andrew preaches is the Son of God.' All were converted except the youth's parents, who cursed him and went home again, leaving all their money to public uses. Fifty days after they suddenly died, and the citizens, who loved the youth, returned the property to him. He did not leave Andrew, but spent his income on the poor.

13. The youth asked Andrew to go with him to Thessalonica. All assembled in the theatre, glad to see their favourite. The youth preached to them, Andrew remaining silent, and all wondered at his wisdom. The people cried out, 'Save the son of Carpianus who is ill, and we will believe.' Carpianus went to his house and said to the boy, 'You shall be cured to-day, Adimantus.' He said, 'Then my dream is come true: I saw this man in a vision healing me.' He rose up, dressed, and ran to the theatre, outstripping his father, and fell at Andrew's feet. The people seeing him walk after twenty-three years, cried, 'There is none like the God of Andrew.'

14. A citizen had a son possessed by an unclean spirit and asked for his cure. The demon, foreseeing that he would be cast out, took the son aside into a chamber and made him hang himself. The father said, 'Bring him to the theatre: I believe this stranger is able to raise him.' He said the same to Andrew. Andrew said to the people, 'What will it profit you if you see this accomplished and do not believe?' They said, 'Fear not, we will believe.' The lad was raised and they said, 'It is enough, we do believe.' And they escorted Andrew to the house with torches and lamps, for it was night, and he taught them for three days.

(3) *Acts of Andrew* 56(6)–64(10)

56(6). When Andrew had said these things, he addressed a general speech to everyone, for even the pagans had hurried to the site, infuriated at Aegeates' unjust decision. 'Men who are present with me, women, children, old, slaves, free, and any others who would hear: if you suppose this act of dying is the end of ephemeral life, leave this place at once. If you understand the conjunction of the soul with a body to be the soul itself, so that after the separation (of the two) nothing at all exists, you possess the intelligence of animals and one would have to list you among ferocious beasts. And if you love immediate pleasures and pursue them above all, in order to enjoy their fruits exclusively, you are like thieves. And if you suppose that you are merely that which can be seen and nothing more, you are slaves of folly and ignorance. And if you perceive that only this nocturnal light exists and nothing in addition to it, you are kindred to this night. And if you think that your earthly food is capable of creating bodily mass and the blood's constitutive power, you yourselves are earthly. And if you suppose that you are happy even though you have an inequitable body, you actually are miserable. And if your external prosperity makes you happy, you truly are most wretched. And if the pleasure and intercourse of marriage please you, and if the corruption which is from them, full of pain, makes you sad, and if you are in need of sustenance for your many children, and if the irritating poverty they cause is known to you, it will upset you. And if the rest of your possessions draw you to themselves as though you belonged to them, may their impermanence reproach you. (57(6).) What benefit is there for you who gain for yourselves external goods but do not gain your very selves? What pride issues from external ancestry if the soul in you is held captive, sold to desires? And why do we desire pleasure and childbearing, for later we have to separate? No one knows what he does. Who will take care of his wife when he is preoccupied merely by the passions of desire? Or why all the rest of the concern for externals, while you yourselves neglect what you actually are? I exhort you all rather to rid yourselves of this life which is painful, vain, senseless, boastful, empty, perishable, transitory, the friend of pleasures, the slave of time, the servant of drunkenness, the neighbour of debauchery, the possession of greed, the kindred of wrath, the umpire of treachery, the ally of murders, the prince of hatred, the patron of desire, the master of adulteries, the mediator of jealousies, the instigator of murders. I entreat you who have come here together for my sake, abandon this entire life and hasten to overtake my soul which speeds toward things beyond time, beyond law, beyond speech, beyond body, beyond bitter and lawless pleasures full of every pain. Observe now, even you, with the eyes of your souls, those things about which I speak. Follow my deep-seated love. Learn of my sufferings about which I am now speaking with you. Take my mind as a deposit. Participate in another fellowship for yourselves. Submit yourselves to my lashes, and cleanse your ears to hear what I say. Flee from everything merely temporal. Even now speed away with me. (58(6).) Even now I know that you are not inattentive to my words. Truly I see you mild as I want it, and to be far away from external forms, for the internal is our unity. I greet you with the grace of God and with love which is due him and even more with your consent to each other, to keep us away from those who do harm, and to apply to him, and to the good, and to the innocence which is to him and to the accord which is in them. For this reason men quietly take courage in the knowledge of our God. On the one hand, I am leaving to prepare routes there for those who align themselves with me and are equipped with a pure faith and with love for him; I am stifling the fire, banishing the shadows, extinguishing the furnace, killing the worm, eradicating the threat, gagging the demons, muzzling and destroying the ruling powers, dominating the authorities, throwing down the devil, casting out Satan, and punishing wickedness. On the other hand, with respect to those who have come here not out of love for God but out of hypocrisy and because of unfruitful pleasures, who have submitted themselves to superstition, disbelief, and every other ignorance, and who suppose nothing else exists after one's release from here, all these monsters fly out, become agitated, rush forth, take wing, ravage, fight, conquer, rule, wreak vengeance, enflame, rage, afflict, punish, and attack. They blaze, enact violence, and do not withdraw or relent, but rejoice, exult, smile, mock, and take their rest and delight in all who are similar to them, possessing those who succumbed to them by not believing in my God. Choose then which of the two paths you prefer, for the choice is yours to decide.'

59(6). When the crowds heard Andrew's speech, they were won over by him, so to say, and did not leave the spot. The blessed one proceeded to speak to them even longer than he had before, to such an extent that those who heard him took it as a sign. He spoke to them for three days and nights, and no one, no matter how weary, separated from him.

On the fourth day, when they observed his nobility, the adamance of his thought, the sheer abundance of his words, the value of his exhortation, the stability of his soul, the prudence of his spirit, the firmness of his mind, and the precision of his reasoning, they were furious with Aegeates and together ran off to the tribunal. As he sat there they cried out, 'What is this judgement of yours, O proconsul? You have judged wickedly! You have made an unjust decision! Your courts are a sacrilege! What crime did the man commit? What evil has he done? The city is in uproar! You are wronging us all! You are grieving us all! Do not betray the city of the emperor! Grant the Achaeans the just man! Grant us this God-fearing man! Do not kill this man possessed of God! Do not destroy this pious man! Even though he has been hanging for four days, he is still alive. Although he has eaten nothing, he has nourished us with his words. Bring the man down and we will all become philosophers! Untie the prudent one, and all Patras will be law-abiding! Release the wise man, and all Achaea will receive mercy!'

60(7). When Aegeates at first disregarded the crowd and gestured for them to leave the tribunal, they were enraged and were gaining courage to oppose him in some way; they numbered about two thousand. When the proconsul saw that they were in some way incensed he was terrified that he might suffer a revolution. He rose from the tribunal and went off with them, promising to release the blessed Andrew.

Some ran ahead to disclose to the apostle this very fact as well as the reason for Aegeates' coming to the place. The crowd was jubilant because the blessed Andrew was about to be untied, and when the proconsul arrived, all the brethren were rejoicing, among them Maximilla.

61(8). When Andrew heard this, he said, 'O the great lethargy of those I have taught! O the sudden fog engulfing us even after many mysteries! O, how much we have spoken up to the present, and we have not convinced our own! O, how much has happened so that we might flee the earthly! O, what strong statements have been spoken against carnal things, and yet they want more of the same! O, how many times I have prayed that I might lift them from these filthy habits, but instead they were encouraged to nothingness! Why this excessive fondness for the flesh? Why this great complicity with it? Do you again encourage me to be put back among things in flux? If you understood that I have been loosened from ropes but tied up to myself, you yourselves would have been eager to be loosened from the many and to be tied to the one. What should I say? I know well that what I am saying will happen, for you yourselves will I tie up with me, and after liberating myself, I will release myself from all things and become united with the one who came into being for all and who exists beyond all. (62(8).) But now that Aegeates is coming to me, I will keep quiet and embrace my children. Whatever I must resolve by speaking to him, these I will speak. Aegates, why have you come to us again? Why should you who are foreign to us come to us? What do you want to attempt now? What do you want to contrive? Whom do you wish to summon? Say something! Have you come to untie us because you changed your mind? Even if you really did change your mind, Aegeates, I would never accede to you. Were you to promise all your possessions, I would stand aloof from them. Were you to say you yourself were mine, I would not trust you. Would you untie the one who is tied up, proconsul? Would you untie the one who has fled? Would you untie the one who was liberated? Would you untie the one recognized by his kindred, the one who received mercy, the one loved by him, the one alien to you, the stranger who appeared so only to you? I possess the one with whom I will always be. I possess the one with whom I will be a compatriot for countless ages. It is to him that I go. It is to him that I speed on, to the one who made me recognize even you by saying to me: "Mark Aegeates and his gifts. Do not let that rogue frighten you, and let him not suppose that he can seize you, for you are mine. He is your enemy. He is a corrupter, a cheat, a destroyer, a slanderer, merciless, a maniac, a plotter, a murderer, an insolent egotist, a flatterer, a magician, terrible, petulant, insensitive, and decorated on all sides by his material veneer." Inasmuch as I recognized you through your turning to me, I am released from you. Proconsul, I know well that you bewail and mourn because of what I am saying to you as I flee to the one beyond you. You will weep, beat your breast, gnash your teeth, grieve, despair, lament, anguish, and behave like your relative the sea, which you now see furiously troubled by waves because I am leaving all of you. The grace which came because of me is delightful, holy, just, true, charming, and articulate, along with all the things by which you seemed to have been adorned through me.'

When the proconsul heard these things he stood there speechless and as if stunned. Andrew looked at him again and said, 'Aegeates, enemy of us all, now you stand there watching. You stand there quiet and calm, unable to do anything you dare. My kindred and I speed on to things our own, leaving you to be what you are and what you fail to understand about yourself.'

63(9). And when Aegeates again attempted to approach the wood to untie Andrew, the entire city was in an uproar at him. The apostle Andrew shouted: 'O Master, do not permit Andrew, the one tied to your wood, to be untied again. O Jesus, do not give me to the shameless devil, I who am attached to your mystery. O Father, do not let your opponent untie me, I who am hanging upon your grace. May he who is little no longer humiliate the one who has known your greatness. But you yourself, O Christ, you whom I desired, whom I loved, whom I know, whom I possess, whom I cherish, whose I am, receive me, so that by my departure to you there may be a reunion of my many kindred, those who rest in your majesty.' When he had said these things and further glorified the Lord, he handed over his spirit, so that we wept and everyone grieved his departure.

64(10). After the departure of the blessed apostle, Maximilla, accompanied by Stratocles, completely disregarding those standing around her, came forward, untied the corpse of the blessed one, and having provided it with the necessary attention, buried it at nightfall.

She separated from Aegeates because of his savage soul and lawless public life. Thereafter, though he simulated good behaviour, she had nothing whatever to do with him. Choosing instead a life holy and quiet, provided for by the love of Christ, she spent her time happily with the brethren. Even though Aegeates often importuned her and offered her the opportunity to control his affairs, he was not able to persuade her. One night, undetected by anyone in his household, he threw himself from a great height and died.

Stratocles, Aegeates' brother according to the flesh, did not want so much as to touch the property Aegeates left—the wretch died childless. He said, 'May your possessions go with you, Aegeates! May Jesus be my friend and I his! Casting from me the entire lot of external and internal evils and entrusting to that one everything I own, I thrust aside everything averse to him.'

C

Stories relating to Life after Death

———————————— ✧ ————————————

Christian writers, Biblical and post-Biblical, concerned themselves, just as their Jewish predecessors had done, with apocalyptic themes and teaching. The word 'apocalypse' means a
revelation of things normally hidden. In general, apocalypses
speak of the signs and portents presaging the end of this world,
and of the nature of the other world.

In the apocryphal literature we may separate these two features. In Chapter 15 are those passages which describe what
heaven and hell hold in store for the faithful and the unbeliever. The texts dealt with in Chapter 7 concern Jesus' descent
to Hades, a realm inhabited by all those who had died prior to
Jesus' triumphant breaking of the power of death and his
bringing of the faithful dead into paradise. The language of the
apocalypses in Chapter 15 is more obviously dualistic and
speaks of two opposing realms: hell, the abode only of the
sinner, and heaven, the home of the believer. Post-Biblical
writers used this genre of literature with its tours of the other
world with great imagination. It could well be that Biblical
texts such as Revelation 21: 1–8 provided the starting-point for
the richly developed imaginative constructions we find in the
apocryphal books. The writings may have been relegated as
'spurious' or 'secondary', in other words as 'apocryphal' in the
common understanding of that term, but they were obviously
regularly read by Christians even after their use was condemned by the ecclesiastical authorities.

In Chapter 16 a text giving warnings about the end time is
translated, but such a theme seems not to have been especially
popular in the apocalyptic literature.

15

Heaven and Hell

--- ✧ ---

Curiosity about the character of heaven and hell fascinated Christian writers from the earliest times. Two of the most influential texts were the Apocalypse of Peter, dating probably from the mid-second century, and the Apocalypse of Paul, probably written in the fourth century. Once again, one finds the names Peter and Paul in use as the supposed authors of apocryphal works. That an apocalypse was written in Paul's name is not surprising given the statement by Paul in 2 Corinthians 12 that he had been 'caught up as far as the third heaven'. In the authentic Pauline literature this baffling statement is not explained. It was an obvious gap that was left to the imagination of a later writer to fill. The Apocalypse of Paul tells what happened to Paul on his other-worldly visits. This apocalypse proved to be the most popular of the Western church's apocryphal apocalypses, and it led to the generally held beliefs about heaven and hell that fuelled the medieval imagination. Much of the art and sculpture in the Middle Ages depicting the afterlife was inspired by this work. Dante's *Inferno* was also influenced by the Apocalypse of Paul and even quotes it.

The first extract below (1) is taken not from one of these apocalypses but from the Acts of Thomas, which includes an apocalyptic passage. The context is a scene in which a woman is restored to life by the apostle, and she then gives an account of her experiences.

This is followed by the pictures of heaven and hell found in the Apocalypse of Peter (2). If a modern reader feels that some of the imagery is commonplace, this familiarity is due to the pervading influence apocalyptic texts such as this one have had on subsequent literature.

The last, and lengthy, extract (3) is from the Apocalypse of Paul where Paul is guided through heaven and hell by an angel whom he constantly questions. One cannot but suspect that it was the descriptions of the punishments meted out to various categories of sinners in hell rather than the images of the heavenly life that interested the sermonizing author and provided his readers with stern but helpful warnings.

(1) *Acts of Thomas* 55–8

55. And the apostle said to her, 'Tell us where you have been.' And she answered, 'Do you, who were with me, to whom also I was entrusted, wish to hear?' And she commenced thus: 'An ugly-looking man, entirely black, received me; and his clothing was exceedingly filthy. And he took me to a place where there were many chasms, and a great stench and most hateful vapour were given forth thence. And he made me look into each chasm, and in the first I saw blazing fire, and fiery wheels running, and souls were hung upon these wheels, dashing against each other. And there was crying and great lamentation and no Saviour was there. And that man said to me, "These souls are akin to you, and in the days of reckoning they were delivered to punishment and destruction. And then others are brought in their stead; in like manner all these are again succeeded by others. These are they who perverted the intercourse of man and wife." And again I looked down, and saw infants heaped upon each other, struggling and lying upon each other. And he said to me, "These are their children, and for this they are placed here for a testimony against them."

56. 'And he brought me to another chasm, and as I looked into it I saw mud and worms spouting forth, and souls wallowing there; and I heard a great gnashing of teeth come from them. And that man said to me, "These are the souls of women who left their husbands and committed adultery with others, and they have been brought to this torment." And he showed me another chasm, and looking into it I saw souls hung up, some by the tongue, some by the hair, some by the hands, others by the feet, head downward, and reeking with smoke and sulphur. Concerning these the man who accompanied me

said the following: "The souls hung up by the tongue are slanderers and such as have spoken false and disgraceful words and are not ashamed. Those hung up by their hair are the shameless, who are not ashamed at all and go about with uncovered heads in the world. Those hung up by the hands are they who took that which did not belong to them and have stolen, and who never gave anything to the poor, nor helped the afflicted; but they did so because they wished to get everything, and cared neither for law nor right. And these hung up by the feet are those who lightly and eagerly walked in wicked ways and disorderly paths, not visiting the sick nor escorting those who depart this life. On this account each soul receives what it has done."

57. 'And again he led me forth and showed me a very dark cavern, exhaling a very bad stench. Many souls were peeping out thence, wishing to get some share of the air. And their keepers would not let them look out. And my companion said to me, "This is the prison of those souls which you saw. For when they have fully received their punishment for that which each has done, others succeed them. Some are fully consumed, others are given up to other punishments." And the keepers of the souls in the dark cavern said to the man that had charge of me, "Give her to us, that we may bring her to the others till the time comes when she is handed over to punishment." But he said to them, "I will not give her to you, because I am afraid of him who delivered her to me. For I was not told to leave her here; I shall take her back with me, till I get an injunction about her." And he took me and brought me to another place, where there were men who were cruelly tortured. He who is like you took me and gave me up to you, saying to you, "Take her, for she is one of the sheep which have wandered away." And received by you, I now stand before you; I beg, therefore, and supplicate you that I may not come to those places of punishment which I have seen.'

58. And the apostle said, 'You have heard what this woman has recounted. And these are not the only punishments, but there are others worse than these. And you too, unless you turn to the God whom I preach, and abstain from your former works and from the deeds which you did in ignorance, shall find your end in these punishments. Believe, therefore, in

Christ Jesus, and he will forgive you the former sins and will cleanse you from all your bodily desires that remain on the earth, and will heal you from the faults that follow after you and go along with you and are found before you. Let every one of you put off the old man and put on the new, and leave your former course of conduct and behaviour. Those who steal, let them steal no more, but let them live, labouring and working. The adulterers are no more to commit adultery, lest they give themselves up to everlasting punishment. For with God adultery is an evil exceedingly wicked above all other evils. Put away also covetousness and lying and drunkenness and slandering, and do not return evil for evil! For all these are alien and strange to the God whom I preach. But walk rather in faith and meekness and holiness and hope, in which God rejoices, that you may become his kinsmen, expecting from him those gifts which only a few receive.'

(2) *Apocalypse of Peter* 7–10, 15–16 (Ethiopic)

7. [Jesus said,] 'Then shall men and women come to the place prepared for them. By their tongues wherewith they have blasphemed the way of righteousness shall they be hanged up. There is spread under them unquenchable fire so that they do not escape it.

'Behold another place: there is a pit, great and full. In it are those who have denied righteousness: and angels of punishment chastise them and there they kindle upon them the fire of their torment.

'And again behold two women: they hang them up by their neck and by their hair; they shall cast them into the pit. These are those who plaited their hair, not to make themselves beautiful but to turn them to fornication, that they might ensnare the souls of men to perdition. And the men who lay with them in fornication shall be hung by their loins in that place of fire; and they shall say one to another, "We did not know that we should come to everlasting punishment."

'And the murderers and those who have made common cause with them shall they cast into the fire, in a place full of venomous beasts, and they shall be tormented without rest, feeling their pains; and their worms shall be as many in number as a dark cloud. And the angel Ezrael shall bring forth the souls of those who have been slain, and they shall behold the torment of those who slew them and say one to another, "Righteousness and justice is the judgement of God. For we heard, but we believed not, that we should come into this place of eternal judgement."

8. 'And near this flame there is a pit, great and very deep, and into it flows from above all manner of torment, foulness, and excrement. And women are swallowed up therein up to their necks and tormented with great pain. These are they who have caused their children to be born untimely and have corrupted the work of God who created them. Opposite them shall be another place where their children sit alive and cry to God. And flashes of lightning go forth from those children and pierce the eyes of those who for fornication's sake have caused their destruction.

'Other men and women shall stand above them, naked; and their children stand opposite them in a place of delight, and sigh and cry to God because of their parents saying, "These are they who despised and cursed and transgressed your commandments and delivered us to death: they have cursed the angel that formed us and have hanged us up and begrudged us the light which you have given to all creatures. And the milk of their mothers flowing from their breasts shall congeal and from it shall come beasts devouring flesh, which shall come forth and turn and torment them for ever with their husbands because they forsook the commandments of God and slew their children. As for their children, they shall be delivered to the angel Temlakos. And those who slew them shall be tormented eternally, for God wills it so.

9. 'Ezrael the angel of wrath shall bring men and women, with half of their bodies burning, and cast them into a place of darkness, the hell of men; and a spirit of wrath shall chastise them with all manner of torment, and a worm that never sleeps shall devour their entrails; and these are the persecutors and betrayers of my righteous ones.

'And beside those who are there, shall be other men and women, gnawing their tongues; and they shall torment them with red-hot irons and burn their eyes. These are they who slander and doubt my righteousness.

'Other men and women whose works were done in deceitfulness shall have their lips cut off; and fire enters into their mouth and their entrails. These are they who caused the martyrs to die by their lying.

'And beside them, in a place near at hand, upon the stone shall be a pillar of fire, and the pillar is sharper than swords. And there shall be men and women clad in rags and filthy garments, and they shall be cast thereon to suffer the judgement of an unceasing torment; these are the ones who trusted in their riches and despised the widows and the women with fatherless children . . . before God.

10. 'And into another place nearby, full of filth, they cast men and women up to the knees. These are they who lent money and took usury.

'And other men and women cast themselves down from a high place and return again and run, and devils drive them. These are the worshippers of idols, and they drive them up to the top of the height and they cast themselves down. And this they do continually and are tormented for ever. These are they who have cut their flesh as apostles of a man: and the women with them . . . and these are the men who defiled themselves together as women.

'And beside them . . . and beneath them shall the angel Ezrael prepare a place of much fire: and all the idols of gold and silver, all idols, the work of men's hands, and the semblances of images of cats and lions, of creeping things and wild beasts, and the men and women that have prepared the images thereof, shall be in chains of fire and shall be chastised because of their error before the idols, and this is their judgement for ever.

'And beside them shall be other men and women, burning in the fire of the judgement, and their torment is everlasting. These are they who have forsaken the commandment of God and followed the (persuasions?) of devils.

15. And my Lord Jesus Christ, our King, said to me [= Peter], 'Let us go to the holy mountain.' And his disciples went with him, praying.

And behold there were two men there, and we could not look upon their faces, for a light came from them, shining more than the sun, and their raiment also was shining and cannot be described and nothing is sufficient to be compared to them in this world. And the sweetness of them . . . that no mouth is able to utter the beauty of their appearance, for their aspect was astonishing and wonderful. And the other, great, I say, shines in his aspect above crystal. Like the flower of roses is the appearance of the colour of his aspect and of his body . . . his head. And upon his shoulders . . . and on their foreheads was a crown of nard woven from fair flowers. As the rainbow in the water, so was their hair. And such was the comeliness of their countenance, adorned with all manner of ornament.

16. And when we suddenly saw them, we marvelled. And I drew near to God, Jesus Christ, and said to him, 'O my Lord, who are these?' And he said to me, 'They are Moses and Elijah.' And I said to him, 'Where then are Abraham and Isaac and Jacob and the rest of the righteous fathers?' And he showed us a great garden, open, full of fair trees and blessed fruits and of the odour of perfumes. The fragrance was pleasant and reached us. And of that tree . . . I saw many fruits. And my Lord and God Jesus Christ said to me, 'Have you seen the companies of the fathers?'

(3) *Apocalypse of Paul* 22–4, 29, 31–40

22. And I [= Paul] looked around upon that land, and I saw a river flowing with milk and honey, and there were trees planted by the bank of that river, full of fruit; moreover, each single tree bore twelve fruits in the year, having various and diverse fruits; and I saw the created things which are in that place and all the work of God, and I saw there palms of twenty cubits, but others of ten cubits; and that land was seven times brighter than silver. And there were trees full of fruits from the roots to the highest branches, of ten thousand fruits of palms upon ten thousand fruits. The grape-vines had ten thousand plants. Moreover in the single vines there were ten thousand thousand bunches and in each of these a thousand single grapes; moreover these single trees bore a thousand fruits. And I said to the angel, 'Why does each tree bear a thousand fruits?' The angel answered and said to me, 'Because the Lord God gives an abounding profusion of gifts to the worthy and

because they of their own will afflicted themselves when they were placed in the world doing all things on account of his holy name.' And again I said to the angel, 'Sir, are these the only promises which the Most Holy God makes?' And he answered and said to me, 'No! There are seven times greater than these. But I say to you that when the just go out of the body they shall see the promises and the good things which God has prepared for them. Till then, they shall sigh and lament, saying, "Have we uttered any word from our mouth to grieve our neighbour even on one day?"' I asked and said again, 'Are these alone the promises of God?' And the angel answered and said to me, 'These whom you now see are the souls of the married and those who kept the chastity of their nuptials, controlling themselves. But to the virgins and those who hunger and thirst after righteousness and those who afflicted themselves for the sake of the name of God, God will give seven times greater than these, which I shall now show you.'

And then he took me up from that place where I saw these things and behold, a river, and its waters were much whiter than milk, and I said to the angel, 'What is this?' And he said to me, 'This is the Acherusian Lake where is the City of Christ, but not every man is permitted to enter that city; for this is the journey which leads to God, and if anyone is a fornicator and impious, and is converted and shall repent and bear fruits worthy of repentance, at first when he has gone out of the body, he is brought and worships God, and thence by command of the Lord he is delivered to the angel Michael and he baptizes him in the Acherusian Lake—then he leads him into the City of Christ alongside those who have never sinned.' But I marvelled and blessed the Lord God for all the things which I saw.

23. And the angel answered and said to me, 'Follow me, and I will lead you into the City of Christ.' And he was standing on the Acherusian Lake and he put me into a golden ship and about three thousand angels were singing a hymn before me till I arrived at the City of Christ. Those who inhabited the City of Christ greatly rejoiced over me as I went to them, and I entered and saw the City of Christ, and it was all of gold, and twelve walls encircled it, and twelve interior towers, and there was a stade between each of the encircling walls. And I said to

the angel, 'Sir, how much is a stadium?' The angel answered
and said to me, 'As much as there is between the Lord God and
the men who are on the earth, for the City of Christ alone is
great.' And there were twelve gates in the circuit of the city, of
great beauty, and four rivers which encircled it. There was a
river of honey, and a river of milk, and a river of wine, and a
river of oil. And I said to the angel, 'What are these rivers
surrounding that city?' And he said to me, 'These are the four
rivers which flow abundantly for those who are in this land of
promise; the names are these: the river of honey is called
Pison, and the river of milk Euphrates, and the river of oil
Gion, and the river of wine Tigris. When they were in the world
they did not use their power over these things, but they
hungered and afflicted themselves for the sake of the Lord
God, so that when they enter this city the Lord will assign them
these things above all measure.'

24. When I entered the gate I saw trees great and very high
before the doors of the city, having no fruit but leaves only, and
I saw a few men scattered in the midst of the trees, and they
lamented greatly when they saw anyone enter the city. And
those trees were sorry for them and humbled themselves and
bowed down and again erected themselves. And I saw it and
wept with them, and I asked the angel and said, 'Sir, who are
these who are not admitted to enter into the City of Christ?'
And he said to me, 'These are they who zealously abstained day
and night in fasts, but they had a proud heart above other men,
glorifying and praising themselves and doing nothing for their
neighbours. They gave some people friendly greeting, but to
others they did not even say "Hail!" And, indeed, they showed
hospitality only to those whom they wished, and if they did
anything whatever for their neighbour they were immoder-
ately puffed up.' And I said, 'What then, sir? Did their pride
prevent them from entering into the City of Christ?' And the
angel answered and said to me, 'Pride is the root of all evils.
Are they better than the Son of God who came to the Jews with
much humility?' And I asked him and said, 'Why is it that the
trees humble themselves and erect themselves again?' And the
angel answered and said to me, 'The whole time which these
men passed on earth, they zealously served God, but on account of the shame and reproaches of men for a time they

blushed and humbled themselves, but they were not saddened, nor did they repent that they should desist from the pride which was in them. This is why the trees humble themselves, and again are raised up.' And I asked and said, 'For what reason were they admitted to the doors of the city?' The angel answered and said to me, 'Because of the great goodness of God, and because this is the entrance of his saints entering this city: for this reason they are left in this place, but when Christ the King Eternal enters with his saints, all the righteous may pray for them, and then they may enter into the city along with them; yet none of them is able to have the same confidence as those who humbled themselves, serving the Lord God all their lives.'

29. And he carried me into the midst of the city near the twelve walls. But there was in this place a higher wall, and I asked and said, 'Is there in the City of Christ a wall which exceeds this place in honour?' And the angel answered and said to me, 'There is a second better than the first, and similarly a third better than the second, as each exceeds the other up to the twelfth wall.' And I said, 'Tell me, sir, why one exceeds another in glory.' And the angel answered and said to me, 'All who have in themselves even a little slander or zeal or pride, something of his glory would be made void even if they were in the City of Christ: look behind you.'

And turning round I saw golden thrones placed in each gate, and on them men having golden diadems and gems; and I looked and I saw inside between the twelve men thrones placed in another rank which appeared to be of greater glory, so that no one is able to recount their praise. And I asked the angel and said, 'My lord, who is on the throne?' And the angel answered and said to me, 'Those thrones belong to those who had goodness and understanding of heart, yet made themselves fools for the sake of the Lord God, as they knew neither Scripture nor psalms, but mindful of one chapter of the commands of God, and hearing what it contained, they acted with much diligence and had a true zeal before the Lord God, and the admiration of them will seize all the saints in the presence of the Lord God, for talking with one another they say, "Wait and see how these unlearned men who know nothing more have merited so great and beautiful a garment and so great glory on account of their innocence."'

And I saw in the midst of this city a great altar, very high, and there was someone standing near the altar whose countenance shone as the sun, and he held in his hands a psaltery and harp, and he sang saying, 'Alleluia!' And his voice filled the whole city; at the same time, when all they who were on the towers and gates heard him, they responded, 'Alleluia!' so that the foundations of the city were shaken; and I asked the angel and said, 'Sir, who is this of so great power?' And the angel said to me, 'This is David; this is the city of Jerusalem, for when Christ the King of Eternity shall come with the assurance of his kingdom, he again shall go before him that he may sing psalms, and all the righteous at the same time shall sing responding "Alleluia!"' And I said 'Sir, how did David alone above the other saints make a beginning of psalm-singing?' And the angel answered and said to me, 'Because Christ the Son of God sits at the right hand of his Father, and this David sings psalms before him in the seventh heaven, and as it is done in the heavens so also below, because a sacrifice may not be offered to God without David, but it is necessary that David should sing psalms in the hour of the oblation of the body and blood of Christ: as it is performed in heaven, so also on earth.'

31. When he had ceased speaking to me, he led me outside the city through the midst of the trees and far from the places of the land of the good, and put me across the river of milk and honey; and after that he led me over the ocean which supports the foundations of heaven.

The angel answered and said to me, 'Do you understand why you go hence?' And I said, 'Yes, sir.' And he said to me, 'Come and follow me, and I will show you the souls of the godless and sinners, that you may know what manner of place it is.' And I went with the angel, and he carried me towards the setting of the sun, and I saw the beginning of heaven founded on a great river of water, and I asked, 'What is this river of water?' And he said to me, 'This is the ocean which surrounds all the earth.'

And when I was at the outer limit of the ocean I looked, and there was no light in that place, but darkness and sorrow and sadness; and I sighed.

And I saw there a river boiling with fire, and in it a multitude of men and women immersed up to the knees, and other men up to the navel, others even up to the lips, others up to the hair. And I asked the angel and said, 'Sir, who are those in the fiery river?' And the angel answered and said to me, 'They are neither hot nor cold, because they were found neither in the number of the just nor in the number of the godless. For those spent the time of their life on earth passing some days in prayer, but others in sins and fornications, until their death.' And I asked him and said, 'Who are these, sir, immersed up to their knees in fire?' He answered and said to me, 'These are they who when they have gone out of church occupy them-selves with idle disputes. Those who are immersed up to the navel are those who, when they have taken the body and blood of Christ, go and fornicate and do not cease from their sins till they die. Those who are immersed up to the lips are those who slander each other when they assemble in the church of God; those up to the eyebrows are those who nod to each other and plot spite against their neighbour.'

32. And I saw to the north a place of various and diverse punishments full of men and women, and a river of fire ran down into it. I observed and I saw very deep pits and in them several souls together, and the depth of that place was about three thousand cubits, and I saw them groaning and weeping and saying, 'Have pity on us, O Lord!', and no one had pity on them. And I asked the angel and said, 'Who are these, sir?' And the angel answered and said to me, 'These are they who did not hope in the Lord, that they would be able to have him as their helper.' And I asked and said, 'Sir, if these souls remain for thirty or forty generations thus one upon another, I believe the pits would not hold them unless they were dug deeper.' And he said to me, 'The Abyss has no measure, for beneath it there stretches down below that which is below it; and so it is that if perchance anyone should take a stone and throw it into a very deep well after many hours it would reach the bottom, such is the abyss. For when the souls are thrown in there, they hardly reach the bottom in fifty years.'

33. When I heard this, I wept and groaned over the human race. The angel answered and said to me, 'Why do you weep? Are you more merciful than God? For though God is good, he knows that there are punishments, and he patiently bears with the human race, allowing each one to do his own will in the time in which he dwells on the earth.'

34. I observed the fiery river and saw there a man being tortured by Tartaruchian angels having in their hands an iron instrument with three hooks with which they pierced the bowels of that old man; and I asked the angel and said, 'Sir, who is that old man on whom such torments are imposed?' And the angel answered and said to me, 'He whom you see was a presbyter who did not perform his ministry well: when he had been eating and drinking and committing fornication he offered the host to the Lord at his holy altar.'

35. And I saw not far away another old man led on by evil angels running with speed, and they pushed him into the fire up to his knees, and they struck him with stones and wounded his face like a storm, and did not allow him to say, 'Have pity on me!' And I asked the angel, and he said to me, 'He whom you see was a bishop and did not perform his episcopate well, who indeed accepted the great name but did not enter into the witness of him who gave him the name all his life, seeing that he did not give just judgement and did not pity widows and orphans, but now he receives retribution according to his iniquity and his works.'

36. And I saw another man in the fiery river up to his knees. His hands were stretched out and bloody, and worms proceeded from his mouth and nostrils, and he was groaning and weeping, and crying he said, 'Have pity on me! For I am hurt more than the rest who are in this punishment.' And I asked, 'Sir, who is this?' And he said to me, 'This man whom you see was a deacon who devoured the oblations and committed fornication and did not do right in the sight of God; for this cause he unceasingly pays this penalty.'

And I looked closely and saw alongside of him another man, whom they delivered up with haste and cast into the fiery river, and he was in it up to the knees; and the angel who was set over the punishments came with a great fiery razor, and with it he cut the lips of that man and the tongue likewise. And sighing,

I lamented and asked, 'Who is that, sir?' And he said to me, 'He whom you see was a reader and read to the people, but he himself did not keep the precepts of God; now he also pays the proper penalty.'

37. And I saw another multitude of pits in the same place, and in the midst of it a river full with a multitude of men and women, and worms consumed them. But I lamented, and sighing asked the angel and said, 'Sir, who are these?' And he said to me, 'These are those who exacted interest on interest and trusted in their riches and did not hope in God that he was their helper.'

And after that I looked and saw another place, very narrow, and it was like a wall, and fire round about it. And I saw inside men and women gnawing their tongues, and I asked, 'Sir, who are these?' And he said to me, 'These are they who in church disparage the Word of God, not attending to it, but as it were making naught of God and his angels; for that reason they now likewise pay the proper penalty.'

38. And I observed and saw another pool in the pit and its appearance was like blood, and I asked and said, 'Sir, what is this place?' And he said to me, 'Into that pit stream all the punishments.' And I saw men and women immersed up to the lips, and I asked, 'Sir, who are these?' And he said to me, 'These are the magicians who prepared for men and women evil magic arts and did not cease till they died.'

And again I saw men and women with very black faces in a pit of fire, and I sighed and lamented and asked, 'Sir, who are these?' And he said to me, 'These are fornicators and adulterers who committed adultery, having wives of their own; likewise also the women committed adultery, having husbands of their own; therefore they unceasingly suffer penalties.'

39. And I saw there girls in black raiment, and four terrifying angels having in their hands burning chains, and they put them on the necks of the girls and led them into darkness; and I, again weeping, asked the angel, 'Who are these, sir?' And he said to me, 'These are they who, when they were virgins, defiled their virginity unknown to their parents; for which cause they unceasingly pay the proper penalties.'

And again I observed there men and women with hands cut and their feet placed naked in a place of ice and snow, and worms devoured them. Seeing them I lamented and asked,

'Sir, who are these?' And he said to me, 'These are they who harmed orphans and widows and the poor, and did not hope in the Lord, for which cause they unceasingly pay the proper penalties.'

And I observed and saw others hanging over a channel of water, and their tongues were very dry, and many fruits were placed in their sight, and they were not permitted to take of them, and I asked, 'Sir, who are these?' And he said to me, 'These are they who broke their fast before the appointed hour; for this cause they unceasingly pay these penalties.'

And I saw other men and women hanging by their eyebrows and their hair, and a fiery river drew them, and I said, 'Who are these, sir?' And he said to me, 'These are they who join themselves not to their own husbands and wives but to whores, and therefore they unceasingly pay the proper penalties.'

And I saw other men and women covered with dust, and their countenance was like blood, and they were in a pit of pitch and sulphur running in a fiery river, and I asked, 'Sir, who are these?' And he said to me, 'These are they who committed the iniquity of Sodom and Gomorrah, the male with the male, for which reason they unceasingly pay the penalties.'

40. And I observed and saw men and women clothed in bright garments, but with their eyes blind, and they were placed in a pit, and I asked, 'Sir, who are these?' And he said to me, 'These are heathen who gave alms, and knew not the Lord God, for which reason they unceasingly pay the proper penalties.' And I observed and saw other men and women on a pillar of fire, and beasts were tearing them in pieces, and they were not allowed to say, 'Lord have pity on us!' And I saw the angel of torments putting heavy punishments on them and saying, 'Acknowledge the Son of God; for this was prophesied to you when the divine Scriptures were read to you, and you did not attend; for which cause God's judgement is just, because your actions have apprehended you and led you into these punishments.' But I sighed and wept, and I asked and said, 'Who are these men and women who are strangled in the fire and pay their penalties?' And he answered me, 'These are women who defiled the image of God by bringing forth infants out of the womb, and these are the men who lay with them. And their infants addressed the Lord God and the angels who were set over the punishments, saying, "Avenge us of our

parents, for they defiled the image of God, having the name of
God but not observing his precepts; they gave us for food to
dogs and to be trodden on by swine; others they threw into the
river." But the infants were handed over to the angels of
Tartarus who were set over the punishments, that they might
lead them to a spacious place of mercy; but their fathers and
mothers were tortured in a perpetual punishment.'

And after that I saw men and women clothed with rags full
of pitch and fiery sulphur, and dragons were coiled about their
necks and shoulders and feet, and angels with fiery horns
restrained them and smote them, and closed their nostrils,
saying to them, 'Why did you not know the time in which it
was right to repent and serve God, and did not do it?' And I
asked, 'Sir, who are these?' And he said to me, 'These are they
who seemed to renounce the world, putting on our garb, but
the impediments of the world made them wretched, so that
they did not maintain a single agape, and they did not pity
widows and orphans; they did not receive the stranger and the
pilgrim, nor did they offer an oblation and they did not show
mercy to their neighbour. Moreover not even on one day did
their prayer ascend pure to the Lord God, but many impediments of the world detained them, and they were not able to do
right in the sight of God, and the angels enclosed them in the
place of punishments. And those who were in punishments
saw them and said to them, "We indeed neglected God when
we lived in the world and you also did likewise; when we were
in the world we indeed knew that we were sinners, but of you
it was said, 'These are just and servants of God.' Now we know
that in vain you were called by the name of the Lord, for which
cause you pay the penalties."'

And sighing I wept and said, 'Woe unto men, woe unto
sinners! Why were they born?' And the angel answered and
said to me, 'Why do you lament? Are you more merciful than
the Lord God who is blessed forever, who established judgement and sent forth every man to choose good and evil in his
own will and do what pleases him?' Then I lamented again very
greatly, and he said to me, 'Do you lament when as yet you
have not seen greater punishments? Follow me and you shall
see seven times greater than these.'

16

The End Time

Whereas the apocalypses of Peter and of Paul are concerned with the current state of affairs in heaven and hell, the Apocalypse of Thomas contains predictions about the ending of the present world. It is thus 'apocalyptic' in its sense of foretelling the future. From the New Testament onwards Christians were made aware that they were already living in the end time. For them Christ was believed to have inaugurated the last age. Christians were not sure how imminent that final day, increasingly thought of as the day of judgement, would be: many hazarded a guess. Nor did the Christians know what warnings would announce or precede the coming of the End. Again, attempts were made to list which events were to be disregarded and which were portentous. Apocalyptic passages in the New Testament Gospels and of course the Book of Revelation are concerned with these warnings and the 'signs of the times'. Such speculation has never ceased. The writer of the Apocalypse of Thomas, dating perhaps from the fifth century, gave a countdown, and describes the events of the final six days before the end of the world. One version of this text is given here.

Apocalypse of Thomas (shorter text)

Hear, O Thomas, for I am the Son of God the Father, and I am the father of all spirits. Hear from me the signs which shall come to pass at the end of this world, when the end of the world shall be fulfilled before my elect depart out of the world. I will tell you that which shall come to pass openly (or, will tell you openly, etc.): but when these things shall be the princes of the angels do not know, for they are now hidden from them.

Then shall there be in the world sharings between king and king, and in all the earth there shall be great famine, great pestilences, and much distress, and the sons of men shall be led captive in every nation and shall fall by the edge of the sword and there shall be great commotion in the world. Then after that, when the hour of the end draws near, there shall be for seven days great signs in heaven, and the powers of the heavens shall be moved.

Then shall there be on the first day the beginning: at the third hour of the day a great and mighty voice in the firmament of heaven and a cloud of blood coming up out of the north, and great peals of thunder and mighty flashes of lightning shall follow it, and it shall cover the whole heaven, and it will rain blood upon all the earth. These are the signs of the first day.

And on the second day there shall be a great voice in the firmament of heaven, and the earth shall be moved out of its place, and the gates of heaven shall be opened in the firmament of heaven toward the east, and the smoke of a great fire shall break forth through the gates of heaven and shall cover all the heaven until evening. In that day there shall be fear and great terror in the world. These are the signs of the second day.

But on the third day, about the third hour, there shall be a great voice in heaven, and the depths of the earth shall roar from the four corners of the world; the pinnacles of the firmament of heaven shall be opened, and all the air shall be filled with pillars of smoke. There shall be an exceedingly evil stench of brimstone, until the tenth hour, and men shall say, 'We think the time draws near that we perish.' These are the signs of the third day.

And on the fourth day, at the first hour, from the land of the east the abyss shall melt and roar. Then shall all the earth be shaken by the might of an earthquake. In that day shall the ornaments of the heathen fall, and all the buildings of the earth, before the might of the earthquake. These are the signs of the fourth day.

But on the fifth day, at the sixth hour, suddenly there shall be a great thunder in heaven, and the powers of light and the wheel of the sun shall be caught away, and there shall be great darkness in the world until evening, and the air shall be sorrowful without sun or moon, and the stars shall cease from their ministry. In that day shall all nations behold as in a sack and shall despise the life of this world. These are the signs of the fifth day.

And on the sixth day, at the fourth hour, there shall be a great voice in heaven, and the firmament of the heaven shall be split from the east to the west, and the angels of the heavens shall be looking out upon the earth through the gaps in the heavens, and all those on the earth shall behold the host of the angels looking forth out of heaven. Then shall all men flee to the tombs and hide themselves from the face of the righteous angels and say, 'Would that the earth would open and swallow us up!' And such things shall happen as never happened since this world was created.

Then shall they behold me coming from above in the light of my Father with the power and honour of the holy angels. Then at my coming shall the fence of fire of paradise be loosed— because paradise is girt round about with fire. And this is the perpetual fire that shall consume the earth and all the elements of the world.

Then shall the spirits and souls of all men come forth from paradise and shall come upon all the earth, and every one of them shall go to his own body, where it is laid up, and every one of them shall say, 'Here lies my body.' And when the great voice of those spirits shall be heard, then shall there be a great earthquake over all the world, and by its force the mountains shall be shattered above and the rocks beneath. Then shall every spirit return to his own vessel, and the bodies of the saints who have fallen asleep shall arise.

Then shall their bodies be changed into the image and like- ness and the honour of the holy angels, and into the power of the image of my holy Father. Then shall they be clothed with the garment of life eternal, out of the cloud of light which has never been seen in this world; for that cloud comes down out of the highest realm of the heaven from the power of my Father. And that cloud shall invest with its beauty all the spirits who have believed in me.

Then shall they be clothed and shall be borne by the hands of the holy angels as I have told you before. Then they shall be lifted up into the air upon a cloud of light, and shall go with me rejoicing into heaven, and then shall they remain in the light and honour of my Father. Then shall there be great gladness for them with my Father and the holy angels. These are the signs of the sixth day.

And on the seventh day, at the eighth hour, there shall be voices in the four corners of the heaven. And all the air shall be shaken, and filled with holy angels, and they shall make war among themselves all the day long. And in that day shall my elect be sought out by the holy angels from the destruction of the world. Then shall all men see that the hour of their destruction draws near. These are the signs of the seventh day.

And when the seven days are passed by, on the eighth day, at the sixth hour, there shall be a sweet and tender voice in heaven from the east. Then shall that angel be revealed which has power over the holy angels, and all the angels shall go forth with him, sitting upon chariots of the clouds of my holy Father, rejoicing and flying in the air beneath the heaven to deliver the elect who have believed in me. And they shall rejoice that the destruction of this world has come.

Epilogue

◇

The fascinating, bizarre, and imaginative stories about Jesus, his family, and his followers which make up the literature known as the New Testament apocrypha, and which we have been sampling in the preceding chapters, give an unrivalled insight into the teachings, practices, and, above all, the entertainment of many Christians from the second century through to the Middle Ages. This type of literature was produced and distributed throughout Christendom, East and West, over several centuries. It has a significant place in the history of Christianity. Despite its extravagances and occasional variations from what emerged as orthodox teaching, this apocryphal literature fuelled and itself reflected theological thinking.

In our own literalist days we inevitably find ourselves asking if any of the stories and sayings in the preceding chapters are true. By that word 'true' we are asking about the historicity of the events described. Did they really happen? Did Jesus actually say this? Did Peter do that? In Chapter 4 I raised the possibility that a few of the sayings attributed to Jesus and perhaps some of the stories, particularly those apparently belonging to the ministry period, may be considered as equivalent to comparable scenes in the canonical scriptures of the church—the New Testament proper—in that they seem to ring 'true' and authentic. But outside the type of material found in Chapter 4, very few of the apocryphal texts merit such consideration. There is little support for those contemporary scholars who wish to place some apocryphal texts, particularly apocryphal Gospels, on a par with the canonical Gospels in terms of their dating and independent witness to the events described or sayings reported.

But we are really asking the wrong questions. In seeking historical value, objective verification, and factuality we are mistaking the nature of the apocryphal literature. Although twentieth-century scholarship quite properly continues to ask similar questions about the historical validity of the New Testament itself, where the Gospels and the Acts of the Apostles in particular are recognized as a complex mixture of historic reminiscence combined with legend, even there such questioning can distort, misinterpret, or cause misunderstandings about the intentions of the writings. Religious literature, Biblical and apocryphal, is concerned with belief and faith and with poetic and theological truths. These need not be rooted only in the verifiable facts demanded of historical research.

What historical value there is to be found is in the theological motives and social conditions that gave rise to the literature, and, of course, in tracing the influence and enduring appeal of its contents.

The introductory remarks at the beginning of this book spoke of the importance of these apocryphal texts as witnesses to the beliefs, prayers, and interests of the society that produced and preserved them. It is only by looking behind the veneer of the story line itself to those Christians who wrote and read these tales that we may legitimately pose questions about historical value. The apocryphal legends may add nothing to our knowledge of the Christianity of the first century, but they can be unparalleled sources of information about the developing traditions of popular folk religion and of Christian faith and practice from the second century onwards. (By contrast, behind the theological motives that gave rise to the canonical New Testament writings, one can occasionally uncover parts of the historical basis of the recently emergent Christianity which it purports to describe.)

Even a cursory comparison of the apocryphal texts with the New Testament material shows that there is a great difference between these two corpora of literature. The first-century Gospels, the Acts of the Apostles, letters, and the Book of Revelation are conspicuously of a different 'type'—less extravagant, terse, more 'spiritual', complex, profound—from the apocrypha, with its verbosity, sensationalism, and occasional deviation from standard teachings. When the church at large, under all kinds of historical and theological pressures, had to pronounce on its corpus of authoritative literature to parallel the Hebrew scriptures, it selected twenty-seven of the earliest Christian writings that had gained the respect and reflected the common usage of all of Christendom. From our vantage-point, it seems obvious that the ecclesiastical authorities in the second, third, and fourth centuries, who debated and eventually selected these twenty-seven books in order to form an exclusive body of approved Christian scriptures, made the correct judgement. In any case, one cannot rewrite history: the canon was a corpus that was eventually promulgated and enforced as an established entity.

Throughout the history of the church these scriptures were irreplaceable, irreducible, and sufficient for the basic needs of Christian theology. My judgement is that the rejected texts were legitimately branded as 'apocryphal', in its sense of 'secondary', 'of dubious quality', and 'inferior' in all sorts of ways. Nevertheless, as I hope this book has demonstrated, the so-called apocryphal legends are no mere side-show in the development of the church, but indispensable guides, giving an insight into post-Biblical Christianity. Their influence was enormous. The apocryphal New Testament deserves recognition and merits study.

Indexes

✧

APOCRYPHAL TEXTS CITED

Acts of Andrew 176–8, 180–6
Acts of John 57–8, 59–64, 148–9, 152–60
Acts of Paul 131–40, 141–3, 144–6
Acts of Peter 121–9
Acts of Thomas 163–74, 190–2
Apocalypse of Paul 195–204
Apocalypse of Peter 192–5
Apocalypse of Thomas 205–8
Arabic Infancy Gospel 28–30, 39–40
Arundel manuscript (404) 17–18

Berlin Codex (8502.4) 119–20

Coptic fragment of Acts of Paul 140–1

Discourse of St John the Divine 42–4

Egerton Papyrus (2) 53–4
Epistle to the Laodiceans 143–4

Gospel of Nicodemus (Acts of Pilate) 73–9, 81–8
Gospel of Nicodemus (Christ's Descent) 94–5, 99–102
Gospel of Peter 69–73
Gospel of Pseudo-Matthew 14–17, 23–8
Gospel of Thomas 55–7

Gregory of Tours, Virtutes Andreae (Epitome) 179–80

History of Joseph the Carpenter 48–50
Homily of Evodius of Rome 40–2

Infancy Gospel of Thomas 20–3

Letter of Lentulus 58–9
Letters of Christ and Abgar 64–5
Letters of Pilate and Herod 95–6

Mors Pilati 94

Narrative of Joseph of Arimathaea 80–1

Oxyrhynchus Papyrus (840) 52–3

Paradosis Pilati 91–4
Protevangelium of James 11–14, 33–8, 46–8, 112–13
Pseudo-Abdias, Virtutes Iohannis 149–51
Pseudo-Titus, de dispositione Sanctimonii 121

Questions of Bartholomew 102–8

Secret Gospel of Mark 54

Vindicta Salvatoris 110–11

GENERAL INDEX

Adoration of the Magi 13–14
Andrew 176–86
  martyrdom 180–6
  miracles 179–80
  and the tale of Euclia 176–8

Beliar questioned 105–8

Corinthians, third letter to 144–6

dance of Christ 60–2

end of world 205–8

harrowing of hell 99–104
heaven described 195–9
hell described 190–4, 199–204
Herod's letter to Pilate 96
Hymn of Jesus, *see* dance of Christ
Hymn of the Soul (Hymn of the
  Pearl) 169–73

Jesus:
  birth in cave 12, 15, 17–18
  cessation of nature at birth 12,
    17
  childhood miracles 20–3, 27–8,
    29–30
  death and resurrrection 62–4, 69–
    73, 80–1, 83–4
  descent to Hades 99–104
  infancy miracles 23–7, 29
  letter by 64–5
  ministry 52–4
  ox and ass at birth 16–17
  physical appearance 57–9
  sayings 55–7
  and schoolmaster 21–2
  transfiguration 59–60
  trial before Pilate 73–9
John 148–60
  and bedbugs 148–9
  and partridge 152
  and the poison cup 149–51
  and the tale of Drusiana 152–60
Joseph of Arimathaea 81–8
  and the burial of Jesus 71, 81
Joseph the carpenter:
  death 48–50
  guardian of Mary 46–7

Joseph and Mary's trial of bitter
  water 48

Mary:
  annunciation 38
  birth 36
  death and assumption 40–4
  miracle-worker 28, 39–40
  nurtured in temple 37
  parents (Joachim and Anna) 33–7
  perpetual virginity 13, 15–16
  pregnancy 47
  presentation in the temple 37
  veil-maker 37–8

Paul 131–46
  baptizing lion 141
  in heaven and hell 195–204
  letters 143–6
  martyrdom 142–3
  physical appearance 131
  and Thecla 131–40
penitent thief 28–9, 80–1, 102
Peter 119–29
  inverse crucifixion 128
  martyrdom 127–9
  miracles 119–21
  and Simon Magus 122–7
Pilate:
  death 91–4
  letter to Claudius 94–5
  letter to Herod 95
  at trial of Jesus 73–9

Quo Vadis? 127

shepherds at Jesus' birth 16
Simon Magus 122–7

Thecla 131–40
Thomas 163–74
  death 173–4
  and Gundaphorus 163–7
  in India 163–74
  relics 174
trial of bitter water 48

Veronica's kerchief 110

Zacharias murdered 113